The Role of AI in Enhancing IoT-Cloud Applications

Authored by

Ambika Nagaraj

St. Francis College,
Koramangala, Bengaluru, Karnataka 560034,
India

The Role of AI in Enhancing IoT-Cloud Applications

Author: Ambika Nagaraj

ISBN (Online): 978-981-5165-70-8

ISBN (Print): 978-981-5165-71-5

ISBN (Paperback): 978-981-5165-72-2

need for a court order if at any point you breach any terms of this License Agreement. In no event will any delay or failure by Bentham Science Publishers in enforcing your compliance with this License Agreement constitute a waiver of any of its rights.

3. You acknowledge that you have read this License Agreement, and agree to be bound by its terms and conditions. To the extent that any other terms and conditions presented on any website of Bentham Science Publishers conflict with, or are inconsistent with, the terms and conditions set out in this License Agreement, you acknowledge that the terms and conditions set out in this License Agreement shall prevail.

Bentham Science Publishers Pte. Ltd.
80 Robinson Road #02-00
Singapore 068898
Singapore
Email: subscriptions@benthamscience.net

BENTHAM SCIENCE

CONTENTS

FOREWORD I

The book focuses on the interesting aspects of the role of Artificial Intelligence in Enhancing Internet of Things-based Cloud Applications. The reader is expected to have some basic knowledge of these three Technical Areas in Computer applications, such as how the sensors sense, connect and convert analog data to the digital formats captured from the physical world data around the human being and the machinery, also, how they interface with Single Board Computers, Micro-controllers, and similar Programmable logic Controllers. The knowledge of the WSN and present state-of-the-art concepts can bring better-added advantages for the readers to understand the contents of this book. The primary knowledge of AI in the broader sense as Machine Learning, Statistical Methodologies, Vision Computing for the feature extraction from images and videos, Text, and Natural Language Processing will be a pre-requisite to a better and easy understanding of the work presented in this book.

The first chapter of the book discusses Expert Systems, NLP, speech recognition and machine vision. AI has well-proven and established methods in soft computing, such as Artificial Neural networks and fuzzy logic, for handling the vagueness, imprecise and ambiguous nature of the data. In addition, the Evolutionary Computing algorithms for optimization provide satisfactory solutions in some cases. The introductory chapter also brings material on the issues and challenges in AI.

The IoT comes with the background of Wireless Sensor Networks, Smart Motes, Dusts, and Unmanned Aerial Vehicles. The Internet of Things, combined with the Industrial setups having SCADA systems, Machine to Machines and Cyber-Physical Systems, bring monitoring and predictions of certain important aspects in the picture for the investigation. IoT brings the opportunity to combine the data from several applications from the Industry, Health, Smart-City, Smart Manufacturing, and ready Digital Twins as Proofs-of-Concept. The huge data that may be characterized by the Bigdata philosophy generated from various sources cannot be converted into useful insights unless the algorithm from Artificial Intelligence is utilized. To amalgamate these technologies, it is important to understand the architecture, applications, and use cases in IoT and AI. Chapter 2 provides the discourse on it.

Cloud-based services and products are an indispensable part of most Manufacturing Industries. The Cloud provides a flexible approach to the users, perhaps to the developers who want to launch microservice-based applications so that the continuous deployment and integration cycles persist. The managed, unmanaged, and Cloud bursts add meticulous flexibility to the Manufacturing Cloud. The Machine Learning, Computer Vision based APIs are accessible from the many established Clouds Services on an on-demand basis. The author has excellently discussed this aspect in Chapter 3.

The Final chapter discusses the approach to integrating the IoT, Cloud, and AI-based services for effective optimization of resource utilization. There are some interesting protocols at the application layer of the IoT, such as MQTT, COAP, and XMPP. The data pushed from the edge is stored in the Cloud through the Telemetry based MQTT in popular Cloud services. After the data is stored in the Cloud, the Machine Learning Methodologies are applied to the text data, image, video, or mixed datasets.

The extensive Research, Innovation, and Academic background of Author Dr. Ambika have made the content of the books interesting for the readers, and the learning for the readers as easy as possible with the necessary knowledge transfer process. Wish you a happy and joyous reading of the book.

Manoj Devare
Amity Institute of Information Technology
Amity University, Maharashtra, India

FOREWORD II

The web of things is a relationship of different gadgets connected with the web, and they can collect and trade information with one another. These IoT gadgets make a great deal of information that should be assembled and looked for essential outcomes by utilizing made mental capacity to coordinate colossal information streams and breaking points of the IoT affiliation. The book subtleties the working of this mixed framework. It has four sections. Chapter 1 deals with Preamble to Man-made Awareness. Chapter 2 inspects the blend of two advances, their plan, applications, and use cases. Troubles and future degrees are fundamental for the readings. Chapter 3 examines the advancement's establishment, applications, use cases, hardships, and future augmentation. Chapter 4 briefs on the system's characteristics, applications, challenges, use cases, and inevitable destiny of the design.

Mansaf Alam
Journal of Applied Information Science
&
DietY, Govt. of India
Department of Computer Science
Jamia Millia Islamia, New Delhi, India

FOREWORD III

The present Machine Learning (ML) is in a mix with the Internet of Things (IoTs)-based cloud applications which assume a critical part in our daily existence. All such associated (intelligent) gadgets produce massive amounts of information that should be inspected and dissected to guarantee that they ceaselessly gain accessible informational indexes and better themselves with no manual impedance. Various ML approaches and strategies that are acquainted in a brief time frame effectively assess enormous information estimations, expanding the IoT's efficiency. It would be hard for intelligent gadgets to progressively pursue smart choices without counting and authorizing ML. The IoT assists with interconnecting different equipment gadgets, such as houses, vehicles, *etc.*, and different gadgets coordinated with actuators and sensors, so information can be gathered and shared. As different associations comprehend the ever-evolving capacity of the IoT, they have started finding different blocks they need to beneficially convey to utilize it. Various associations and organizations use ML to take advantage of the IoT's inert limit. The book introduces 4 chapters that discuss many interesting and intelligent ideas that show how artificial Intelligence helps to tackle situations in the manufacturing and operational ecosystem and machine learning solicitation for IoT and Cloud applications.

Jyotir Moy Chatterjee
Department of Information Technology
Lord Buddha Education Foundation
Kathmandu-44600, Nepal

PREFACE

Artificial intelligence has a place in the evolution of human intelligence, complicating teleological explanations in which symbolic artificial intelligence is a natural and inevitable result of attempts made over many years to reduce human reasoning to a logical formalism. Due to this, the history of artificial intelligence is not merely the chronicle of mechanical attempts to mimic or replace some fixed idea of human intelligence but also a developing narrative of what intelligence is. IoT can communicate without the need for a human. The related items will gain new capabilities thanks to the Internet of Things. Some early Internet of Things applications have already been created in the healthcare, transportation, and automotive industries. IoT technologies are still in their infancy.

In contrast, there have been a lot of new advancements made in the integration of items with sensors in the cloud-based Internet. The term "cloud computing" has recently become popular among people who work in distributed computing. It is a concept for providing accessible, on-demand grid admission to a standard, programmable collection of computer aids that can be quickly delivered and discharged with little administration work or service provider involvement. Multiple people think that the cloud will revolutionize the IT sector.

This textbook is a collection of the authors' suggestions regarding cloud, integration techno-logy, artificial intelligence, and the Internet of Things. The chapters summarize the technology's applications and drawbacks, and suggest future paths by various authors. As it provides greater insight into different technologies, researchers, and students, the collection is profitable for young readers. I want to express my gratitude to Bentham Science Publications for allowing me to write this book. I want to express my appreciation to the management of my college for their help and support. I also want to thank my friends and family for their support.

Ambika Nagaraj
St. Francis College,
Koramangala, Bengaluru, Karnataka 560034,
India

CHAPTER 1

Introduction to Artificial Intelligence

Abstract: The term manufactured brilliance connotes both opportunities and threats to humanity. As a global trend, intelligence is becoming relevant at almost every level of social behavior, raising both high expectations and serious concerns. Numerous algorithms, models and methods, as well as machine learning, databases, and visualizations, are reflected in artificial intelligence. One of the main benefits is that AI-driven machines adhere to consistently rational algorithmic rules without being biased. Ethical considerations aim to instill morality in machines and make AI-driven robots more human. The process of simulating human intelligence using machines, particularly computer systems, is known as artificial intelligence. Expert systems, natural language processing, speech recognition, and machine vision are some specific applications of cleverness. This chapter explains its working, issues faced by the same and challenges of the technology.

Keywords: Artificial intelligence, Challenges, Expert systems, Human intelligence, Intelligent behaviour, Machine learning, Taxonomy.

1.1. INTRODUCTION

In ways that complicate teleological accounts of how attempts over centuries have been made to reduce human reasoning to a logical formalism, it led to the natural and inevitable development of symbolic artificial intelligence (AI); artificial intelligence belongs in the history of human intelligence. At various times, human cognitive faculties have been theorized, divided, valued, and devalued in multiple ways. The past also shows that attempts to make human behavior more like a machine often co-occur with efforts to make machines more intelligent. Automation efforts frequently parallel the discipline of human minds and bodies for the efficient execution of tasks, from the metronome's disciplining of factory workers' bodies in the 19th century to De Prony's search for the automatic and unthinking performance of arithmetic in his human computers.

Real-world applications are increasingly being used by AI programs that lack common sense and other essential human understanding. Even though some people are concerned about super-intelligent, the most dangerous aspect of AI systems is that we will trust them too much and give them too much autonomy without fully understanding what they can and cannot do.

The artificial intelligence landscape [2] consists of economic agents with R&D or industrial AI-related activities and is covered and categorized by the proposed taxonomy, which addresses political, research, and industrial perspectives. As a result, a wide range of core AI-related scientific subdomains and transversal topics, such as applications of the former or ethical and philosophical considerations, can be detected by this taxonomy. The concept of rational agents, which are entities that make decisions and act about their environment, including interaction with other agents, is also detected by this taxonomy. Rather than being distinct intelligence subsets, the domains and subdomains are related. The process by which machines convert data into knowledge or infer facts from data is the subject of the reasoning environment. Providing solutions and efficiently representing them, several classifications address knowledge representation and automated reasoning as a field of intelligence. Creating and implementing strategies to carry out some activity, typically by intelligent agents, autonomous robots, and uncrewed vehicles, is the primary objective of automated planning. Without being explicitly programmed, learning aims to learn, decide, predict, adapt, and respond to changes automatically. A machine's ability to identify, process, comprehend and generate information in written and spoken human communications is referred to as communication. The power of systems to sense their surroundings is called perception - hearing, vision, and manipulation. The combination of perception, reasoning, action, learning, and interaction with the environment—as well as characteristics like distribution, coordination, cooperation, autonomy, exchange, and integration—is the focus of the transversal domain of Integration and Interaction. Any infrastructure, software, and platform provided as services or applications—possibly in the cloud—that are available off the shelf and executed on demand to reduce the management of complex infrastructures is referred to as the transversal domain of intelligent services. As intelligent systems, philosophical and ethical issues become more prevalent, attracting citizens' and governments' policy interests. Fig. (**1**) portrays Taxonomy- Artificial intelligence techniques.

There are three main ideas in the proposed taxonomy [3]. Artificial intelligence technology is a collection of techniques, algorithms, and methods that allow systems to carry out tasks frequently associated with intelligent behavior. The AI Research Field represents fields of study dependent on AI methods and would not be possible without them. The term application refers to cross-domain applications that use AI to boost performance and ease of use.

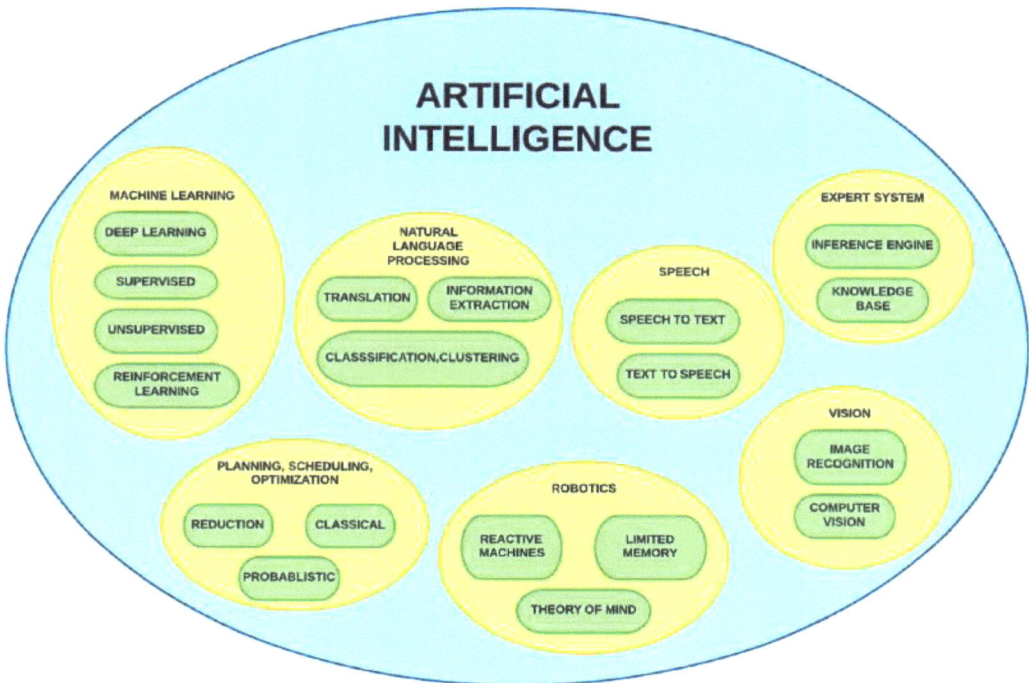

Fig. (1). Taxonomy- Artificial intelligence techniques [1].

The work [4] gives mathematical structures for ART, CNN, and SVM networks. The used taxonomy provides an overview of the literature on the various algorithms of artificial intelligence used to solve this problem, ranging from military applications to other areas of application. Logistics, transportation, armed attack analysis, and communication are areas where they can use artificial intelligence in the military. Fig. (**2**) depicts the same.

The study [5] looked at four criteria for how intelligence could be used in Iranian library systems- public services, technical services, and management services. Exploratory Factor Analysis is used in work. It is a statistical technique that depicts the variability of observed, correlated variables in terms of potential factors. It looks for such related variations to combine them into a group of variables. In the numerical taxonomy analysis method, the four intelligence techniques groups were identified as evaluation criteria.

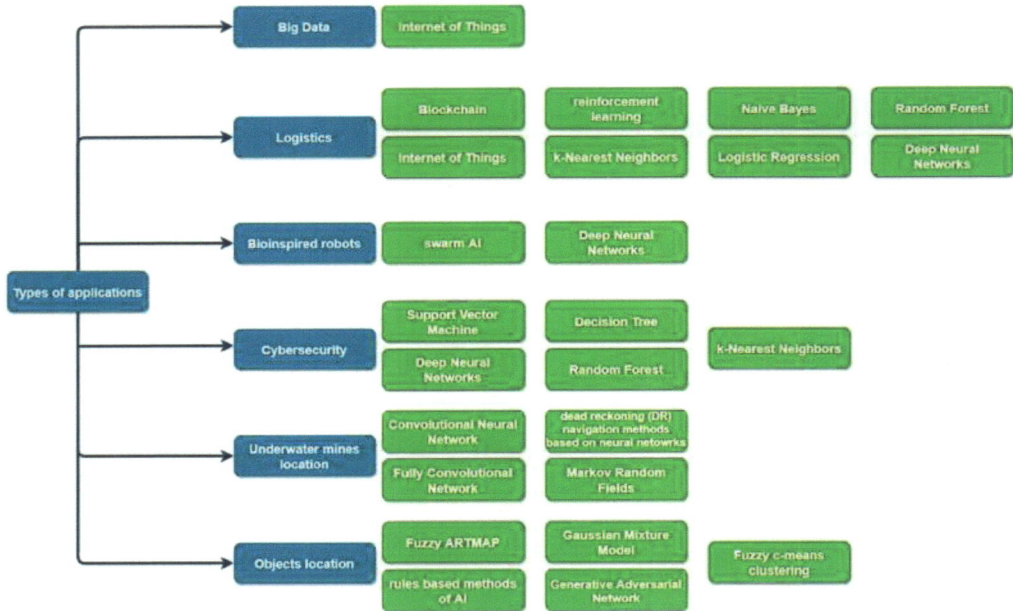

Fig. (2). Proposed taxonomy [4].

The writing [6] suggests using technology to make data easier to read and more accessible through unnatural brilliance. It makes things more straightforward. The report recommends using technology to make data easier to read and more accessible through artificial intelligence. XBRL is a component of the choice architecture for government regulation, which uses nudging to sway mass consumers toward a preferred option. A taxonomy connects to XBRL. The article incorporates ethical considerations and develops a taxonomy to increase public understanding of artificial intelligence applications. The taxonomy is inductively derived from the offerings on the robot-advice market or includes the existing ethical codes for using robots and artificial intelligence.

1.2. BACKGROUND

Compared to interacting with a computer, cell phone, or other smart device, humans perceive and interact with robot machines with a higher physical appearance. Robots must not only meet a level of strength, robustness, physical skills, and improved cognitive ability based on intelligence to succeed in a human-driven environment; they also need to complete a social impetus and be ethically conscientious. There are a lot of obstacles in the way of designing and building social robots. One of the most important is making robots that can meet the needs and expectations of the human mind by having cognitive capabilities and being friendly. Socio-Cognitive Robotics is the interdisciplinary study and application of robots that can teach, learn, and reason about how to behave in a complex world. It has evolved and verified through a series of projects to develop advanced and modern technology-based systems to support learning and knowledge functions. It is beginning to play an influential role in societies worldwide. The technology of social robotics offers several advantages, but it also presents obstacles that it must prepare organizations to overcome through legal and ethical means. Fig. (**3**) represents the Evolution of Artificial Intelligence.

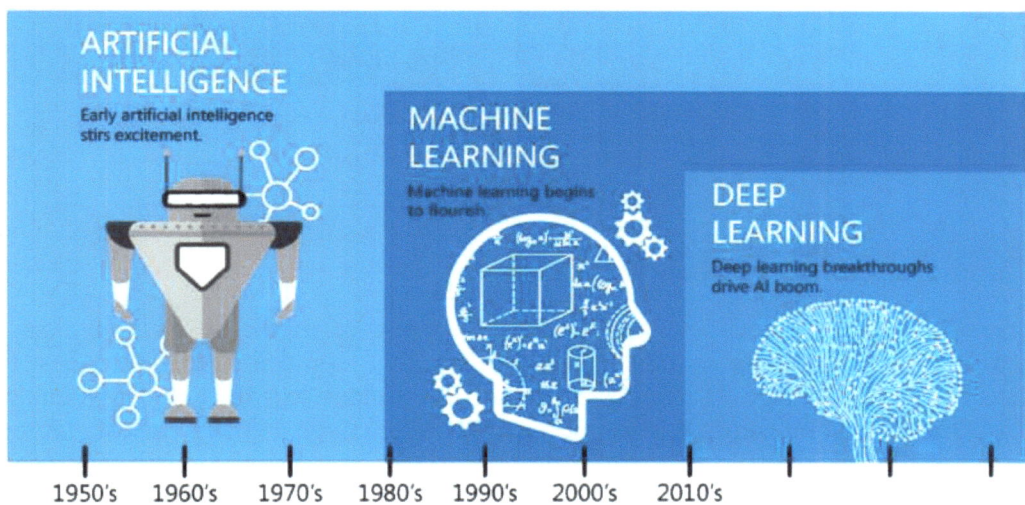

Fig. (3). Evolution of Artificial Intelligence [7].

1.2.1. Medicine

Human-shaped mechanical artistry constructed of leather, wood, and artificial organs was presented to the Emperor Mu of Zhou in the third century in China when the first humanoid automaton was first mentioned. The US Department of Defense quickly grew interested in the numerous challenging mathematical problems that computers began to tackle over the years. Artificial cleverness is regarded as an area of engineering that employs fresh ideas and creative approaches to tackle complex issues. Computers may one day be as clever as people if advancements in technological speed, capacity, and software coding are made in the future. Fig. (**4**) depicts the Evolution of Artificial Intelligence in medicine.

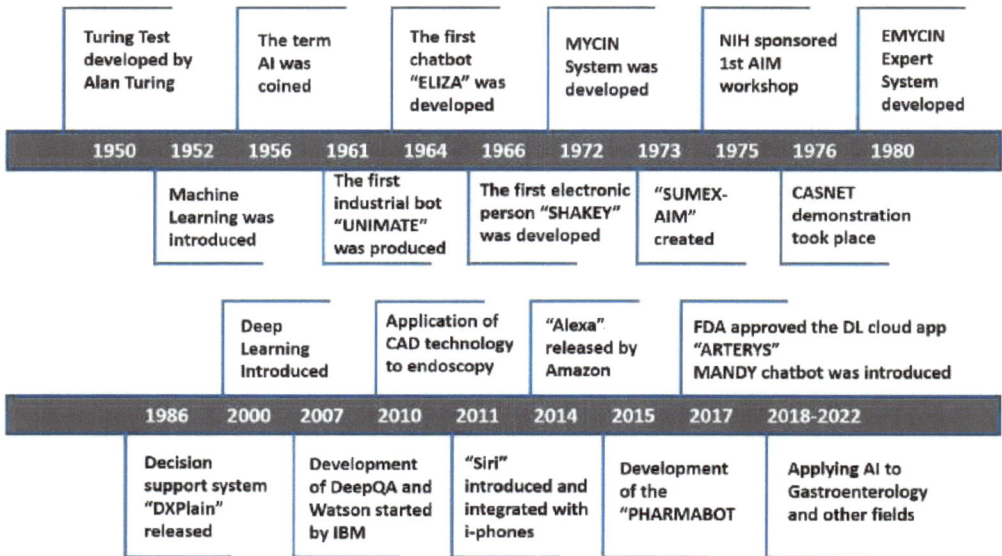

Fig. (4). Evolution of Artificial Intelligence in Medicine [8].

Over the past five decades, artificial intelligence in medicine has developed significantly. The development of machines that could make inferences or decisions that could previously only be made by humans was the primary focus of early intelligence. Joseph Weizenbaum introduced Eliza [9]. Its use of natural language processing was able to mimic human speech through pattern-matching and substitution techniques. It was the foundation for chatterbots in the future. Shakey [10], the first mobile robot capable of interpreting instructions, was developed at the Stanford Research Institute. Shakey could comprehend more detailed instructions and carry out the necessary actions.

In 1973, a time-shared computer system called the Stanford University Medical Experimental–Artificial Intelligence in Medicine SUMEX-AIM [11] was developed to improve networking capabilities among numerous clinical and biomedical research institutions. Three distinct programs make up the causal-associational network known as the CASNET system [12] - model-building, consultation, and the collaboration's creation and upkeep of a database physician could benefit from this model's guidance on patient management by applying information about a specific disease to individual patients.

MYCIN [13] might be able to provide a list of potential bacterial pathogens and then suggest antibiotic treatment options that are tailored to the patient's weight. Using the same framework as EMYCIN [14] and a more extensive medical knowledge base, INTERNIST-1 [15] assists primary care physician diagnoses.

The University of Massachusetts released the decision support system DXplain [16]. A differential diagnosis helps with the symptoms you enter into this program. In addition, it serves as an electronic medical textbook with additional references and in-depth disease descriptions. DeepQA [17] analyze unstructured content data using natural language processing and various searches to generate probable answers. Fig. (**5**) represents applications of Artificial intelligence in healthcare. Table **1.1** represents the development of healthcare technology by 2026.

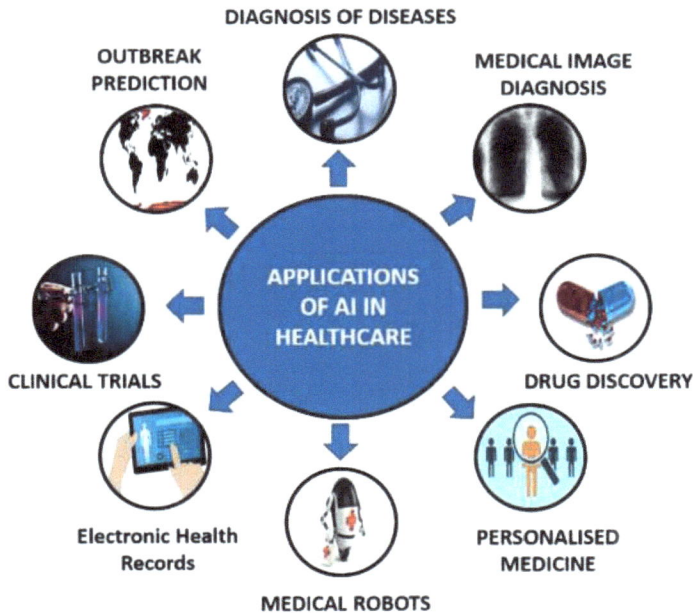

Fig. (5). Applications of Artificial Intelligence in Healthcare [8].

Table 1.1. Development of technology by 2026 [18].

Areas of Development	Percentage	Countries Incorporating the Methodologies
Hospital surgical centres and clinics	40%	North America; Europe; Asia Pacific; South America; Middle East and Africa
Clinical research organization	20%	
Government defence institutions	15%	
Research and diagnostic laboratories	22%	

1.2.2. Education

The objective of present and future educational initiatives should be to improve students' preparedness for a world with artificial intelligence [19]. The rhetoric around its complexity and progress may sound both inspiring and terrifying for primary children because it is a young and developing technology. The goal of its education should be to demystify technology, close the gap between it and daily life, and assist students in acquiring fundamental knowledge and abilities. According to studies, students' perceptions of their intelligence preparation can significantly impact how they learn and decide to study in the future. Students should be prepared for an AI-infused future by teaching and learning synthetic brilliance. Fig. (6) portrays the structural model of measured variables.

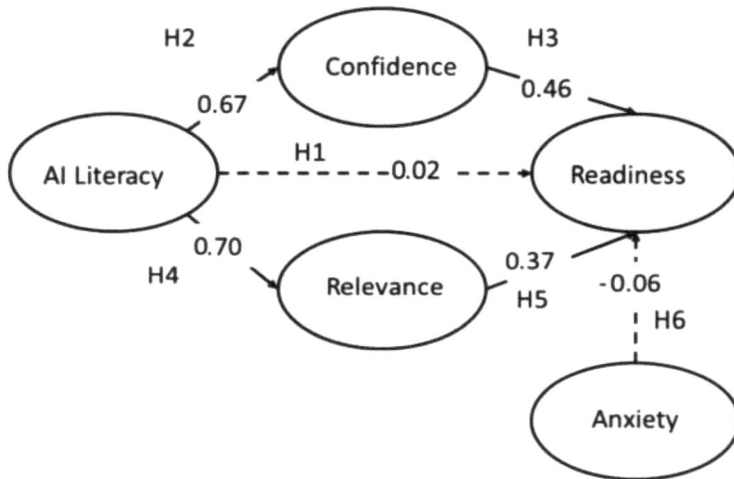

Fig. (6). Structural model of measured variables [20].

In 1998, some works expanded the definition of education to include informal learning and workplace training [21]. This comprehensive viewpoint is provided by the Cognitive Tutor ecosystem [22], which in 2006, introduced the technology and a curriculum. Cultural traditions, systems, and ways of knowing are considered in an interactive learning environment. Education is a socio-cultural phenomenon [23], and it was one illustration of the variety of applications for technology in 2012.

1.2.3. Engineering

Generally, acquiring domain information to add to an expert system's knowledge base is a significant undertaking. It has occasionally proven to be a bottleneck while creating an expert system. An inductive learning method for automatically acquiring knowledge is the extraction of knowledge in the form of IF-THEN rules. A series of examples act as input for an inductive learning program. The goal of the inductive learning program is to identify sets of characteristics that models in particular classes have in common and then use those characteristics to create rules with the IF part acting as conjunctions and the THEN part working as the classes. The hybrid technique uses predicate logic, which is more potent, to program inductive reasoning, while propositional logic describes examples and represents new concepts. Fig. (**7**) depicts the System Engineering Lifecycle comprised of the AI modelling cycle.

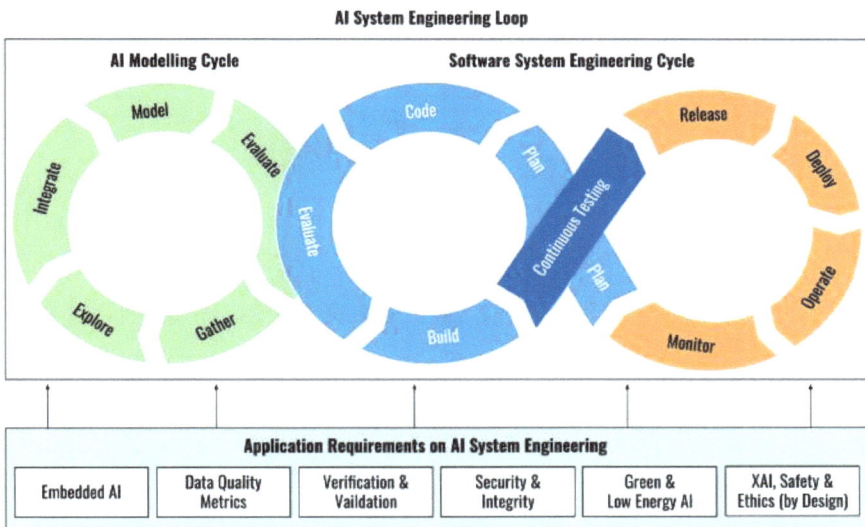

Fig. (7). System Engineering Lifecycle comprised of AI modelling cycle [24].

Another population-based global optimization technique is particle swarm optimization [25], which permits several individual solutions, or "particles," to wander around a hyper-dimensional search space in search of the optimum. Every particle has a location vector and a velocity vector, which are modified after each iteration by learning from the local best that each particle independently discovered and the most recent global best discovered by the entire swarm. PSO techniques incorporate problem-solving attempts in a social network and are suitable for optimizing exceedingly complex systems and have thus been successfully implemented. These approaches model a scenario where several candidate solutions coexist and collaborate simultaneously.

The ant colony optimization method [26] imitates how real ants behave in their colonies, using pheromones to communicate with one another and completing complicated tasks like finding the quickest route from the nest to food sources. An expert system [27] is based on the knowledge of human specialists established through established knowledge systems; in artificial intelligence research, the expert system develops the earliest and most effectively. The expert system is frequently utilized in the engineering fields of construction, geological exploration, material engineering, geotechnical engineering, underground engine-ering, petroleum chemical industry, and others. Table **1.2** represents the details of the development of the automobile industry by 2026.

Table 1.2. Development of technology (automobiles) [28].

Areas of Development	Percentage	Countries Incorporating the Methodologies
Bus transportation	28%	North America; Asia Pacific regions
Train transportation	45%	
Troll usage	27%	
Car utilization	19%	

1.3. WORKING OF ARTIFICIAL INTELLIGENCE

Machine learning, natural language processing, and robotics are all subfields of artificial intelligence using practically any area of medicine. Artificial intelligence has seemingly endless potential to advance biomedical research, medical edu-cation, and healthcare provision. Artificial intelligence can play a role in diagnostics, clinical decision-making, and customized medicine thanks to its robust capacity to integrate and learn from massive volumes of clinical data. The ability of the sophisticated virtual human avatars to hold meaningful conver-sations has implications for the identification and management of psychiatric disorders. Since synthesized intelligence technology has a great potential to endanger patient preference, safety, and privacy, a fresh set of ethical concerns is created by the powerful technology that must be discovered and managed. Fig. (**8**) represents the dimensions of Artificial Intelligence. Fig. (**9**) re-presents developing AI models.

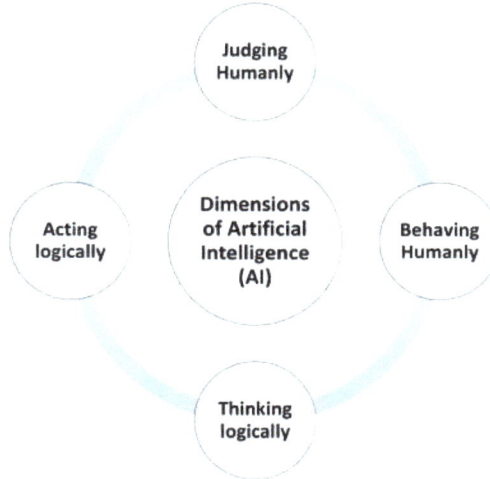

Fig. (8). Dimensions of Artificial Intelligence [29].

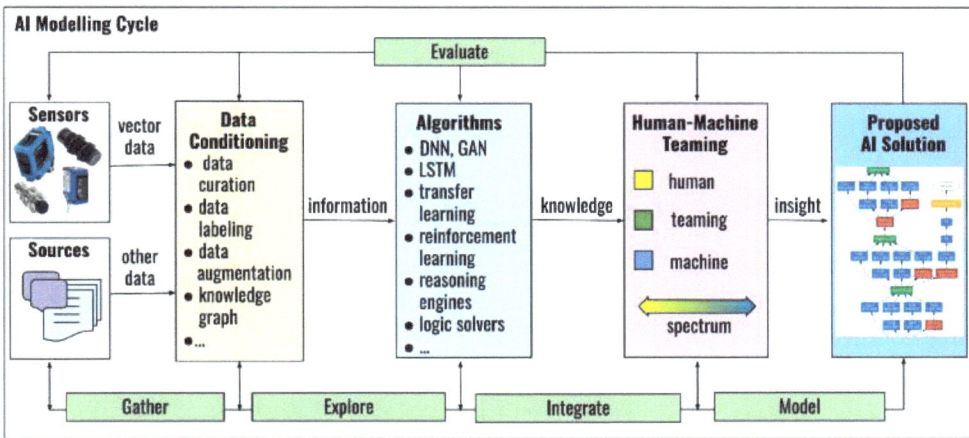

Fig. (9). Developing AI models [24].

The work [30] addresses some moral problems of applying artificial intelligence in healthcare and medical education. The most challenging issues include managing the increased risk to patient privacy and confidentiality. It defines the lines between the doctor's and the machine's roles in patient care and changes how future doctors are educated to prepare them for impending medical practice changes. The discussions on these issues will help stakeholders build realistic perceptions of what cleverness can and cannot achieve, enhancing physician and patient knowledge of AI's role in health care. Intelligence-trained physicians will benefit from anticipating potential ethical issues, finding feasible remedies, and suggesting legislative recommendations.

The questionnaire survey [31] was carried out using Wenjuanxing, a mainland Chinese online survey platform that serves the same purpose as Amazon Mechanical Turk. Each participant who knew intelligence received 3 yuan. The survey returned four hundred ninety-four valid samples. 46.1% of the respondents were female, and 53.8% were between 18 and 22. All fears were assessed in-dependently, including those related to privacy violation, discriminatory behavior, job replacement, learning, existential risk, ethics violation, artificial consciousness, and lack of transparency. The factor model of AI anxiety was evaluated using first-order confirmatory factor analysis. The model's fundamental adaptation index was considered and found to meet the requirements of factor analysis. It was assessed how well the model fits the overall system, including Internal coherence, dependability, and convergence.

1.4. ISSUES AND CHALLENGES FACED BY AI

1.4.1. Legal Issues

The legal system faces both practical and conceptual difficulties due to AI's growing influence on society and the economy. Two of the fundamental conceptual challenges are the real problem of controlling the actions of autonomous machines and the difficulties in assigning moral and legal respons-ibility for harm caused by autonomous machines. It must confront the issues of foreseeability and causation, but courts have always had to adjust the rules for proximate causation as technology has changed and developed. Although limiting the harm caused by AI systems after they have been designed is difficult due to the control issue, it is not more difficult to regulate or direct AI development before its development. Distinctness and opacity can be dealt with through the legal system. Numerous other technologies, both modern and less so, share AI's discreteness. Fig. (**10**) depicts the Ethical management of AI framework.

1.4.2. Building Trust

Many aspects of our lives are supported by trust [34], and some of the most fundamental relationships in a person's life require it. Without faith, it would jeopardize many critical social bonds, and trust may be one of the most basic attitudes or behaviors in human interaction. We would become paranoid and isolationist if we did not have even a tiny amount of trust in other people because we would be afraid of being tricked and hurt. A belief in a person's trustworthiness is often necessary for placing trust in them, but the two are not the same. For confidence to work, one or more skills may be required.AI used in healthcare should accurately predict the onset of tumors, AI used in self-driving vehicles should be able to transport individuals to their destinations safely, and AI used in the insurance industry should accurately detect fraudulent claims. Fig. (**11**) represents the Hybrid artificial intelligence model.

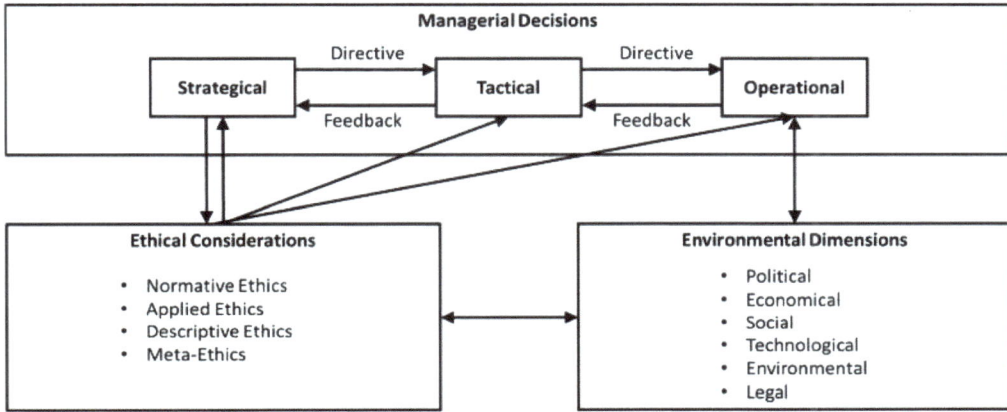

Fig. (10). Ethical Management of AI Framework [32].

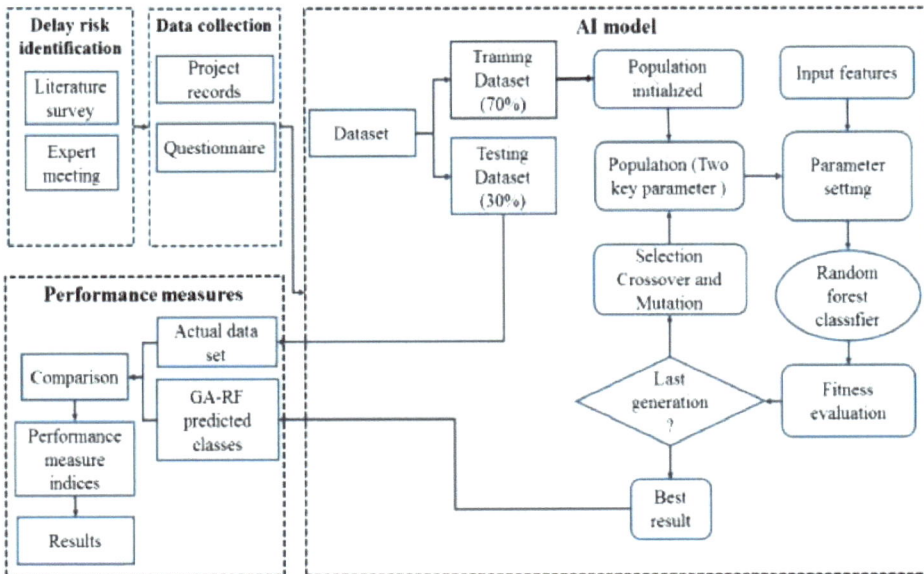

Fig. (11). Hybrid artificial intelligence model [33].

1.4.3. Software Malfunction

Organizations are adaptive systems that constantly work to push the boundaries of their efficiency to get closer to perfection. Organizations dealing with complex tasks, uncertainty, and the significant and apparent penalties of irreversible error are especially susceptible to this. Human weakness is frequently seen as the root of organizational inefficiency or failure [35].

For two decades, artificial intelligence researchers invented new branches, used them, and solved difficulties to improve performance. Artificial intelligence has been around since the dawn of time. Scientists have attempted to employ it in many fields since its inception. Expert systems—with various definitions-;emulate human experts' work in computer models or programs using five key elements: a knowledge base, working memory, inference engine, external inference, and user inference. Despite its lengthy history, artificial intelligence is being actively used today.

With various ML techniques and artificial intelligence, the current effort [36] intends to provide a non-invasive and affordable diagnostic tool for the early detection of a minor bearing problem in an induction motor. Scratches and holes are regarded as defective factors. A three-phase engine serves as a study sample. First, an experiment is carried out under various load conditions, and the fast Fourier transform analysis is used to determine the frequency spectrum of the load current. The machine learning and deep learning algorithms are trained using the features that were retrieved. Finally, the distinction between machine learning and deep learning is assessed, and its application to identify motor faults is examined. Fig. (**12**) represents the same.

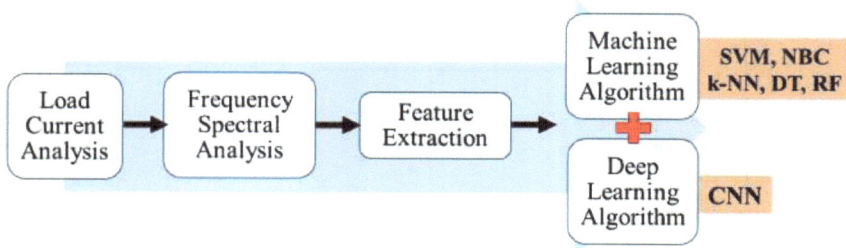

Fig. (12). Proposed model [36].

1.4.4. AI-human Interface

The Human-Centered Artificial Intelligence framework [37] explains how to design for high levels of human control. The high levels of computer automation improve human performance, recognize situations where complete human control or full computer control is required, and steer clear of the dangers of too much human power or computer control. The new objective is to achieve high levels of both human control and automation, making it more likely that computer applications will be reliable, safe, and trustworthy. By utilizing unique computer features like sophisticated algorithms, advanced sensors, information-rich displays, and potent effectors, designers are more likely to develop technologies. These methods enhance human performance as they move beyond thinking of computers as our teammates, collaborators, or partners. By clarifying human responsibility, designers can also support the human capacity to invent creative solutions in novel contexts with incomplete knowledge. Fig. (**13**) portrays architecture of Smart Campus.

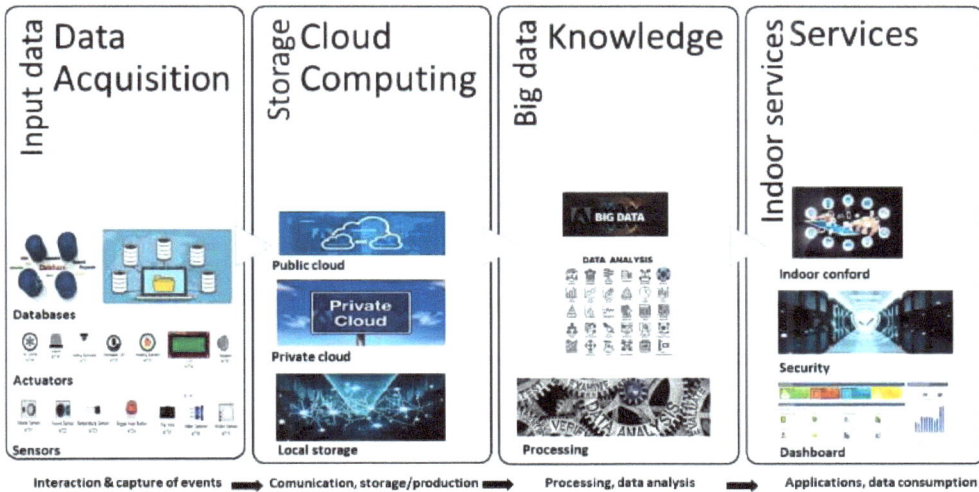

Fig. (13). Architecture of Smart Campus [38].

1.4.5. Productivity

An intense debate has erupted regarding the present and future effects of AI on society due to the profound social and economic shifts brought about by the implementation and growth of AI applications in the production of goods and services, transportation and logistics, or the provision of services. There are clear indications that almost all other industries are increasingly taking advantage of the opportunities presented by a new level of automation by AI technologies, even though developments in AI concentrate on the telecommunications, software services, and electronics manufacturing sectors. Quantitative analyses to measure the effects of AI on economic outcomes like growth, productivity, and employment are becoming increasingly necessary in light of these contradictory predictions. However, the requirement for high-quality firm-level data is a significant obstacle. A more upbeat body of research asserts that it can leverage the disruptive nature of AI technology through task automation, uncertainty reduction, the recombination of existing innovations, and the generation of new ones. Economic theories predict that technological advancement will have a positive effect on productivity. Hopes for reversing the persistently negative productivity trend and revitalizing the economy as a whole were raised by recent advances in AI technology and its vast applicability. Through a variety of channels, AI has the potential to increase productivity. These channels include the automated recombination of existing technologies, the reduction of uncertainties due to increased forecast precision, and, more generally, the generation of inno-vations. Fig. (**14**) portrays the Artificial intelligence framework.

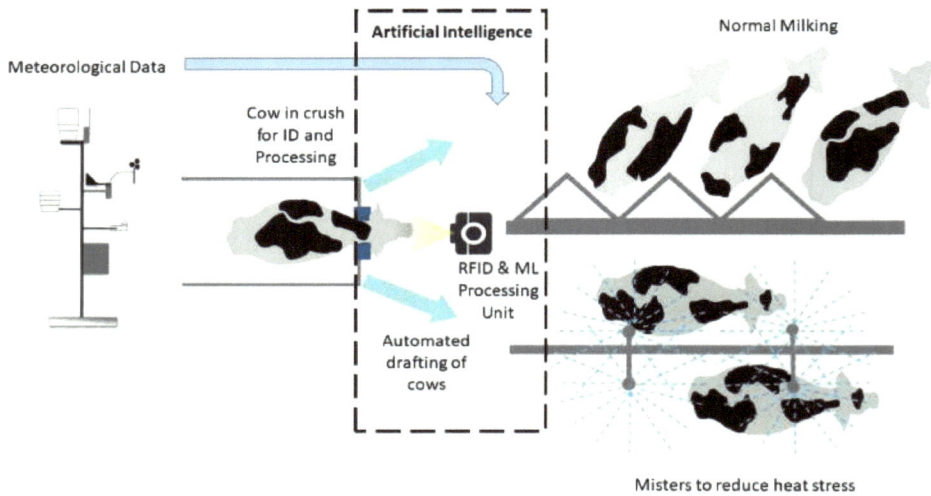

Fig. (14). Proposed Artificial intelligence framework [39].

1.5. OVERVIEW OF THE BOOK

Industry 4.0 refers to several advancements, including the Internet of Things and artificial intelligence. While the last alternative can combine artificial intelligence and its methods, these support points account for the contemporary web of things, information, and inquiry. The process of developing intelligent machines that carry out tasks requiring human understanding, such as direction, speech acknowledgment, *etc.*, is known as artificial intelligence. This cycle needs to think and be able to correct itself. Learning is the acquisition of knowledge and the application of rules; thinking is the application of rules to reach approximate or precise conclusions. Decentralized AI, blockchain thinking, the intellectual prowess of objects, machines, and other cutting-edge advancements all use AI in some way. The most significant way to collect data, analyze it, and see how it is used for applications like medical care, housing, smart farming, and intelligent vehicles, is through the coordination of AI and IoT. The second chapter describes the integration's architecture, applications, difficulties and open issues.

In today's culture, distributed computing is crucial and enables various applications, from virtual entertainment to framework. As long as it complies with the requirements of the Nature of Administration, such a framework should be able to adjust to shifting demands and expanding usage while reflecting social orders' communication and reliance on robotized figuring frameworks. Along with practical advancements designed to meet the demand for developing registration applications, these frameworks are becoming empowered. Future appli-cation licensing has to distinguish between fundamental advances. Cloud service providers like Facebook, Google, and Amazon deploy many cloud server farms to meet various nature administration needs. As Web of Things applications rely on the dependability of cloud administrations, cloud registering platforms can provide a cohesive connection point over the diverse assets in those applications. The cloud-AI architecture, applications, difficulties, and future perspectives are covered in the third chapter.

Modern approaches include the cyber of items, stockpiles, datasets, and artificial intelligence. They revolve around the means of knowledge transfer. It includes several communal functions like business, education, recreation, housing, finance, healthcare, business, administration, and production. IoT uses cyber to connect the entire world to cyberspace and a virtual planet, producing some information. The environment of the repository calibration encourages the approach to knowledge and builds conclusions using dataset analysis and equipment training. The fourth chapter describes the integration's traits, uses, and open problems. The fifth chapter discusses the use cases of the amalgamation of sub-systems.

CONCLUSION

Artificial intelligent systems are programs that give computers the ability to behave in ways that give the impression that a person is competent. A subfield of computer science called artificial intelligence is capable of analyzing complex data. It can utilize its ability to find significant relationships in data collection to anticipate outcomes in various situations. Intelligent behavior is a discipline of science and engineering involved with computational understanding. In every subject, academics have looked into the possible uses of intelligent methods since the middle of the previous century.

REFERENCES

[1]   C. Gupta, I. Johri, K. Srinivasan, Y.C. Hu, S.M. Qaisar, and K.Y. Huang, "A systematic review on machine learning and deep learning models for electronic information security in mobile networks", *Sensors (Basel)*, vol. 22, no. 5, p. 2017, 2022.
[http://dx.doi.org/10.3390/s22052017] [PMID: 35271163]

[2]   S. Samoili, M.L. Cobo, E. Gomez, G. De Prato, F. Martinez-Plumed, and B. Delipetrev, AI Watch. Defining Artificial Intelligence. Towards an operational definition and taxonomy of artificial intelligence.*Joint Research Centre (JRC)* the European Commission's science and knowledge service: Sevilla, Spain, 2020.

[3]   N. Bešinović, L. De Donato, F. Flammini, R. Goverde, Z. Lin, R. Liu, S. Marrone, R. Nardone, T. Tang, and V. Vittorini, "Artificial intelligence in railway transport: taxonomy, regulations and applications", *IEEE Trans. Intell. Transp. Syst.*, vol. 23, no. 9, pp. -15, 2021.
[http://dx.doi.org/10.1109/TITS.2021.3131637]

[4]   M. Bistron, and Z. Piotrowski, "Artificial intelligence applications in military systems and their influence on sense of security of citizens", *Electronics (Basel)*, vol. 10, no. 7, p. 871, 2021.
[http://dx.doi.org/10.3390/electronics10070871]

[5]   A. Asemi, and A. Asemi, *Artificial Intelligence (AI) application in Library Systems in Iran: A taxonomy study*. Library Philosophy and Practice, 2018, p. 2.

[6]   D. Beerbaum, and J.M. Puaschunder, "A behavioral approach to irrational exuberances–an artificial intelligence roboethics taxonomy", *Scientia Moralitas-International Journal of Multidisciplinary Research*, vol. 4, no. 1, pp. 1-30, 2019.

[7]   D. Lee, and S.N. Yoon, "Application of artificial intelligence-based technologies in the healthcare industry: opportunities and challenges", *Int. J. Environ. Res. Public Health*, vol. 18, no. 1, p. 271, 2021.
[http://dx.doi.org/10.3390/ijerph18010271] [PMID: 33401373]

[8]   S. Pandya, A. Thakur, S. Saxena, N. Jassal, C. Patel, K. Modi, P. Shah, R. Joshi, S. Gonge, K. Kadam, and P. Kadam, "A Study of the recent trends of immunology: key challenges, domains, applications, datasets, and future directions", *Sensors (Basel)*, vol. 21, no. 23, p. 7786, 2021.
[http://dx.doi.org/10.3390/s21237786] [PMID: 34883787]

[9]   S. Natale, "If software is narrative: Joseph Weizenbaum, artificial intelligence and the biographies of ELIZA,", *new media & society*, vol. 21, no. 3, pp. 712-728, 2019.

[10]   A. Kirsch, "Shakey ever after? questioning tacit assumptions in robotics and artificial intelligence", *KI - Künstliche Intelligenz*, vol. 33, no. 4, pp. 423-428, 2019.
[http://dx.doi.org/10.1007/s13218-019-00626-w]

[11]   G. Freiherr, *The seeds of artificial intelligence: SUMEX-AIM*. US Department of Health, Education, and Welfare, Public Health Service, National Institutes of Health, 1980.

[12]   C.A. Kulikowski, and S.M. Weiss, Representation of expert knowledge for consultation: the casnet and expert projects.*Artificial Intelligence in Medicine*. Routledge: New York, 2019, pp. 21-55.
[http://dx.doi.org/10.4324/9780429052071-2]

[13]   E. Shortliffe, *Computer-based medical consultations: MYCIN*. vol. 2. Elsevier: new york, 2012.

[14]   W. Van Melle, E.H. Shortliffe, and B.G. Buchanan, EMYCIN: A knowledge engineer's tool for constructing rule-based expert systems.*In: Rule-based expert systems: The MYCIN experiments of the Stanford Heuristic Programming Project*. Maidenhead, Berkshire: U.K Pergamon-lnfotech state, 1984, pp. 302-313.

[15]   R.C. Parker, and R.A. Miller, Using causal knowledge to create simulated patient cases: CPCS Project as an extension of INTERNIST-1.*Selected topics in medical artificial intelligence*. Springer: New York, 1988, pp. 99-115.
[http://dx.doi.org/10.1007/978-1-4613-8777-0_8]

[16]　P.L. Elkin, M. Liebow, B.A. Bauer, S. Chaliki, D. Wahner-Roedler, J. Bundrick, M. Lee, S.H. Brown, D. Froehling, K. Bailey, K. Famiglietti, R. Kim, E. Hoffer, M. Feldman, and G.O. Barnett, "The introduction of a diagnostic decision support system (DXplain™) into the workflow of a teaching hospital service can decrease the cost of service for diagnostically challenging diagnostic related groups (DRGs)", *Int. J. Med. Inform.,* vol. 79, no. 11, pp. 772-777, 2010.
[http://dx.doi.org/10.1016/j.ijmedinf.2010.09.004] [PMID: 20951080]

[17]　D. Ferrucci, E. Brown, J. Chu-Carroll, J. Fan, D. Gondek, A.A. Kalyanpur, A. Lally, J.W. Murdock, E. Nyberg, J. Prager, N. Schlaefer, and C. Welty, "Building watson: an overview of the deepQA project", *AI Mag.,* vol. 31, no. 3, pp. 59-79, 2010.
[http://dx.doi.org/10.1609/aimag.v31i3.2303]

[18]　M. M. R. P. Ltd*Global internet of things (iot) in healthcare market forecast 2018-2026* Maximize market research pvt. ltd.: Pune, Maharashtra, India., 2018.

[19]　J. Knox, W. Yu, and M. Gallagher, *Artificial intelligence and inclusive education.* Springer: Singapore, 2019.
[http://dx.doi.org/10.1007/978-981-13-8161-4]

[20]　Y. Dai, C.S. Chai, P.Y. Lin, M.S.Y. Jong, Y. Guo, and J. Qin, "Promoting students' well-being by developing their readiness for the artificial intelligence age", *Sustainability (Basel),* vol. 12, no. 16, p. 6597, 2020.
[http://dx.doi.org/10.3390/su12166597]

[21]　P. Hager, "Recognition of informal learning: challenges and issues", *J. Vocat. Educ. Train.,* vol. 50, no. 4, pp. 521-535, 1998.
[http://dx.doi.org/10.1080/13636829800200070]

[22]　N. Matsuda, E. Yarzebinski, V. Keiser, R. Raizada, G.J. Stylianides, W.W. Cohen, and K.R. Koedinger, "Learning by teaching SimStudent–An initial classroom baseline study comparing with Cognitive Tutor", *International Conference on Artificial Intelligence in Education,* 2011 Christchurch, New Zealand
[http://dx.doi.org/10.1007/978-3-642-21869-9_29]

[23]　E.G. Blanchard, "Socio-cultural imbalances in AIED research: Investigations, implications and opportunities", *Int. J. Artif. Intell. Educ.,* vol. 25, no. 2, pp. 204-228, 2015.
[http://dx.doi.org/10.1007/s40593-014-0027-7]

[24]　L. Fischer, L. Ehrlinger, V. Geist, R. Ramler, F. Sobiezky, W. Zellinger, D. Brunner, M. Kumar, and B. Moser, "AI system engineering—key challenges and lessons learned", *Machine Learning and Knowledge Extraction,* vol. 3, no. 1, pp. 56-83, 2020.
[http://dx.doi.org/10.3390/make3010004]

[25]　B. Akay, and D. Karaboga, "Artificial bee colony algorithm for large-scale problems and engineering design optimization", *J. Intell. Manuf.,* vol. 23, no. 4, pp. 1001-1014, 2012.
[http://dx.doi.org/10.1007/s10845-010-0393-4]

[26]　J.E. Bell, and P.R. McMullen, "Ant colony optimization techniques for the vehicle routing problem", *Adv. Eng. Inform.,* vol. 18, no. 1, pp. 41-48, 2004.
[http://dx.doi.org/10.1016/j.aei.2004.07.001]

[27]　C.S. Krishnamoorthy, and S. Rajeev, *Artificial intelligence and expert systems for artificial intelligence engineers.* CRC press: Boca Raton, Florida, 2018.

[28]　M. M. R. P. Ltd*oT in Automotive Market – Global Industry Analysis and Forecast (2022-2029)* Maximize market research pvt. ltd.: Pune, Maharashtra, India., 2019.

[29]　M. Tanveer, S. Hassan, and A. Bhaumik, "Academic policy regarding sustainability and artificial intelligence (AI)", *Sustainability (Basel),* vol. 12, no. 22, p. 9435, 2020.
[http://dx.doi.org/10.3390/su12229435]

[30]　M.J. Rigby, "Ethical dimensions of using artificial intelligence in health care", *AMA J. Ethics,* vol. 21,

no. 2, pp. E121-E124, 2019.
[http://dx.doi.org/10.1001/amajethics.2019.121]

[31]   J. Li, and J.S. Huang, "Dimensions of artificial intelligence anxiety based on the integrated fear acquisition theory", *Technol. Soc.,* vol. 63, p. 101410, 2020.
[http://dx.doi.org/10.1016/j.techsoc.2020.101410]

[32]   A.B. Brendel, M. Mirbabaie, T.B. Lembcke, and L. Hofeditz, "Ethical management of artificial intelligence", *Sustainability (Basel),* vol. 13, no. 4, p. 1974, 2021.
[http://dx.doi.org/10.3390/su13041974]

[33]   Z.M. Yaseen, Z.H. Ali, S.Q. Salih, and N. Al-Ansari, "Prediction of risk delay in construction projects using a hybrid artificial intelligence model", *Sustainability (Basel),* vol. 12, no. 4, p. 1514, 2020.
[http://dx.doi.org/10.3390/su12041514]

[34]   R. Mittu, D. Sofge, A. Wagner, and W.F. Lawless, *Robust intelligence and trust in autonomous systems.* Springer: US, 2016.
[http://dx.doi.org/10.1007/978-1-4899-7668-0]

[35]   D. Patterson, *Introduction to artificial intelligence and expert systems.* Prentice-Hall, Inc.: Hoboken, New Jersey, 1990.

[36]   S. Esakimuthu Pandarakone, Y. Mizuno, and H. Nakamura, "A Comparative study between machine learning algorithm and artificial intelligence neural network in detecting minor bearing fault of induction motors", *Energies,* vol. 12, no. 11, p. 2105, 2019.
[http://dx.doi.org/10.3390/en12112105]

[37]   A.V.D.L. Gardner, *An artificial intelligence approach to legal reasoning.* MIT press: Cambridge, Massachusetts, 1987.

[38]   W. Villegas-Ch, A. Arias-Navarrete, and X. Palacios-Pacheco, "Proposal of an architecture for the integration of a chatbot with artificial intelligence in a smart campus for the improvement of learning", *Sustainability (Basel),* vol. 12, no. 4, p. 1500, 2020.
[http://dx.doi.org/10.3390/su12041500]

[39]   S. Fuentes, C. Gonzalez Viejo, B. Cullen, E. Tongson, S.S. Chauhan, and F.R. Dunshea, "Artificial intelligence applied to a robotic dairy farm to model milk productivity and quality based on cow data and daily environmental parameters", *Sensors (Basel),* vol. 20, no. 10, p. 2975, 2020.
[http://dx.doi.org/10.3390/s20102975] [PMID: 32456339]

[40]   L. Munkhdalai, T. Munkhdalai, O.E. Namsrai, J. Lee, and K. Ryu, "An empirical comparison of machine-learning methods on bank client credit assessments", *Sustainability (Basel),* vol. 11, no. 3, p. 699, 2019.
[http://dx.doi.org/10.3390/su11030699]

CHAPTER 2

Internet of Things (IoT) with AI

Abstract: The web of things and man-made brainpower are a couple of innovations that together structure, alluded to as Industry 4.0. These support points incorporate the modern web of things, information, and investigation, whereas the last option can incorporate synthetic intelligence and its techniques. Artificial intelligence is the cycle of creating clever machines and performing assignments of human knowledge, for example, direction, discourse acknowledgment, *etc*. This cycle has to think and be capable of self-remedy. Learning is the securing of data and rules for employing the information; thinking is rules to arrive at rough or distinct resolutions. AI is utilized in different areas of trend-setting innovations, for example, blockchain thinking, decentralized AI, the intellectual prowess of things, machines, *etc*. Coordination of AI and IoT gives the best approach to gathering the data, examining it, and observing the proper realization of utilized for applications like medical care, home, shrewd cultivating, and astute vehicles. This chapter explains the architecture, applications, use cases, challenges and open issues of the integration.

Keywords: AI-IoT integration, Applications, Communication networks, IoT.

2.1. INTRODUCTION

The Internet of Things may integrate the natural world and computer communication networks more efficiently [1, 2]. As a result, applications like infrastructure management and environmental monitoring make privacy and security measures essential for upcoming IoT systems. The Internet of Things [3] can be defined as connected things/objects in our surroundings that offer contextual services and seamless communication. IoT is more sophisticated and dynamic than the Internet because it involves many connections between machines and humans and between devices and other appliances. All intelligent systems capable of doing particular tasks without being specifically programmed to do so, are considered to be AI [4, 5, 6]. It is a versatile type of intelligence that can pick up new skills for various jobs. The IBM Institute for Business Value has noted the Internet's full potential. Fig. (**1**) represents the smart city scenario.

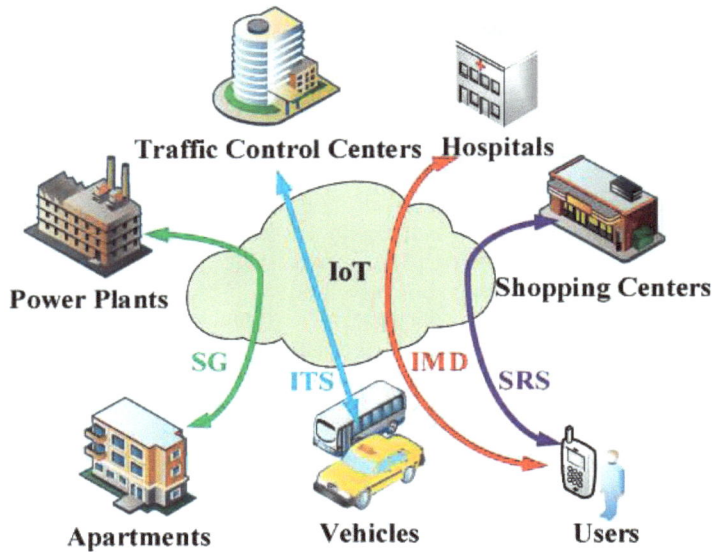

Fig. (1). Smart city Scenario [7].

2.2. ARCHITECTURE AND WORKING OF IOT-AI

The work [7] has three layers. The framework layer has shrewd gadgets. The IoT-got to the savvy gadget is the premise to develop the IoT. The brilliant widget has three distinct sorts: sensors, actuators, and cross-breed devices. The adminis-tration of the executive layer is answerable for gadget the board, information examination, and administration arrangement. It conveys to the Cloud [8] and the assistance region. It connects the client with the Cloud. The IoT stage is the available entry of the IoT for shrewd devices. These IoT stages control the got to gadgets and gather gadget information. The IoT stage has two related submodules. One submodule is conveyed around the brilliant gadgets to guarantee their admittance to the IoT, and it gives the passages. The other submodule gives the distant administration, information examination, and expanded services. The AI module contains five submodules- information investigation, client ID, conduct acknowledgment, administration development, and administration provision. The semantic examination module gives essential data of semantic examination for client distinguishing proof, conduct acknowledgment, and admi nistration development in the AI module. The asset arrangement layer contains asset suppliers in the scheme. Fig. (**2**) represents the same.

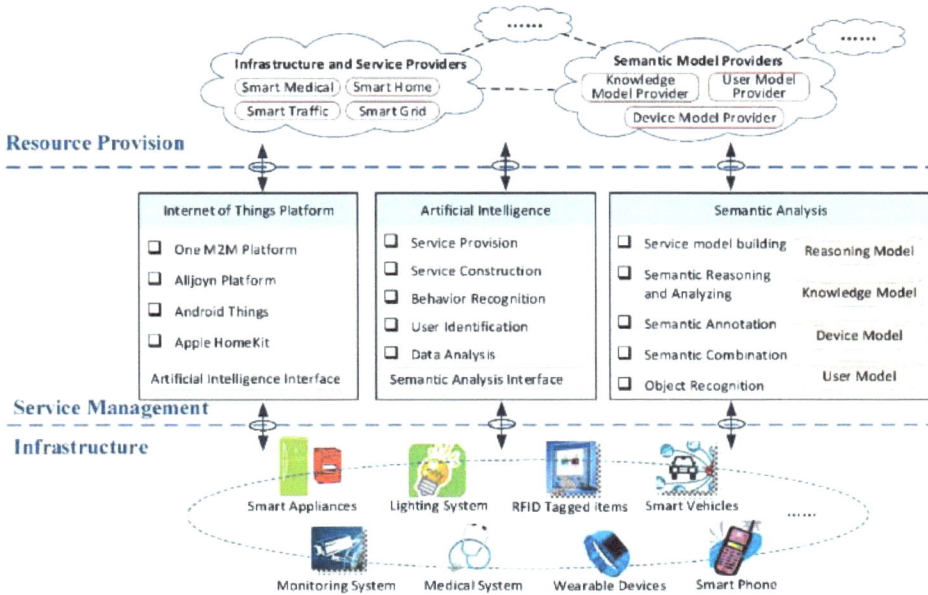

Fig. (2). AI-SIoT Architecture [7].

The proposed engineering [9] has four levels. Cloud Intelligence is the primary level of the proposed BlockIoTIntelligence Architecture of uniting Blockchain and AI for IoT where AI-empowered server farm is associated with one another with Blockchain. Artificial intelligence-empowered server farm dissects and handles the information starting with one hub and then onto the next hub in the framework. The second level of the proposed BlockIoTIntelligence Architecture combines blockchain and AI for IoT. Man-made intelligence empowers fog hubs with blockchain, where the fog hub shares the data with the next one of blockchain innovation. Computer-based intelligence and blockchain innovation-empowered base stations are utilized in the third level of decentralization and security to move the calculation to the edge layer. Correspondence is performed to various IoT gadgets with AI and blockchain applications to perform huge information examinations at the gadget layer and circulated blockchain networks.

The commanding device [10] is responsible for all application workload deployment, scheduling, and placement decision. It detects and manages changes to the state of deployed applications. It assigns the application to a chosen node depending on its need. The agent creates and starts an application pod on the worker and monitors the state of health of workers and all running pods to the leading node *via* the API server. The Container Engine Docker manages the life cycle of containers - getting the images, starting and stopping containers, *etc*. The dataset contains 54,303 healthy and unhealthy leaf images divided into 38 categories by species and disease.

The fundamental engineering [11] is a three-layer structure covered by an unavoidable security layer for the edge layer. CoAP-DTLS CoAP capacities as a kind of HTTP for obliged gadgets, empowering part-level hardware such as sensors or actuators to impart on the IoT, controlled and passed along their information. The convention has unwavering quality in low transfer speed and high clog through its low power draw and low organization upward. The engineering takes on firewalls, Network-based IDS components. Digital Threat Hunting relegates a mark as an irregularity or typical for the dubious way of behaving. An information channel handles information gathered in the various layers for taking care of the AI motors. The help-situated engineering should deal with the business movement and afterward give an appropriate convention for taking care of business methods. The framework has three fundamental parts the executive's server, MN door and end-client. The three parts are AI4SAFE engineering. The security modules apply in each layer.

In the primary phase [12] of the cycle, the system fabricates Artificial Intelligence. These models utilize AI calculations with a bunch of prepared information. It handles regular language reports or encoding human aptitude. The best models work with preparing information by handling an enormous corpus of archives. The expected handling limits access focal area, server farm, or cloud site. Utilizing a brought-together methodology, drones associated with catastrophe recuperation would send all their data back to the focal area for handling. Mental Processing Elements chains incorporate numerous components sequenced together to frame a more complicated program. In the Discover stage, a client will transfer preparing information, naming it, and testing different AI models. In the Deploy stage, the picked models are retrieved, serialized, and bundled as Docker holders stack into a store from which they can be gotten to by the edge components. In the Operate Phase, a miniature help running on the edge gadget is liable for starting up the stream and executing the related Docker compartment on the edge gadget upon demand by the client. The retraining stage catch data about the adequacy of the CPEs.

The principal part of the system [13] contains seven layers. The actual equipment and Storage layer comprise virtualized machines, devoted conventional capacity medium, distributed storage arrangements, *etc.*, focussing on three principal exercises arrangements. The network Layer contains every one of the various kinds of organization associations. The security Layer is liable for information security moved among divergent layers. Applications Layers assemble various applications connected with manageable horticulture. Web of Things and Sensing

Layer frame the association layer with SSA locations. SSA Domain Layer has different Smart Sustainable Architectural areas and structures as the fundamental source. The securing and catching of information happen at the layer (containing sensors and actuators). It trails by information characterization, changes of the broken down and handled information before it moves to information under-standing and the coming about building choices. The last stage is to store the information for future recovery.

The element extraction stage [14] completes with the stage WEKA. It contains AI and profound learning devices obtained through a Graphical User Interface, standard terminal applications, or a Java Application Programming Interface. It utilizes LSTM organizations to order the information. The models are prepared by employing back-spread.

The responsibility [15] comprises three normal vision-based picture handling and discourse-based sound enduring assignments emerging in many edge-based AI applications. The photograph grouping doles out a text mark to a photo given its items. Object discovery includes deciding all objects of interest available in the picture. It figures a jumping box around each such article and moves out a probabilistic mark to each object. Keyword spotting includes handling a sound stream to distinguish and perceive the event of catchphrases.

The system [16] first trains the unaided organization, using the spatial setting data to get highlights of articles from the large crude IoT information (in the cloud). The system is solo pre-preparing. Then, the extricated highlights move to execute an objective surmising network, such as item acknowledgment. The derivation network plays out the exchange learning in light of the solo organization. The precision of the induction network corresponds to the exactness (of the unaided network). The gadgets convey the edge-figuring hubs, which process information from various sensors.

The actual layer has a few gadgets, and their responsibility is to continually gather face picture information from the neighbourhood, particularly at the entry [17]. The most reduced layer is known as the gadget layer. It is an assortment of actual gadgets associated together to accomplish specific work allocated to them by the application layer through the edge layer. The edge layer is the foundation of the framework residing between the actual layer and the application layer and has computational units. It comprises cloud engineering having an application server and cloud data set, which persistently gets information from layer gadgets. The application layer is constrained by people for their expected positions.

Introductory access [18] is a method where clients start remote associations with a remote radio head structure. IoT client endeavours to begin the strategy and selects an irregular access asset, including a prelude and an actual arbitrary access channel, from an irregular access asset pool. IoT clients will send the arbitrarily chosen introduction on the haphazardly picked PRACH. IoT clients need to complete irregular access freely. The laying out associations with the radio head structure organizations and the cloud follows. Each IoT client has free brain organizations to perform profound support advancing exclusively.

The IoT gadgets [19] with the multiple jobs of the two-information assortment information pre-handling layout is a versatile edge processing layer. It has three layers. The top layer is the modern distributed computing stages adjusted to help the scope of IIoT applications. The centre layer is the edge passage accountable for overseeing information assortment processes from edge gateways and adjusting systems administration, figuring, and capacity assets. The base layer comprises edge servers. The IoT gadgets are versatile and vehicular organizations might encounter changing organizational conditions and the nature of administration while getting across edge servers.

The proposed CIoT-Net design [20] depends on five layers. The Smart City stage comprises many sub-layers. The information created here is both organized and unstructured information. Brilliant homes and structures give knowledge gathered from sensors that incorporate numerous human perspectives like feelings, voice, and cerebrum action. The IoT layer portrays the data from sensors set in various gadgets. These sensors give beginning information to the mental processing calculation and continuous ongoing perspective on how sufficiently the hardware performs. The information layer indicates the information gathered from sensors concerning human movement. These are imperative for the plan of the mental figuring fuelled consciousness framework. The mental registering layer characterizes the interaction following the mind-to-figure estimation. This layer delivers a calculation given picked highlight determination which empowers customized arrangements in shrewd urban communities. The assistance layer talks about the different utilizations of mental processing. These incorporate the areas of Law, firefighting, police office, clinical consideration, independent vehicles, retail industry, and media industry.

Every User Equipment [21] executes at least one IoT administration that procures information from their current circumstance. The information handling offloads to Edge Data Centre. Edge Data Centre is situated at the edge of the organization. It is known as the Radio Access Network and has strong figuring capacities to work on the nature of calculation experience apparent by every User Equipment. Passageways go about as entryways and lay out remote correspondence channels between User Equipment and the Radio Access Network. User Equipment generally interfaces with their nearest Access Point. As User Equipment hubs can change their area, handovers start with one Access Point, then the next set off. Passage forwards information bundles sent by User Equipment to the Edge Data Centre through Point-to-Point optical fibre correspondence joins. The Internet Service Provider that possesses the Radio Access Network performs different organization the executives related assignments utilizing Core Network Functions.

The work proposes QoS-based energy and entropy streamlining calculation [22] during interactive media transmission in a savvy robotization framework over an AI-based 6G network. The proposed 6G-based layered engineering includes three fundamental layers, IoT gadgets, 6G-driven visionary layers, and independent frameworks. Layer 1 assumes a striking part in information assortment, examination, and assessment, with a safe association with layer 2 to accomplish a savvy. It is energy-effective, universal, consistent, top to bottom, holographic correspondence. Layer 3 is shaped by one and two tiers that are dependable, energy-proficient, and versatile frameworks. The mixed-media content is caught through a dish radio wire to put away in the servers and then moved to the video encoder to lessen overt repetitiveness. The encoded video moves to the AI-based 6G organizations regarding the base station. The server will inspect the information and forward it to the traffic connector, which will change the information traffic by focusing on the undertakings with fair asset assignment to the clients.

The rules [23] are characterized and divided among all hubs in the blockchain. It aims the network to control access and deal with this organization. Orders and the executive's norms need not be approved for all machines partaking in the organization. They are allowed to have a specific arrangement of believed systems having specialists. Diggers have likewise agreed on hubs in the organization and the main elements that have the position to make, authorize and incorporate new squares into the blockchain. Down-to-earth, Byzantine Fault Tolerance is the collective agreement convention for this kind of blockchain. Access and consent rules give an extra security layer to the proposed IoT organization. The gadgets are part of the blockchain network with confined specialists and control to limit information spillage from the IoT gadgets. The proposed approach depends on executing productive and complex AI modules to naturally identify presumptive exercises and safeguard all hubs partaking in the blockchain network. The information cleaning and handling methods are applied to the dataset to manage this issue during information addition and transport data into the data set. The strategy recognizes fragmented entries, irregular qualities, and missing elements.

Engineering [24] has three principle useful squares- end gadget, passage, and cloud. The registering abilities of end gadgets can be diverse. The connectivity deliberation layer is liable for interfacing widgets with an organization. The layer incorporates a solitary module called Connectivity SDK that stows away the hidden organization innovation and gives the normalized correspondence capacities for the upper layers. The device administrations layer characterizes administrations vital for every gadget to use its resources. The custom application tier serves a specific errand. It improves the upheld functionalities to have sufficient registering resources. The passage contains three principles of functionalities-network, end gadget for the executives, and information on the board.

The work [25] presents the plan of a coordinated testbed design that includes IoT and IIoT frameworks and gadgets of edge, fog, and cloud layers. It offers a dynamic testbed network and empowers the interchanges of the three layers. It produces heterogeneous datasets from different appropriated information sources. The datasets contain crude and handled information sources gathered from Telemetry datasets of IoT services. The testbed was planned in light of associating network and IoT/IIoT frameworks with the three layers of edge, fog, and stockpile portrayed underneath to mimic the sensible execution of late certifiable IoT/IIoT organizations. The information sources are sent from endpoints to an entryway, where they are then moved to hotspots for handling and return transmission at the fog level. An edge layer places knowledge, examination, and handling power in gadgets, such as installed robotization regulators and lightweight IoT devices. The Cloud layer incorporates the cloud administrations designed online in the testbed. Table **2.1** presents a List of implementation details of various contributions.

Table 2.1. List of implementation details of various contributions.

Contribution	Implementation Details
[9]	BlockDeepNet system is used to detect an object. PASCAL VOC 2012 dataset comprises 27,450 trainval cases, and 13841 approval occurrences of 20 item classes are utilized.
[7]	The item retires furnished with RFID perusers. The client utilizes the RFID card to enter the room. The forced air system is created by C++ in the control framework, and it can distinguish and control indoor temperature. The RFID peruser and the forced air system interface with the savvy door through WiFi. The semantic models are created by JSON.
[10]	The proposed edge engineering is interconnected gadgets made out of three parts. Three Nvidia Jetson Nano (472 GFLOPS) with 128-center CUDA Maxwell, a Quad-center ARM A57@1.43 GHz,4GB 64-bit LPDDR4@25.6 GB/s outfitted with an extra M.2 SSD through a connector M.2 Key-E to Mini PCI-E connector. Jetson Nano utilizes JetPack 4.3 containing (NVIDIA L4T1, TensorRT2, cuDNN3, CUDA4, OpenCV5) and is introduced on a ScanDisk Extreme 32GB Micro SDHC UHS-3. The point of Jetson Nano is to prepare AI models on gathered IoT information. It has four Odroid N2 incorporating a quad-center ARM Cortex-A73 CPU group and double center Cortex-A53 bunch, and another age Mali-G52 GPU that processes information on the Edge. It has an 8-port Gigabit Network Switch that oversees interchanges between all components of the heterogeneous group (Jetson Nano, Odroid N2). Kubernetes is an open-source holder organization stage that oversees containerized responsibilities and administrations at scale.

(Table 2.1) cont.....

Contribution	Implementation Details
[14]	The system uses the CICDDoS2019 dataset. Evaluation analysis is done with CICFlowMeter-V3.`
[15]	The system uses Pi3, x86 server-based nodes, and GPU-equipped x86 servers. For image classification and object detection, CAVIAR test case datasets are used. Four edge accelerator platforms used are Intel Movidius NCS2 VPU, Google Edge TPU, Nvidia Jetson Nano GPU, and Nvidia TX2 GPU.
[16]	NVIDIA Titan X is used to perform the training. FPGA is used.
[17]	Raspberry Pi device is used to collect image data. WIDER FACE dataset is a face detection benchmark dataset used. All these servers are Linux-based POSIX. SQLite is used as a database for faster retrieval of data and communication purposes.
[25]	The NSX vCloud NFV platform of Software Defined Network (SDN), Network Function Virtualization (NFV) and Service Orchestration (SO) was utilized at the IoT lab of the University of New South Wales (UNSW) at Canberra

2.3. APPLICATIONS OF IOT-AI

Man-made consciousness methods empower innovations in various applications of IoT situations. Computer-based intelligence is utilized for the purchaser. Other applications include modern IoT, industry 4.0, intelligent urban areas, savvy structures, clever homes, savvy transportation, medical services, natural checking, farming and brilliant grids.AI strategies are primarily applied to investigate server-side information gathered from IoT detectors. The rising accessibility of computational assets in IoT gadgets regularly handles multi-faceted signs utilizing AI-based techniques. Each IoT application involves explicit correspondence advancements and can embrace security assurance. Artificial intelligence strategies assume a significant part likewise for these parts of IoT.

2.3.1. Smart Transportations

Wise transportation [26] in a shrewd local area comprises two primary parts-intelligent traffic light administration and independent vehicles. A definitive objective of the thoughtful traffic light is to have a framework wherein automobiles, traffic signs, and control bases could divide the information between themselves to settle on an appropriate choice in an improved climate. Other significant prerequisites in the clever transportation framework [27] are wise traffic signs and savvy roads. In a brilliant city, all the traffic signs and the street offices can settle on choices in light of the information coming from the vehicles and the cameras covering every one of the streets and convergences.

The brilliant vehicle framework [28] requires numerous partners to speak with one another progressively for the smooth activity of the public vehicle system. The functionalities of the clever vehicle frameworks are checking standard support of transports, observing continuous traffic conditions, and finding traffic crises in accurate regions. Neighbourhood transport authority gathers the nearby traffic information from vehicles, side-of-the-road units, and different elements. It distributes meaningful information to a blockchain and sends accumulated data to territorial vehicle specialists. The upkeep group is the extraneous body that has a concurrence with the neighbourhood transport expert for the support of the public vehicle. They are liable for ordinary support. The provider is in concurrence with the support group and supplies the parts once requested. The territorial Transport Authority and State Transport Authority are the policymakers and administrative bodies and can get to the upkeep report from blockchain if necessary. Fig. (**3**) represents the same.

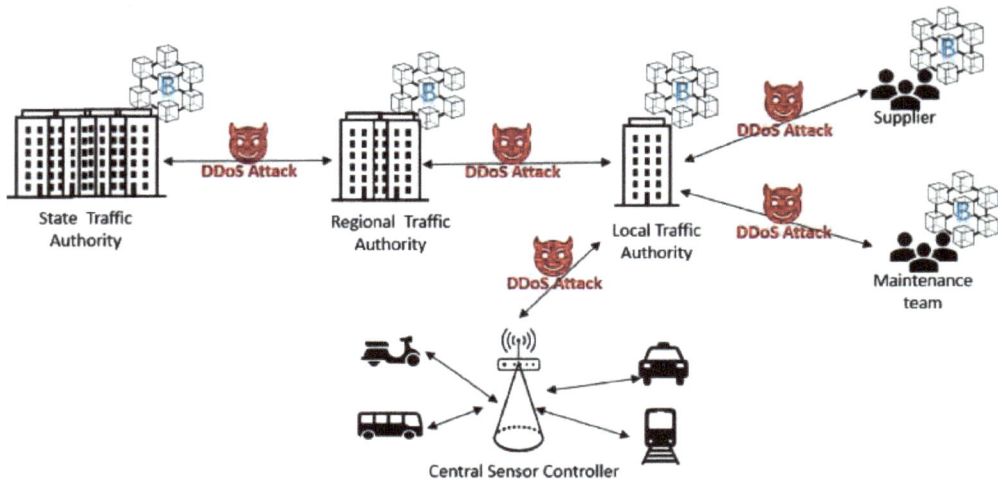

Fig. (3). Smart transportation Architecture [28].

A brain network [29] combines with the chosen input boundaries for a decent presentation of the savvy semaphores. The system is introduced in Bogotá. The work carries out brain networks as a type of control and expectation around the variety of the vehicular stream. Simultaneously the current traffic on the fundamental lane of Bogotá was analysed as a kind of perspective through internet-based traffic re-enactment programming called road traffic test system. It permits getting information for the brain network planned in MATLAB. Bogotá had 2,180,000 personal automobiles traveling on its roads, showing a chart of the development of private vehicles in the capital. A preparation was picked for 87% and approval information 13% of the data.

The framework [30] has two phases. In the preparation stage, the improved profound learning network can process a caught street IoT sensor picture without eliminating the commotion. The actual organization has a capacity that predicts the name worth of the info picture, as it previously had a self-growing experience from the past investigation. The data from the preparation are handled in the testing stage, and breaks are recognized by applying the bio-propelled profound learning organizations. A few dataset subtleties analyse the bio-roused learning-based break identification process (dataset description stage).

The recommendation [31] partitions into layers for data assortment, handling and direction. The first layer is the information layer. It is an information assortment layer from different sources like reconnaissance cameras, savvy traffic signals, GPS, RFID, and the Internet. The knowledge is gathered from divergent sources and put away for examination in the capacity tier. The details will be brought from the capacity layer and investigated utilizing various data scientific devices on equal or lattice registering climate in the investigation slab. The deduction is sent to the correspondence layer When the investigation finishes. The activity is for ongoing distributing utilizing different correspondence mediums like portable, radio, television, or web.

The proposed design [32] of IoT-empowered STSS has three layers. The upper and halfway layers are responsible for digital protection. The lower layer stresses on geospatial security of the board. The halfway layer is the instrument through which IoT-empowered networks span the control and standard frameworks of public infrastructural and geospatial plans. Online protection executives allude to the structure of components. It recognizes accidental dangers of end-client administrations, including digital assaults, security infringement, and data revelation. The third layer will apply spatial-transient effects on security at a full scale. It underlines the conversion of public foundations in working with transportation security and savvy correspondence advancements. It contains a bunch of geospatial factors that work synergistically with 5G-empowered foundations.

The gridlock likelihood [33] of an area is a typical traffic stream in each square region. The metropolitan transportation organization can be thought to be projected onto a 2-D Cartesian plane. SDN regulators can assemble measurable data about the gridlock likelihood esteem. The practical blockage is arranging strategy assuming the metropolitan traffic demands delay-touchy planning or navigation. In an SDN-empowered network, the regulators can procure the situation with the organization and finely grained change the size of the network square.

The framework [34] has camera hubs, IoT gadgets, cell information transmission modules, and an incorporated server. The general plan is the harmony between computational burden and information transmission volume. It has the unwavering quality and versatility of the framework. The changed SORT calculation is carried out on the server-side. Foundation-based inhabitancy identification and SSD-based discovery results are consolidated. There are two gatherings of pipelines in camera-based stopping inhabitancy location strategies. The paired inhabitancy classifiers decide the situation with each parking spot district in the camera view in the principal bunch. The (subsequent) gathering applies vehicle recognition to limit vehicles in the entire camera view and afterward decides the situation with parking spots in light of the matches of identification results and parking spot areas. This naming system has a little distinction between order and discovery concerning adaptability or responsibility in conventional server-based stopping recognition frameworks.

2.3.2. Industry 4.0

IoT is a term that alludes to any gadget with network access. Present-day gadgets of frameworks are furnished with sensors, programming, and organization gear. The organization hardware and these sensors are equipped for arranging and handling information clusters utilizing web conventions.5G colossally affects IoT innovation and the economy because of its predominant degree of network and further developed usefulness. The key 5G innovation drivers are superfast broadband and low idleness correspondence. It also has gigantic machine-type interchanges, high accessibility, and proficient energy use. The primary area of utilization of 5G-empowered IoT is merchandise and materials, resource checking, self-administration frameworks, remote assistance conveyance frameworks, *etc.*

Most current businesses use displaying and recreations for process observing, control, analysis, advancement, and plan. Industry 4.0 [35] and monstrous digitization have made it conceivable to gather and handle enormous varieties of information, improving information-driven choices and demonstrating apparatuses. Fig. (**4**) depicts the building block of Industry 4.0.

Industry 4.0 is the fourth modern unrest, which can satisfy modified prerequisites during the COVID-19 emergency [37]. The accessible advances of Industry 4.0 could likewise assist in the identification and determination of COVID-19 and other related issues and symptoms. Industry 4.0 plants have machines that are upheld by remote networks and sensors. These sensors are associated with a framework that can picture and screen the whole presentation line and likewise settle on its own choices. Industry 4.0 intends shrewd assembling processes of fundamental expendable things to satisfy the lack of the COVID-19 pandemic. It gives a brilliant inventory network of clinical disposables and hardware during this emergency by which the patients can get the expected fundamental clinical things.

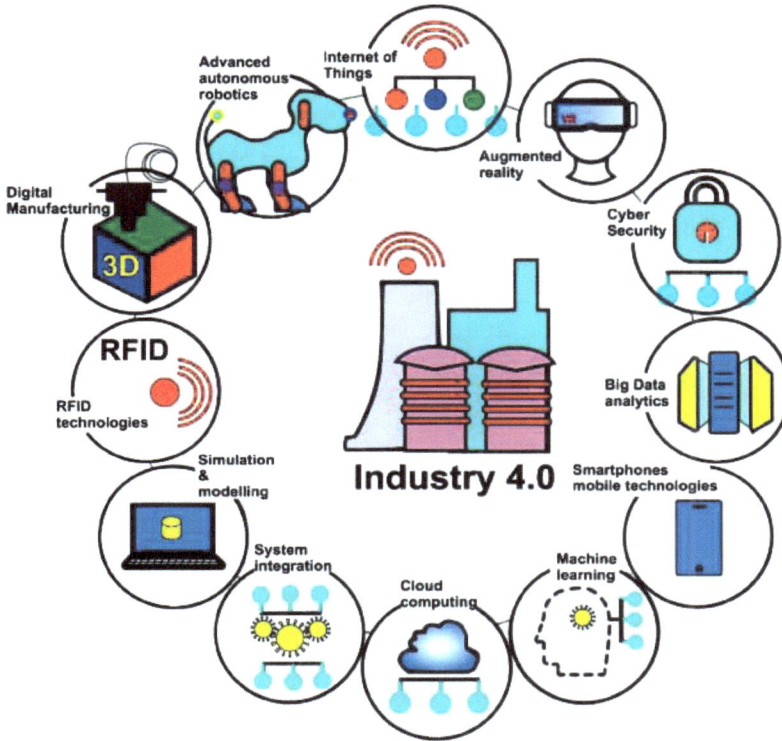

Fig. (4). Building block of Industry 4.0 [36].

The insightful structure [38] drives the most common way of intensifying information from existing store network models and adjusting the total discoveries to the idea of supply chains in Industry 4.0. The holes and main elements in current innovative patterns for I4.0 production network configuration coordinate IIoT standards obtained from the ordered review. The contextual analysis configuration thinks about individual issues received from the writing with the mechanical practices in the industry today. The relative investigation includes the five driving I4.0 drives and innovative patterns. The Défense for choosing the particular I4.0 drives was their lavishness of exhaustively and unequivocally expressed methodologies. The contextual investigation research at first surveyed 15 drives.

The work [39] utilizes URL-based highlights to browse for an email's authenticity. The proposal partitions the approaching traffic into little bunches.

The primary clump is a preparation dataset, and the other groups are the premise of past clusters. The standard report portrayal utilized in text characterization is the vector space model. An assortment of reports addresses a bunch of archive vectors. The principal phase of the approach characterizes the approaching traffic into authentic and dubious messages. It separates elements from approaching messages and makes a component vector for each example. The work involves a progressive grouping calculation for bunching the messages. The classifier utilizes the marks by preparing information, and it gives two classes specifically, ham and spam thus. The ham messages are isolated, and spam messages are taken to the following stage of the order. For the second level of strategy, the initial step again is the choice of the most plausible highlights for phishing email detection. The arrangement of the next approaching clumps likewise integrates the results from the past bunches to work on the exactness.

The overhauling and change of existing SME fabricating [40] include plan, acquirement, creation, operations, deals, authoritative administration, and venture methodology. It includes viewpoints like modern chain cooperation. The assembling ventures have two fundamental frameworks. It creates and manages the architecture overseen by MES and undertakes asset arranging (ERP). It has five layers-gear layers, creation line layer, studio layer, venture layer, and modern layer. The redesigning and modification of assembling use shrewd assembling innovations to finish updating and change at some or all levels and understanding the keen assembling interaction and the executives. The reconciliation of the gear layer and the control layer of fabricating endeavours needs the help of new technology. An efficient data stream can speed up item design, production, deals, promotion, and venture activity, and what's more, the executives. The clients are nearer to the maker of innovations like the Internet, dexterous assembling and administration, and the client to manufactory mode. The composition digitization makes the creation process more straightforward and works on the process checking.

While deciding the impact of the action on the utilization of human insight and AI on the productivity of the exercises of social business venture, the technique [41] for relationship investigation is utilized in this work. The association between the signs of personal satisfaction is determined by Numbeo. The rationale of the examination comprises deciding the distinctions in the irrelevance of human and fake scholarly funds for the arrangement of development of personal satisfaction today. The impact of the marks of the degree of improvement of human and counterfeit capital on every sign of personal satisfaction will be more grounded, assuming the pessimistic worth of the connection coefficients is low. The work is a review showcasing preparation and interest in these bearings among every closely involved individual: social business visionaries, representatives of organizations, and customers of their labour and products. The extraordinary structures for each different class involve individuals. The accompanying six viewpoint bearings of the utilization of AI in friendly business are recognized. First heading: automatization of promoting studies. The use of AI is a speedy and exact division of the business sectors of social labour and products and assurance of the place of a social organization in these business sectors, viewpoints of advancement. Computer-based intelligence decides changes in the requirements and inclinations of customers. The second course is the automatization of the advancement of social labour and products. It promotes informal organizations or messages in versatile applications. The third course is the automatization of an assortment of social merchandise and services. The fourth bearing is the automatization of the passion for ventures. The fifth heading is the automatization of the fascination of representatives and volunteers. The sixth course is automatization of the creation of social labour and products.

The design structure [42] makes direct proposals for components by incorporating best practices from the observational study. It coordinates gathering methods from scholarly reports on the CPS combination structure, with functional drives from observational examinations and strategies with a flowing system that relates reasoning to CPS advancements. An ordered gathering of future and present procedures is with the current various leveled flowing plan. The contention for this interaction is a fake perception in CPS. The main phase of the study distinguishes the connected components and standards from scholarly writing. These are gathered and joined with present and future difficulties from the late report. In the subsequent stage, the progressive flowing interaction forms using pragmatic drives. There is a reflection on the information that an inventory network view is vital for acquiring the business 4.0 qualities associating the need to initially coordinate socially into the business 4.0 idea before the inventory network digitizes and the execution stages. The mental input instrument provides a legitimate arrangement incorporating the NRS centre advancements. It details the reconciliation of AI and robotized conduct in the NFI key innovations list.

The work [43] joins the IoT and blockchain with cutting-edge profound learning. It is a model of repetitive brain network calculations. It figures the market interest of food, involving long memory and gated intermittent units as an expectation model and the Genetic Algorithm streamlining mutually to enhance the boundaries of the mixture model. The proposed framework lays out a blockchain-based advanced record for every food item. The clients can rapidly find out about creation data, quality data, market data, cost data, and so forth through the framework. The blockchain records the beginning, exchange time, and examination and quarantine data of every item that enters the market. The end client has to enter the number of exchanges or sweep the standardized tag, and they will want to follow the beginning of the food. According to this framework, every one of the partners can utilize their cell phones to include knowledge into this framework. It gathers information from IoT gadgets without the intercession of some other individual. The rancher can make faculty documents and obligation record records for each segment. They can involve shrewd agreements and occasion notice capacities for upper and lower cut-off points of stock data. The subsequent member is the handling unit of the stockroom in the creation and handling join, the information recognized by the ear tag in the rearing unit moving to the innovation and handling unit. The handling unit is answerable for the data concerning various hubs of the creation and handling, which is gathered agreeing to the administration norms and details and particularly distinguished through the standardized identifications. The information moves to the conveyance unit. The dissemination unit is liable for moving resources for the retailers. This data is composed on the bed of the conveyed merchandise or the standardized tag of the bundling box as per the predefined guidelines of the beginning, amount, quality, grade, *etc*. The scanner tag framework can give point-by-point information to the genuine products in the inventory network and layout an actual association between the items and their total personality. Fig. (**5**) depicts the same.

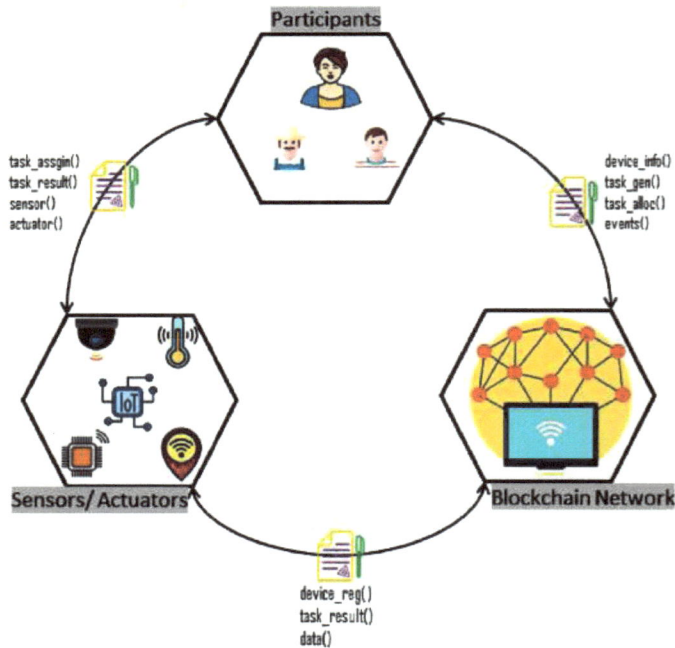

Fig. (5). Structure of IoT with Blockchain [43].

The philosophy is an advancement of the development model [44]. Stage 1 is the blend of meanings of the extension. It arranges the outside outskirts for the application and use of the model. The characterized interest group is scholastic analysts, organizations engaged with change, and experts that need to be aware of industry 4.0 abilities and development levels. Stage 2 comprises the appreciation of the ideal interest group's necessities. In the third stage, the model is compounded and approved, pondering the exercises of the idea and populace of its substance. It distinguishes the estimation in the development assessment and how it tends to be measured. Stage 4 is the test stage of confirming its sufficiency of structure. Stage 5 is sending. After the model is approved, it is into testing by its crowd. It may be accessible for use. Stage 6 is the support of the development model that is affected by the assets required for its refreshing and usage over the long haul. The proposed model has four key components the aspects, the change abilities, the development levels, and the estimation instrument. Table **2.2** portrays the implementation details of various contributions.

Table 2.2. Portrays the implementation details of various contributions.

Contribution	Implementation Details
[39]	• Spam detection stage was tested using four classification algorithms - Naïve Bayes, SMO, Random Forest. • The work selected 5 features for suspicious and legitimate email classification. • The initial dataset into eight batches of about 1000 emails.
[41]	• The highest quality of population's life is peculiar for Denmark (196.47 points) and Switzerland (195.06 points). • Correlation between the health care index and the level of development of human intellectual capital is high (-0.69). • Correlation between the cost of life index and the level of development of human intellectual capital is moderate (-0.22). • Correlation between the cost of life index and the level of development of artificial intellectual capital is high (-0.63). • Correlation between the climate index and the level of development of human intellectual capital is moderate (-0.23). • Correlation between the level of development of artificial intellectual capital (-0.27).
[43]	• Uses BCT Network Cloud Platform. • Uses byzantine fault tolerance (iPBFT) algorithm. • Use food trading system with consortium blockchain (FTSCON).
[44]	• The proposed maturity model has 41 variables. • Each dimension and each transformation capability are evaluated in six levels of maturity (from level 0 to level 5). • The analysed model 1 and model 3 have six levels of maturity and model 2 has five levels.
[32]	• The system uses GB/T 33356-2016 national standard system. • It uses ArcGIS is a geographic information system (GIS) tool.

2.3.3. Healthcare Applications

Wearable gadgets [45] and the availability between these gadgets and PCs are crucial ideas behind the innovative changes in medical services. IoT is a bunch of advancements that empower objects - ordinary buyer items or modern machines - to associate with each other and with the web, impart information about their properties, and give instant information investigation and savvy activity. IoT makes esteem in all ventures through an assembly of the modern, purchaser, and public area applications. The ascent of IoT has brought about the reappearance of AI, an assortment of innovations and frameworks ready to detect their climate, think, learn, and make a move. IoT assumes a critical part in gathering and checking facts. AI is answerable for examining the developing measures of details and making a move given what it gains from the information. These innovations can assist medical services associations with taking advantage of the capability of the capability of an undeniably interconnected and responsive world.

IoT-CPS applications incorporate components that speak with confounded actual environmental factors. Such an incorporated encompassing is a requesting revelation that could change existing endeavours. The structure [46] works on the Quality of Life of a more seasoned individual whose child is in the workplace during the daytime and recoveries clinical expenses. The day-to-day physical and clinical data of a more seasoned grown-up is gathered and put away in an outsider cloud using an in-home WSN-Cloud Gateway. The child in the workplace and emergency clinic specialists can routinely look at such clinical records and apply AI to identify sicknesses and give a few ideas and remedies utilizing a wired or remote association with the cloud in a verified manner. In a pressing circum-stance, such emanant data will be sent instantly to both the specialists and their relatives with the goal that quick moves can initiate to help the fallen elder. The security and confidence in connected gadgets are two issues for the acknowledgment of IoT-CPS. The calculation takes Patient Disease Testing Data from patients' or older people's wearable gadgets and characterization rules. This calculation separates all property estimations from the got information. It contrasts characteristic qualities and arrangement runs and figures out what choice it should take. Fig. (6) depicts the same.

The wearable sensor [47] is practically any part of the human body. The sensor recognizes and forecasts illnesses in human beings. The patient data is gathered, for example, segment information, attributes of the malignant growth analysis, heart illnesses, diabetes, and pulse. They answer physiological signs, body developments, and natural substances. Information is a pipeline of progressive advances like information pre-processing and knowledge investigation. A unique beacon from the loud signal is recuperating in the pre-handling unit. The recurrence and time-space are investigated. Highlight extraction extricates the component by utilizing the optimality rule. The data of infections information acquire the very much resolved the illnesses data set to get a better investigation of navigation.

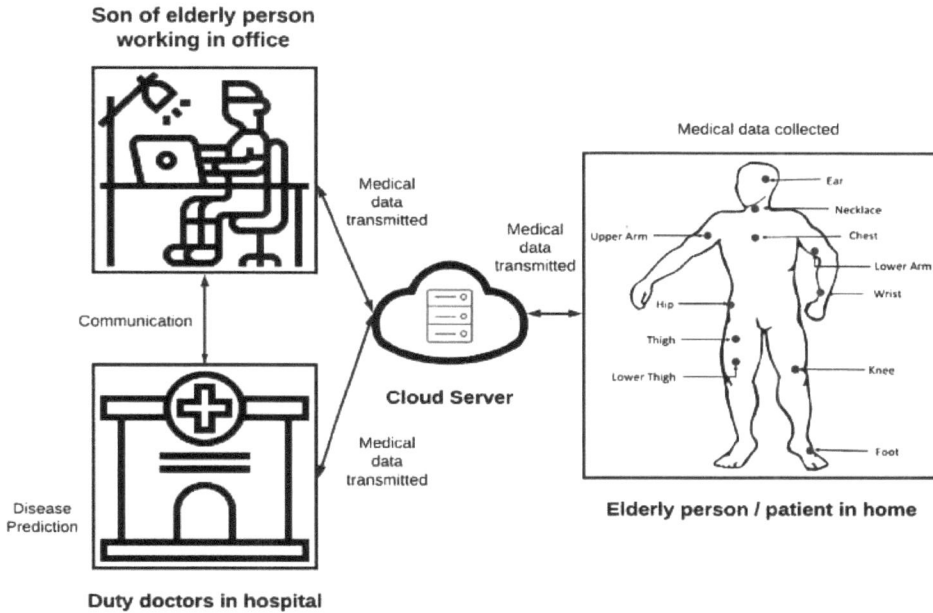

Fig. (6). AI-enabled IoT-CPS [46].

The work [48] utilizes six purposes - Blockchain, IoT, AI, Drone, Robot, and auto-sterilization. Disinfection can be performed through a GPS-IoT-AI-empo-wered drone framework with no human intercession. The robotized robot can deal with the everyday requirements of patients in clinics. Reception of these innovations will decrease the mediation of HCWs. It lessens the possibilities of contamination. The transitory testing community is in a far-off area with appropriate assets and improved transportation organizations. Improvement of IoT-empowered computerized management instruments and Dieses the executive's device expects to give on the web and disconnected geo-following administrations. The client-server model allows access while incorporating stock administration devices with continuous information access. It apportions the assets for productive coordination, mechanical development, diminishing defilement, and asset double-dealing. Table **2.3** represents the implementation details of various contributions.

Table 2.3. Represents the implementation details of various contributions.

Contribution	Implementation Details
[47]	The work uses Generalized Approximate reasoning-based Intelligence Control (GARIC) implement a neuro-fuzzy system. Methodologies are executed in MATLAB version 2018.
[46]	Fourteen volunteers do standardized movements, including 20 voluntary falls and 16 daily life activities (ADL), resulting in a huge dataset with 2520 trials.

2.3.4. Environmental Monitoring

IoT is a robust worldwide organization framework with self-designing capacities in light of standard and interoperable correspondence conventions, where physical and virtual "things" have characters, actual traits, and virtual characters and utilize sharp connection points. They flawlessly coordinate in the data organization. IoT can see, think, and control the world by gathering, handling, and breaking down information.

IoT-based marine climate checking and insurance framework [49] have five layers. The discernment and execution layer are the base layer of the design. It incorporates sensor and actuator gadgets with the goal of sensor information assortment and order invitation. In IoT-based marine climate observing and security frameworks, this layer includes GPS sensors, energy reaping devices, standard water conditions, and quality checking sensors. The information transmission layer sends the different gathered information to the information handling layer using correspondence organizations, generally versatile or remote correspondence organizations. The pre-handling information layer is in the IoT framework engineering, where the crude information can be put away and pre-handled utilizing progressed information mining advancements. Depending on the situation, it also finishes data accumulation or disaggregation, information cleaning, fitting or screening, and sharing. Sometimes, it triggers cautions or alerts because of pre-characterized rules. The application layer offers types of assistance as indicated by various applications mentioned by clients. The business layer is the top layer and deals with the general IoT framework exercises and administrations, including making plans of action, business rationale flowcharts, and realistic portrayals per the application layer's information. It likewise screens and checks the results of the other four layers per the plans of action to upgrade benefits and keep up with the client's security. Fig. (7) represents the same.

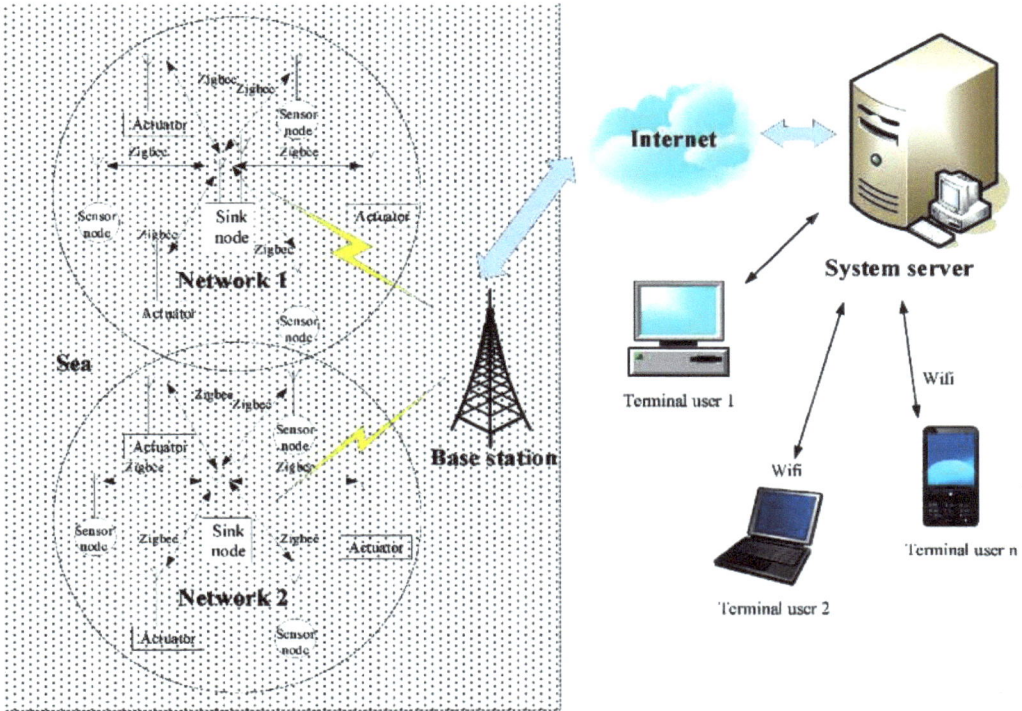

Fig. (7). IoT-based marine environment [49].

The proposition [50] is a model of workspace observing in savvy producing, in light of arising remote sensor advances and the message lining telemetry transport convention. It is a five-layer design. The information assortment layer is answerable for detecting, securing, and handling information. The organization and correspondence layer is responsible for the start-to-finish availability of the wellbeing checking applications. The information handling layer is answerable for necessary computations and accurate estimations on totaled information. The board layer is liable for managing results and results of information handling. The administration layer is responsible for end-client availability for clinics, crisis divisions, ambulances, police headquarters, and insurance agencies. The framework execution empowered checking states of being in the workspace and the state of being boundaries of assembling laborers. The assessment of the proposed framework was produced using the point of view of protection and pay for gathering laborers. The execution results uncovered that the proposed engineering added to further developing wellbeing checking and specialist wellbeing in antagonistic working circumstances. Fig. (8) depicts the same.

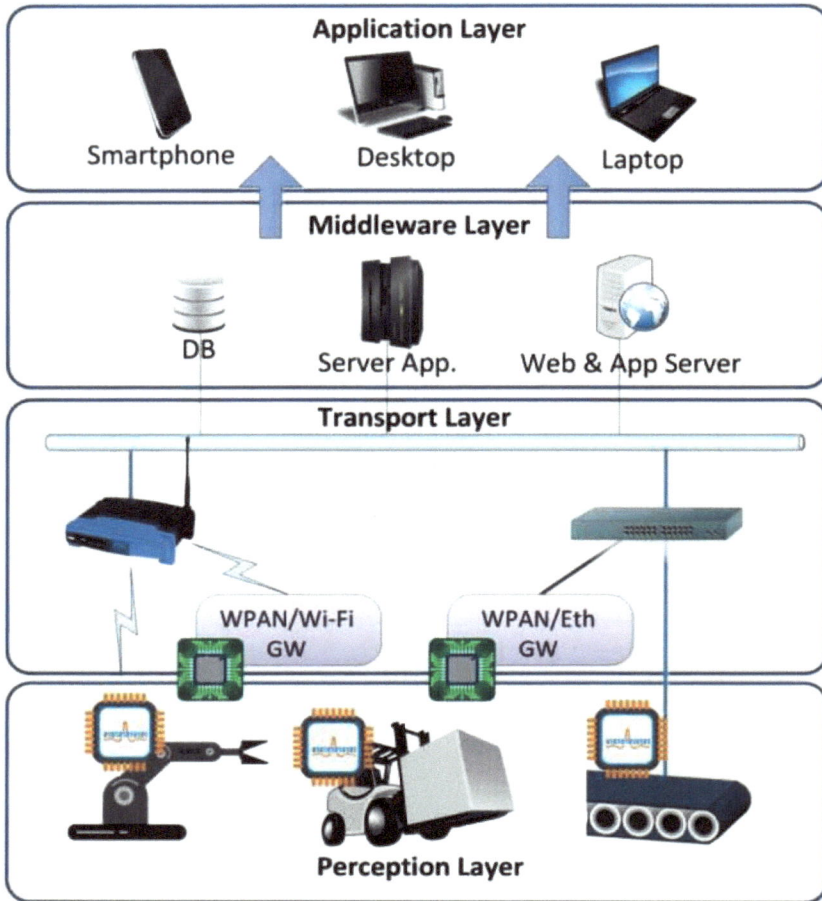

Fig. (8). Five-layered architecture [50].

The strength of soil, dampness investigation, tainting water level, water amount level, and a few different variables are fundamental in acquiring reasonable efficiency in the agribusiness area. The savvy horticulture checking framework [51] incorporates every such variable, controlled and observed with the assistance of IoT gadgets, affordable sensors catching the farming information, then communicated to the cloud through a WSN. The work utilizes a relapse model of the third degree and gives an expectation precision of 98%. The yield quality evaluation uses SAR information to screen paddy rice quality. Support vector machines with back-dissipating highlights assessment of the rice quality, with a restricted example size. Leaf region and aspect likewise assume a fundamental part in the appraisal of different sorts of yields to decide whether the development is palatable. It estimates the leaf region record involving SVM as the AI strategy with a Gaussian cycle model, and the estimation exactness is viewed as 89% with a restricted example size likewise for this situation. A specialist framework utilizing AI uses the Naive Bayes strategy and AI, which works on sensor information caught in agribusiness. This work helped check the nature of compost, pesticides, and how much water flooded in the harvests. The ecological circumstances influence the strength of yields. The elements engaged with farming, for example, soil condition, dampness condition, water contamination, air quality, temperature, and so on, have been thought about while evaluating the advances in brilliant climate observing techniques.

The proposed work [52] is separated principally into two expansive classes. First is getting the sensor information from the sensor hub utilized at the information transmission end and transferring every sensor worth to thingspeak to screen it for additional assessment. Besides, in the wake of getting sensor information values, using it for breaking down the crop yield creation will have the high ground from now on the expectation of harvest creation. The client characterized the site to screen the subtleties. The dampness content of the dirt is estimated with the utilization of a cathode manufactured. A chip is likewise manufactured inside it to switch the adjustment of opposition to some simple voltage completely. The datasets were gathered from the recently detected esteem from the sensors utilized at the perception site.

The work [53] is the insightful framework for water quality grouping utilizing the Pollution Index strategy. Actual Devices and Controllers are the hubs furnished with water quality sensors dissipated at a few focuses along the stream that goes through the city of Surabaya. It has six-point seats dispersed along the creek and recovers information from the sensors every 5 seconds. The information correspondence convention utilizes MQTT. The sensor hubs will go about as MQTT distributors who send the information to the MQTT broker. The 4G modem interface between the implanted framework and the server. The cycle of information acknowledgment in the server utilizes an MQTT representative by Mosquitto. The water information is drunk/bought in from Kafka Broker, so there is a system for directly conveying information from MQTT Agent to Kafka Broker. The proposed framework comprises three stages. Growing experience portrays the structure of the arrangement model utilized in the framework. The constant arrangement depicts the composition of continuous investigation. Continuous perception represents the continual representation process toward the front web client interface.

The framework [54] portrayed improves water usage based on plant's water need rather than cultivator's presumptions by chipping away at static information, for example, plant and soil type and climate dynamic information assembled from sensors. The framework splits into two stages - the Green House unit and the server unit. The downsized form of the mechanized greenhouse unit comprises a local microcontroller. A controlled climate development requires constant track of significant variables influencing the yield's quality. A downpour drop sensor module, which is a water-saving gadget, flags the safeguard of the greenhouse to open utilizing a stepper engine when a downpour fall happens.

The SAFe task [55] expects to introduce a bunch of imaginative exercises in locales with the potential to start the fire in the region of Braganca. The proposed framework hopes to develop the nature of further checking and to help the current reconnaissance frameworks through Wireless Sensor Networks. The organization shaped by the arrangement of sensors can distinguish wood starts and alarm the specialists through LoRaWAN correspondence. The proposed framework has four fundamental components. Given manufactured brainpower, the mix of these four components and an administration framework will enable a proficient and keen examination of the information. This information investigation will produce the making of woodland start cautions and thus, ought to alarm the salvage and battle groups.

The work [56] presents a brilliant and secure structure for emergency clinic climate utilizing the Internet of Things and Artificial Intelligence. It helps defeat the current issues of treatment, determination, patient checking, and upkeep of medical clinic records in the electronic organization. The IoT-empowered AI framework comprises an application and administration layer that incorporates the board applications and choice and medical clinic data application. The information like monetary administration, clinical administration, material and gear the board, drug the executives, active recuperation the board, pathology, radiology, assessment, and short-term administration data is put away in this layer. Security has a guideline and strategy layer that centers mainly around the basic design's trust parts.

The work [57] constructs an innovative IoT framework for agrarian climate observation by incorporating edge figuring and manufactured brainpower. This framework coordinates sensors, RFID, video, and other detecting and observing gadgets to gather detailed data about the ranch. This framework presents a cloud-edge coordinated effort system to process, break down, and store information to work on the proficiency of organization transmission capacity usage and assurance of the top-notch of the stage's outer administrations. The framework incorporates remote sensor organizations and accomplishes steady and dependable information transmission through 5G organizations. The proposed design utilizes planning innovation to perform similarity with different IoT character guidelines and takes on redid personality inside the framework. The stage gives the data assortment capability, with which we can see the continuous status of the plot on the guide. The stage communicates the pictures gathered by top-quality cameras to the server farm through the organization and empowers constant review and playback. The point of interaction counter can screen the absolute number of connection point calls and the achievement pace of the end of interaction calls. The framework administrator can peruse and deal with the data of base stations in each block and sensor data. The framework has some control over the hardware on the ranch, for example, turning on/off the gadgets, including the fan, the fill light, the shade screen, and the programmed sprinkler water system. The framework can likewise uphold the offices' exhibition checking, for example, the administration of M2M cards and SIM cards on the board.

2.3.5. Agricultural Applications

IoT (internet of things), big data, and AI are possibly outdated terms in the tech sector that have only recently begun to impact. A large portion of the world's population continues to integrate AI successfully into their life in one way or another as the number of communication devices grows. Making the most of these new information technologies to feed the world sustainably is a natural area of interest for agri-food scientists and engineers. Fig. (**9**) depicts Smart sensors for Agriculture.

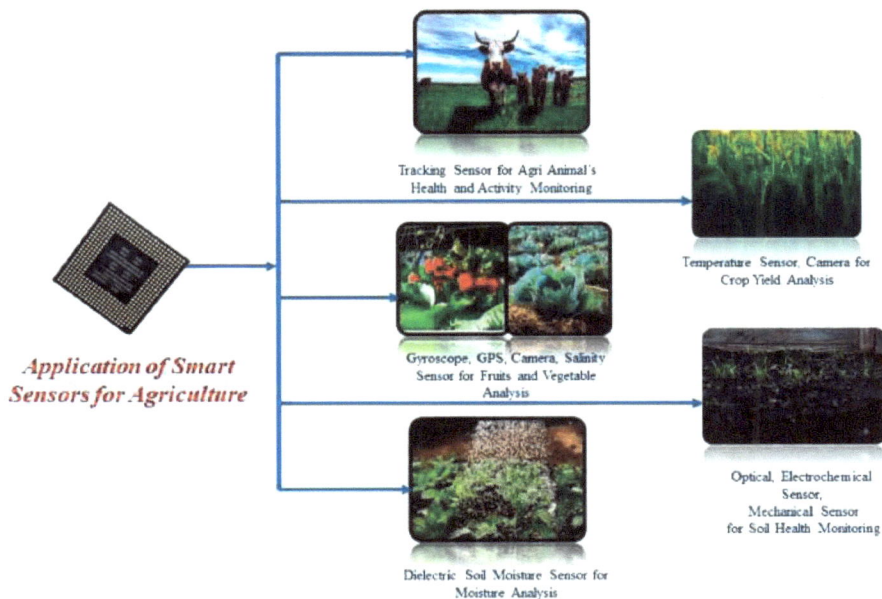

Fig. (9). Smart sensors for Agriculture [58].

The framework [59] will assist the ranchers with evaluating the farming area for development as far as four choice classes, particularly more appropriate, reasonable, respectably reasonable, and unsatisfactory. This appraisal views the information gathered from the different sensor gadgets utilized for preparing the framework. Sensor-based information assortment requires three fundamental stages: information obtaining, correspondence, and handling. Additional sensors gather the different boundary values concerning soil properties appropriate for agribusiness improvement. The transmission utilizes other sensor gadgets like the pH sensor, soil dampness sensor, saltiness sensor, and electromagnetic sensor. The raspberry Pi 3 framework deals with inputs from numerous sensors, and the information moves to a cloud for capacity. A wi-fi office is likewise accessible and transfers the data from distant farming land. The cloud office utilized here is Amazon Web Service and the put-away information for AI with the end goal of the analysis. Electromagnetic sensors estimate soil surface, interior waste, accessible water content, natural matter, cation trade limit, carbonates, and level of immersion. pH sensors acquire the pH worth, and saltiness sensors get the saltiness esteem. Fig. (**10**) represents the same.

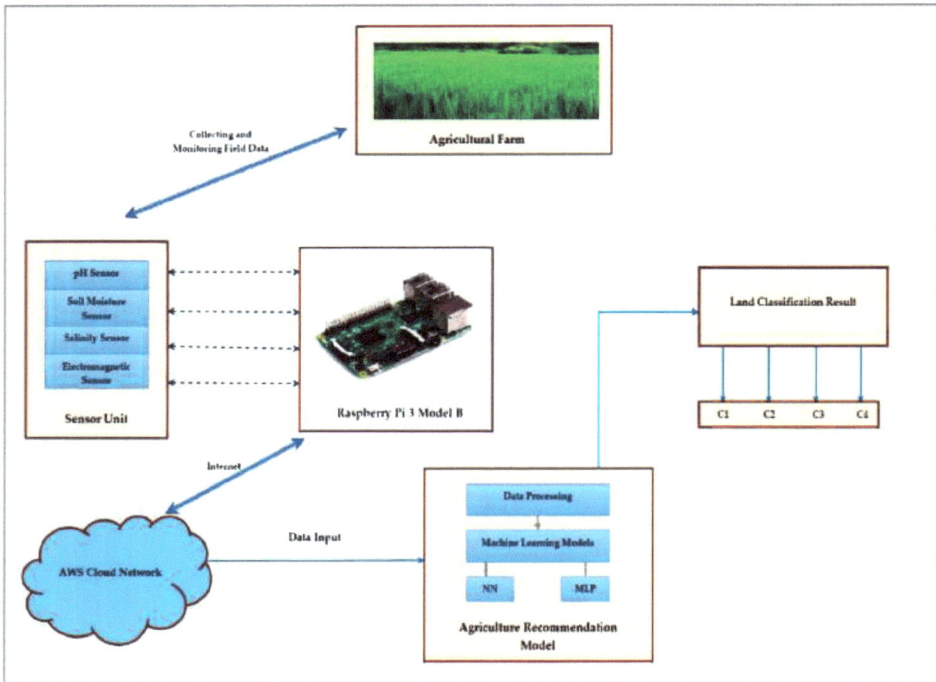

Fig. (10). Framework of the system [59].

The proposal is an AIoT framework [60] for savvy horticulture in light of the idea of front-backside partition and the system of the ModelView-View Model, through which it is feasible to deal with complex business rationale and makes the reconciliation of the AI calculations considerably more available. The discernment layer incorporates different remote detecting hubs based on the inserted frameworks to gather the sensors' information. The information collected by the detecting hubs communicates to the distant server through remote connections in the organization layer. The application layer comprises the server and explicit capabilities in shrewd farming applications. The application layer takes on front and back detachment design. The Controller layer was answerable for front-end demands, yet additionally expected to parse and call Model layer information and communicate the information to the View layer for show. The design isolates the View and the Model, and the ViewModel layer typifies the properties and interfaces for information showing and manipulation. After getting a client demand, the ViewModel receives the information that the Model answers and yet again delivers the comparing view page through knowledge restricting.

The work [61] proposes an AI sound responsive shortcoming location and checking framework for arising end-gadgets, which uses the generated sound close to the parts and sends valuable data after examination to the approved help places. To foster such a model, we made a research center arrangement of water-driven AgM. It incorporates an engine, oil siphon, sump, channel, and pull valves to emulate the progression of oil in a pressure-driven framework. Information assortment is the primary phase of this examination work. The information was gained through the receivers situated around the oil siphon. This technique gives financial arrangement, where amplifiers are the most financial sensors worldwide. The gathered soundtracks are, for sure, the sound commotion around the oil channel when in a functioning state. Sounds close to the portable pieces of the framework are the rich hotspot for getting data for the typical finding of framework conditions before disappointment. In all accounts, the AgM is in the normal working state of 900 revolutions for every moment. After having the soundtracks of the underlying clean oil condition, various degrees of contaminating residue add to the pressure-driven framework in light of the norm of ISO4406. The contamination levels are set from one to six. In preparing the fake brain organization, the quantities of data sources are addressed by a parallel number. For each info, if there is 1, it is accessible to the counterfeit brain network for preparing, generally dismissed by the generic algorithm.

AgriSegNet [62] is a profound learning structure for the programmed discovery of farmland irregularities utilizing multiscale consideration semantic division of UAV procured pictures. It is a semantic division of farmland from an ethereal view. The proposed model is valuable for checking farmland and yields to expand the proficiency of cultivating techniques. The dataset contains various abnormalities, for example, cloud shadow, twofold plant, standing water, *etc*. It utilizes two picture scales for preparing and three picture scales during derivation. The consideration component chooses task-explicit highlights from the multiscale highlights extricated using the spine organization, which fundamentally beats max-pooling and average pooling. It also helps us envision elements' meaning at various scales and positions.

The work [63] is AI sensor plays out a job along the edge of savvy cultivating, gives more precision and shows better in general execution to advantage a more evident mastery about farming improvement and develop productiveness. Parametric assessments in AI might be highly advantageous in fixing issues in horticulture. The sensors gather the plant conceal records and soil reflectance. It decides mud regularly and the dampness content material of the soil. Electrochemical Sensors get strategy, guide, and soil compound records. This sensor gives the measurements needed for the accuracy agribusiness, soil supplement degree, and PH. HTE MIX Sensors decide the dampness content and temperature from both soil and ecological perspective. Cloud-based IoT gathers the information cycle and examination the presentation of the harvest to give improved respect to the ranchers. IoT-based Simulated intelligence sensors with a combination of distributed computing administrations like field planning, and information capacity can be gotten anywhere and empower the live observing. It will live from start to finish connection. The AI-based sensor can consistently check a crop improvement and transmits using cloud-based IoT agriculture. This detected information is sent to the cloud, and the information ships off the ranchers' portable through SMS using the GSM module.

The work [64] comprises different parts, specifically the dampness and temperature sensor, Soil Moisture sensor, Microcontroller unit, wifi module, switch, thingspeak cloud, and versatile application. There are two terminals in the cathode. DHT 11 is a solitary gadget with both a dampness sensor and temperature. It senses moistness utilizing capacitive detecting innovation and faculties temperature using a thermistor implanted inside the little bureau. It gives yield in mechanical beat structure, so it is associated with the automated contribution of MCU. Soil dampness information deciphers. Arduino IDE programming does the programming of the MCU. For testing reasons, the wifi area of interest tying of the wireless is used as a wifi switch.

2.3.6. Smart Grids

Shrewd frameworks incorporate processing and two-way correspondence capacities with existing power foundations. They cover all levels of the energy esteem chain and utilize sensors, implanted registering, and advanced correspondences to make the power organization perceptible, controllable, computerized, and completely incorporated. It is self-recuperating, has a better nature of power, dispersed age and request reaction, shared activity, and client interest. Fig. (**11**) portrays Cyber-attacks in smart grid systems. Fig. (**12**) represents Artificial Intelligence in Distributed Smart grids.

Fig. (11). Cyber-attacks in smart grid system [65].

A HEM framework [66] is an equipment and programming program that permits the end clients to screen their energy use and creation and deal with the energy inside a home. A HEM framework is an essential piece of SG that might empower demand response applications for end clients. It oversees and controls energy usage by booking the home apparatuses as per the scheduler strategy implanted in the HEM regulator. It assists the end-client with cost-putting something aside for society assets preservation and environment assurance in the enormous circle by coordinating and organizing different energy assets without compromising work processes. The intelligent grid presents an organization of smart meters that can gather, share, and update. The smart meter learns the customer's way of life, machines the exchanging design, and discusses the data with the utility. Fig. (**13**) depicts the same.

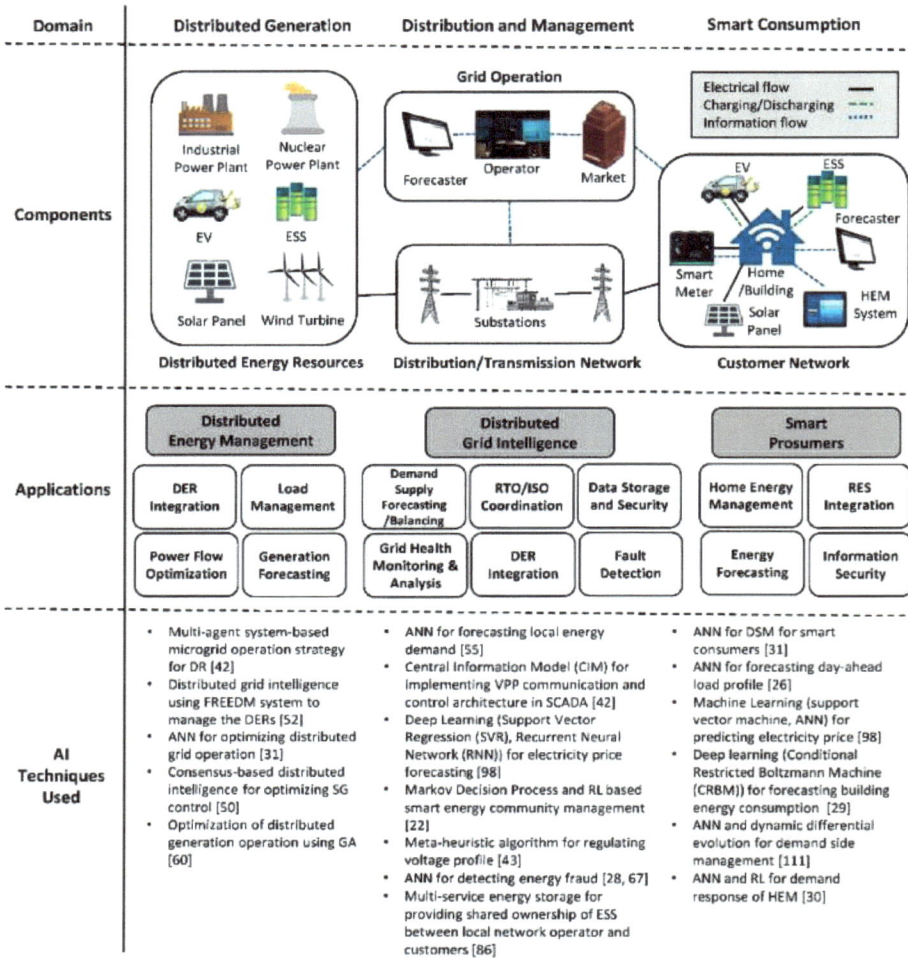

Fig. (12). Artificial Intelligence in Distributed Smart grids [66].

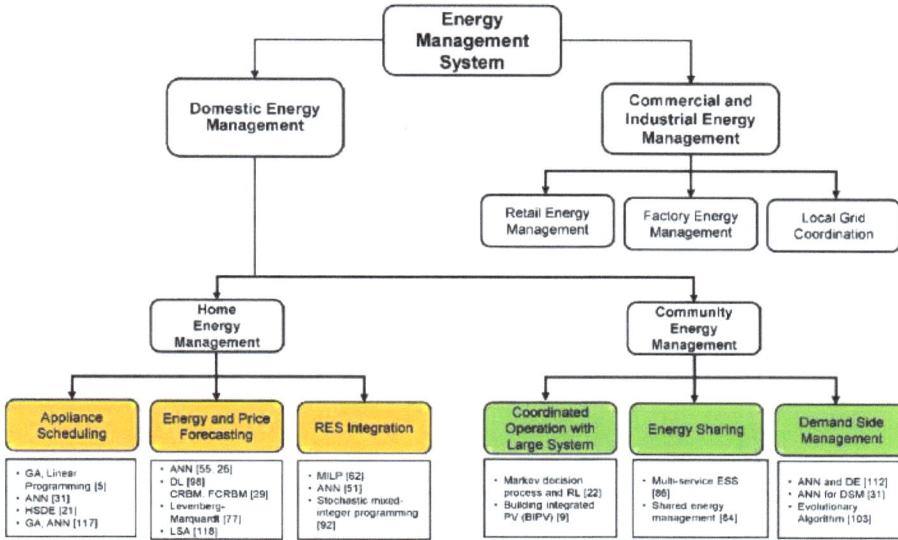

Fig. (13). Energy management system in SG system [66].

The work [67] is a cross-breed blockchain instrument given the 5G MEC savvy network, where both public and private blockchains are sent on the MEC entryway/server. A blockchain framework contains numerous parts, including web, agreement, application, and meta-application layers in the blockchain system. Meta application layer covers the application layer and consolidates the blockchain with different applications. The application layer is the semantic understanding of the blockchain framework, and its vital capability is to create blockchain answers for various applications and industries. The consensus layer upholds the dispersed agreement instrument of the blockchain framework. This layer confirms each blockchain's rightness, decides the blockchain's structure, and accomplishes the consistency expected by the system. The network layer is predominantly liable for adding blockchain chains, refreshing and trading data on the blockchain, and other functions. The design embraced in the brilliant framework will advance the correspondence between various associations.

The work [68] is an intelligent framework with their design, the IoT with the part engineering and the Smart Meters, which assume a pertinent part for the assortment of data of electrical energy continuously. The AI strategies for anticipating electrical power in structures. It has three building blocks: Home Area Networks, Neighborhood Region Networks, and Wide Area Networks.

The recommendation [69] is an abnormality-based IDS mainly intended for the intelligent grid using available information from a genuine power plant. It depends on a regulated learning system that integrates a preparation and a testing stage. The information assortment module has Programmable Logic Controllers and Remote Terminal Units that screen and control the tasks of modern hardware like power generators and transformers. The ground truth was given by the power plant engineers demonstrating the peculiarities and the occasions that set off them. The dataset has to prepare and test subsets and basic k-crease Cross-Validation. The complex highlight vectors use a sliding time window for many approaches. During the preparation stage, all techniques utilize ordinary information. The Euclidean distance gets the disparity lattice and T-disseminated Stochastic Neighbor Embedding to ascertain the proclivity grid for Stochastic Outlier Selection. The working measure of the typical way length between the root and each leaf with the unusual information focuses on the ones with moderately short distinct paths. The response module gets the result of the Anomaly Detection Module. It attempts to illuminate the security administrator or the security head about potential cyberattacks by separating the proper security occasions.

The work [70] is a new productive, provably secure, confirmed necessary arrangement conspire for savvy lattice. It accomplishes notable security functionalities, including shrewd meter qualifications' protection and SK-security under the CK-enemy model. Suppose the session-specific vaporous insider facts are uncovered startlingly to an enemy by meeting openness assaults. In that case, they can recover the related smart meter confirmation certifications and mimic that smart meter afterward. The proposed verification plot utilizes the ECC-based El-Gamal type signature technique to produce the intelligent meters' mysterious accreditation and the personality-based encryption strategy to create the specialist organizations' qualifications. Accordingly, the proposed plot accomplishes SK-security and areas of strength protection under the CK-foe alongside the decreased calculation costs.

The work [71] is a protected interest side administration machine sending AI for the Internet of Things approved stage. These home region networks with an intelligent grid, an auxiliary committed to demand-side management inside the Smart Phase. These incorporate interest reaction and energy capability. Its screens deal with the committed organization's home's power utilization using the home region network. Deals with its guests and brilliant gadgets in the shrewd metering climate. The home region network screen the entire framework. The safe demand-side management machine in the intelligent grid keeps up with possible use securely, contingent upon inclinations and energy needs. High-power-consuming and favored gadgets are picked and conveyed instantly with endorsement inside the boundaries of explicit requirements or burden and cost limits. The message beneficiary on the demand-side management machine gets this data, and safeguarding the message from Intrusive persons is approved. The handling data results are sent back to the home region network for productive asset use. The results are utilized for the method called pattern investigation for impending gauging. The provider administrator is liable for keeping up with every supplier's profile. The elements of customer chief rely upon a quality assortment.

2.4. CHALLENGES OF IOT-AI

2.4.1. Compatibility

Sensors built into equipment or the environment capture raw data for real-time data extraction. Today, the Internet of Things ecosystem is leveraged to promote autonomous data collection by minimizing human participation. The analysis of such information is challenging, especially when using real-time sensors. To improve quality of life, industries, society, enterprises, and education can be integrated *via* the IoT environment. IoT is a group of dispersed innovative entities and items that can communicate with one another using sensors.

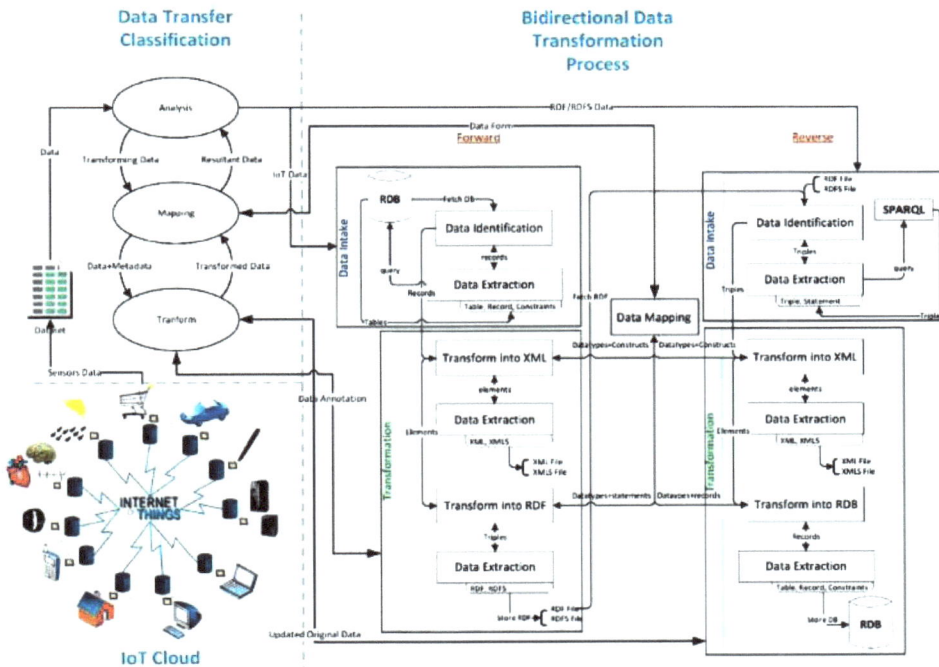

Fig. (14). Procedure of BDTM using IoT [72].

The work [72] gives a total computerized system to change from inexactly organized information put away in Relational Database into Resource Description Framework. The data of a table's section is characterized as a perplexing kind, while imperative data is described as an essential sort component. A circle is begun that chooses the names of a table individually from the rundown. A question brings the table's record set alongside some fundamental data regarding segment names and their information type. Another circle gets data in the segments of the concerned table. If the worth is a number kind, it is the type given to store a role as a string. All data is stored in ArrayList for later use to keep in touch with an XML record. This data is a rundown of the string type. A class tag of RDF is made that contains a reference ID from the XML component tag while perusing the XSD document. It encloses labels named marks, remarks, and subclass of titles. Names of tables with component labels get data about tables. The component tag has table data after data. Fig. (**14**) depicts the same.

The proposal [73] gives shared confirmation among members and permits a client and an end gadget to lay out a solid meeting key between themselves without genuinely confiding in the Network Server genuinely and totally. It is a secure meeting key foundation between a client and an end-gadget over a LoRaWAN organization. This plan utilizes the LoRaWAN standard, as it were the security natives that are determined in the norm. The program incorporates four stages: client enrollment stage, end-gadget enrollment stage, login, and verification stage. Furthermore, biometric and secret word refreshing phase. A client planning to profit from the proposed design needs to enroll with the Network Server NS of the LoRaWAN network. After an end-gadget is registered and actuated on the LoRaWAN organization, given the LoRaWAN particular. The validation stage gives confirmation and critical foundation administrations through which the client and end-gadget can commonly verify one another and set up a meeting key. In the Biometric and Password Update Phase, the framework updates its biometrics layout furthermore secret word.

The proposal [74] is a lithe AI-Powered IoT-based minimal expense stage for mental observing for brilliant cultivating. The crossover Multi-Agent framework constantly studies agribusiness boundaries like temperature, dampness, and strain to furnish end clients with ongoing ecological information and AI-based figures. The light-footed approach empowers a cooperative climate in which partners like ranchers, specialists, and designers constantly work on the framework through its different deliveries and emphases. The methodology begins with the necessity assortment stage. In this step, we accumulate the framework necessities that ought to be executed by the partners, like information perception, framework support, and savvy-based bits of knowledge. The conditions are then focused on as indicated by their importance and timetable inside the investigation stage. The planning stage uses an equipment and programming configuration approach. It is a complete arrangement with the framework gauge, like the minimal expense technique, the compactness, the versatility, the interoperability, and so on. The improvement stage comprises the framework execution, which changes from a plan into a model. The delivery stage is the broad activity and double-dealing of the ongoing model variant for execution investigation. Finally, the screen stage measures and tracks the framework execution and distinguishes any likely issue or improvement for therapeutic activities. This final stage directs proactively to permit the framework's nonstop upgrade. Fig. (**15**) depicts the same.

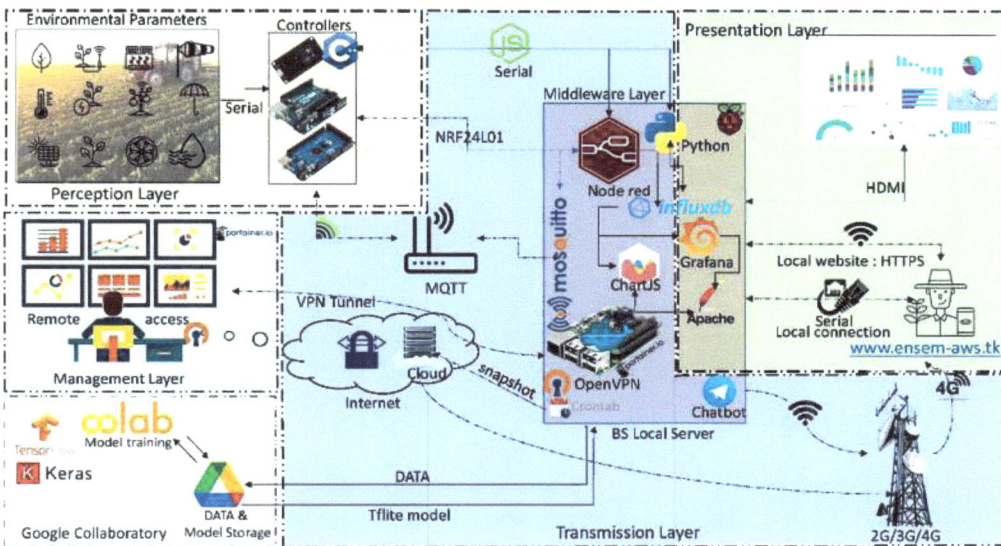

Fig. (15). Proposed Agro-weather station [74].

2.4.2. COMPLEXITY

The Internet, as we currently know it, will likely be integrated into many devices thanks to IoT technologies. As a result, everyday items like clothing, food packaging, toothbrushes, *etc.*, will be fitted with some Internet-addressable AI. Depending on their processing capacity and power consumption limitations, these IoTs will share some level of pseudo-intelligence and offer context awareness and communication functions. New channels of communication between things and between things themselves will emerge as a result of this development.

The proposition [75] proposes a particular arrangement as a various leveled layered ICT-based foundation that handles ICT issues connected with the "huge difficulties" and consistently coordinates IoT, smart homes, and savvy city structures into one lucid unit. It explains a dream for a smart city ICT-based foundation that partitions into layers. These layers give means to communicating and incorporating the singular critical advances into one joined help system. Specifically, the layers that arrange with the complex IoT gadgets regarding brilliant homes and Cloud-of-Things advances are in focus. It contains four layers that exemplify IoT, smart homes, Cloud-of-Things, and savvy city advancements and administrations. The IoT layer incorporates complex IoT gadgets, which make bunches by communicating with one another and with the intelligent home Artificial Intelligence AI framework. At the savvy home level, the smart homes are coordinated and joined into Cloud-of-Things groups which comprise the super sharp city spine. Also, the Cloud-of-Things and the brilliant city layers exemplify the intelligent home, its advancements, and its services. The model reproduces the capability of collecting energy from wastewater by planning and controlling the elaborate assets and its clients. Fig. (**16**) depicts the same.

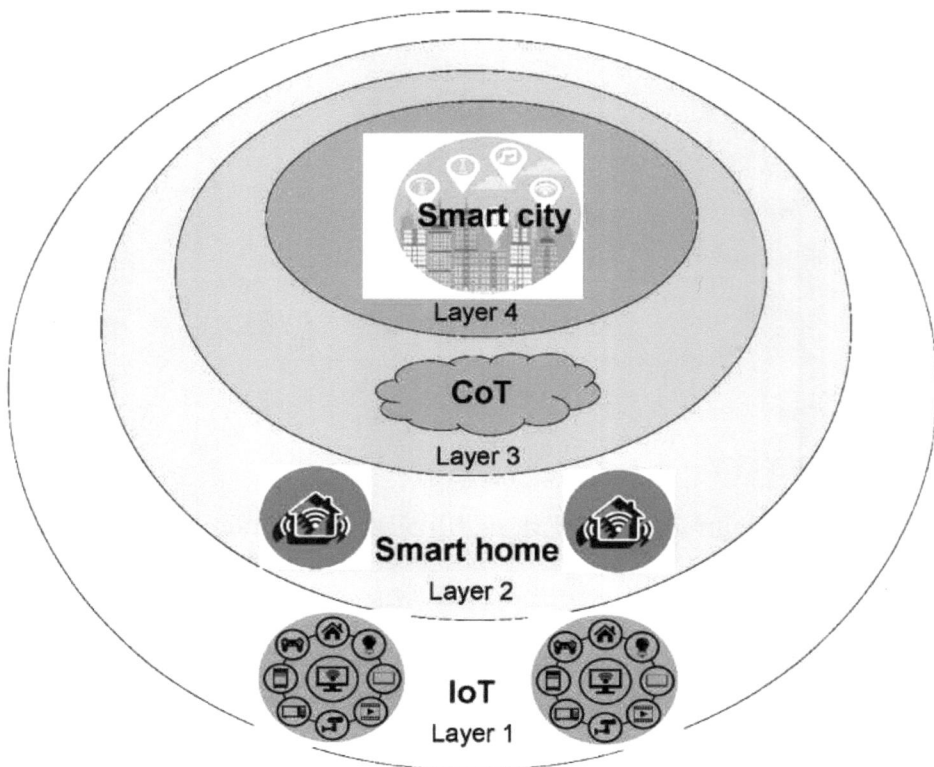

Fig. (16). ICT-based infrastructure [75].

2.4.3. PRIVACY AND SAFETY

Among the significant issues facing the Internet of Things are privacy and security. IoT is confronting several difficulties, including incorrect device updates, a lack of adequate and reliable security mechanisms, user ignorance, and well-known active device monitoring. IoT, or the Internet of Things, has become increasingly popular due to its use in communication, transportation, education, and corporate development, among other applications. With the introduction of the hyperconnectivity idea *via* IoT, businesses and individuals can easily communicate with one another from a distance. These businesses can gain a competitive advantage. Professionals are required to address these threat issues, create thorough security procedures and policies to safeguard their company's assets, and guarantee the continuation and stability of their services.

The proposition [76] is a new design that can uphold a few IoT-empowered shrewd home use cases with a predefined level of safety and protection preservation. The information is gathered from different heterogeneous IoT sources, then, at that point, anonymized, handled, and broken down utilizing Artificial Intelligence-based methods. Given the result of this examination, a few moves enhance the boundaries of interest to accomplish the ideal security and execution goals of the intelligent home application. It guarantees a security-savvy home climate with enhanced utilization of accessible assets. Security Parameters Configuration stage another IoT gadget before interfacing it with the savvy home framework. The Data Sensing and Reporting gadget detects at least one boundary and sends the information readings occasionally or when certain circumstances are met, contingent upon its configuration. Data Aggregation and Relaying information will either hand off to their objective through the transfer organization or stored first and, afterward, totaled with different readings before handing off the amassed values. Cloud-Based Data Analytics stage store, process, and break down the collected information sent by the IoT Gateways. Optimal Decisions deliveries convey to the activation framework through the IoT Gateway. The invitation framework will train the concerned gadgets to make the mentioned changes by sending a refreshed setup record. Fig. (**17**) represents the same.

The proposition [77] is a blockchain-based framework to give the safe administration of home quarantine. The protection and security credits depend on cutting-edge cryptographic primitives. The home has a security framework, like cameras, infrared sensors, and savvy attractive entryway pull gadgets, which are associated with the rest of the world through brilliant passage gadgets. The framework doesn't permit unapproved gadget admittance to keep the toxic way of behaving from consuming social assets. Savvy passages in a similar local area structure a group and have a similar bunch name. Each family's brilliant entryway gathers related data and finishes designing and conglomeration. It consistently sends the total data to the significant intelligent agreement. The official gave this clever agreement and connected it with the quarantine guidelines. It has two phases. The introduction process is like giving testaments. In Operation Phase, sensors in the brilliant home send apparent data to the intelligent door. The savvy passage can choose the public keys of gadgets in a similar local area to sign the data and send it to the related shrewd agreement for examination. Fig. (**18**) depicts the same.

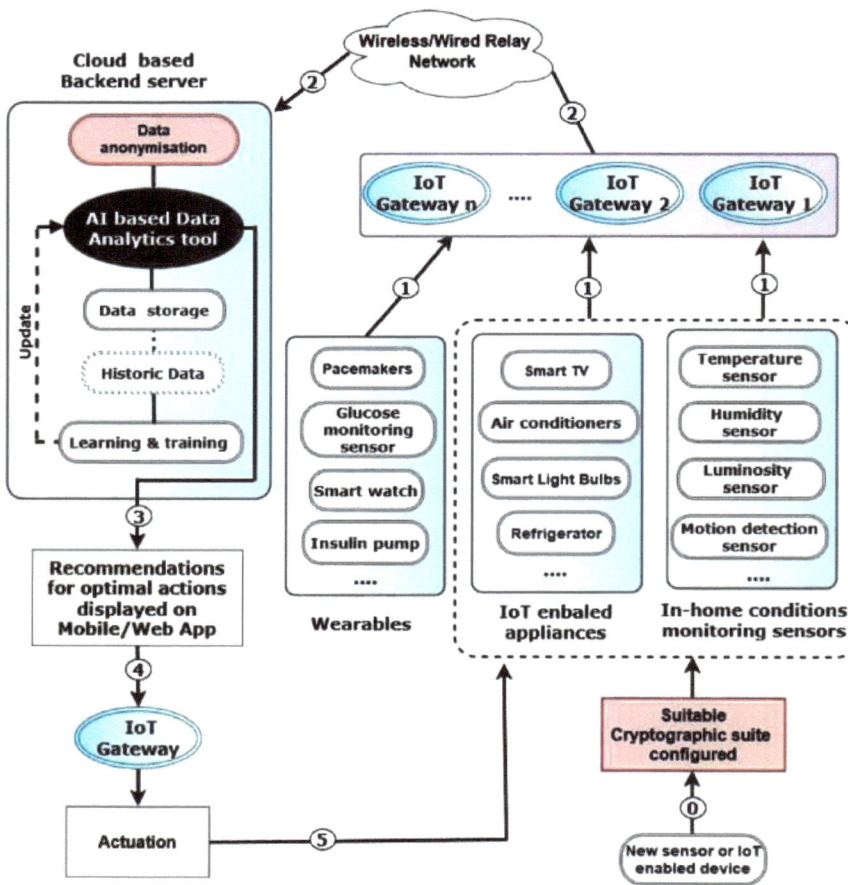

Fig. (17). System Architecture [76].

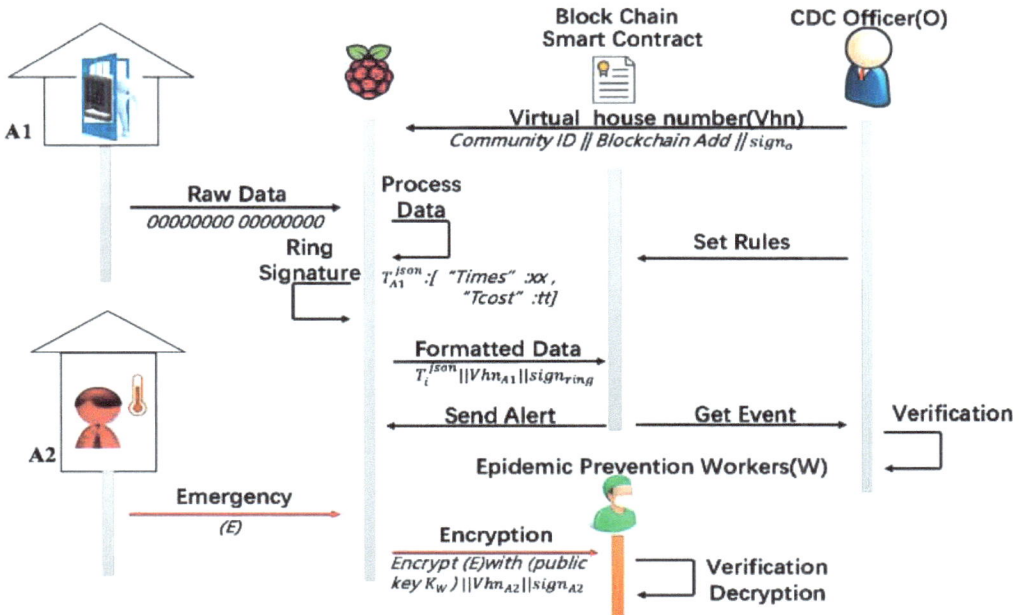

Fig. (18). System execution [77].

The review [78] is a protection safeguarding phrase with multi-watchword positioned looking through that presents upgraded sifting, parallel tree record design, and conjunctive catchphrase search to accomplish secure looking through productivity. The wearable sensor gadgets gather information in the scrambled clinical records over the IoT entryway. The clinical documents are sent to distributed storage. It gets the papers and related questions to store in another distributed storage. It contains six continuous elements. Information proprietor rethinks private and delicate information to accomplish helpful access, unwavering quality, and on-request information admittance to approved users. Data use sends the looking through catchphrases to the information proprietor and gets a secret entrance relating to the looking through watchwords from the proprietor. Believed specialists gather the properties to produce the public keys and appropriate the keys to other entities. IoT-Gateway collects the clinical records from the owner to total the clinical information. Cloud − Server stores the scrambled archives and the relating encoded BMS tree from the proprietor. The continuous substances, including IoT entryway, cloud-server, information proprietor, and client, ensure information classification to rethink the scrambled information documents. It can construct accessible records to empower productive and secure access commands over encoded information. Each list makes a safe-looking-through record to characterize the client types and strategies. It approves information clients that execute secret inquiry entrance, which depends on encoded catchphrases. Table **2.4** Portrays the implementation details of various contributions

Table 2.4. Portrays the implementation details of various contributions.

Contribution	Implementation Details
[50]	• The work uses Arduino/Genuino and TI Launchpad. • UNO Rev3 clones with integrated ESP8266 module. • Hosting computer has CPU Intel(R) Core(TM) i3-4005U CPU @ 1.70 GHz, 4 GB RAM, DDR3 450 GD SATA HDD, internal WLAN adapter (optionally with TP-Link 722N external USB WLAN adapter).
[52]	• It uses NodeMCU. It functions on ESP8266 Wi-Fi module.
[53]	• The nodes use Raspberry Pi 3, type B. • Hive is used for data saving.
[54]	• The work uses LPC2138 microcontroller. • The ESP8266 was used for giving the green house unit native controller WiFi connectivity. • Mysql 5.5.29 was used for database management. • The attribute file was created using data from FAO.
[55]	• It uses ATmega328p microcontroller. • It is powered by 18650 lithium-ion cell battery.
[60]	• The system consists of a remote data service platform, data collection terminals build on Raspberry Pi and wireless data transmission using narrow-band Internet of Things (NB-IoT) modules. • The front-end is built using Vue.js and Element. • The front-end and rear-end data transmission layer uses Axios
[59]	• It uses raspberry Pi 3 system
[61]	• Conjugate gradient descent backpropagation (SCGB) trained ANN is used.
[62]	• The work uses DeepLabV3+ with ResNet50. • The work consisted 21,061 farmland images captured across the United States during the year 2019. • The model is implemented in PyTorch framework.
[63]	• It uses ATMEGA2560. It includes 12V DC voltage battery-powered battery with 600mah yield.
[64]	• NodeMCU microcontroller is used. • prototyping kit is based on ESP8266. • The work is visualized in the thingspeak platform.
[71]	• Naive Bayes (NB)- ML algorithm is used to identify correspondence as safe or unsafe.
[79]	• It combines an embedded processor (CPU) or a microcontroller (MCU) with on-board memory, sensor/actuator interfacing and analog inputs/outputs—and basic connectivity.
[80]	• It uses OpenVPN. • It uses Python language with API commands. • It uses the Raspberry Pi platform.

Contribution	Implementation Details
[81]	• It uses VOSviewer software.
[73]	• The system uses On-the-Fly Model-Checker (OFMC) and the Constraint-Logicbased Attack Searcher (CL-AtSe) backends. • The simulation is performed using the Security Protocol ANimator (SPAN) tool for AVISPA.
[76]	• The work uses Raspberry Pi 3.
[77]	• The setup has a desktop computer, laptop, and Raspberry Pi single-board computer.
[78]	• 1024 − bits Paillier cryptosystem has been implemented using Python 3.6.

2.4.4. ETHICAL AND LEGAL ISSUES

Artificial intelligence has undergone extraordinary technological advancements, which now influence our daily lives through smartphones and the Internet of Things. AI evaluates credit and loan applications. It frequently influences parole decisions: the black box dilemma, machine bias, and autonomous transportation present substantial ethical and legal challenges. Additionally, there are worries about the quick advancement and expanding application of intelligent technologies, specifically their effects on fundamental rights. Concerns have also been raised about the rapid rise and growing application of smart technologies, particularly how these developments could affect fundamental rights. Fig. (**19**) represents Characteristics of IoT causing Ethical problems.

The work [82] tackles this issue by fostering a reasonable moral system for combined AI, IoT, and blockchain. The emotional cycle, including morals, follows a predefined and organized approach to accomplishing a goal and settling upon a choice. The structure depends on the communication between the three tomahawks to be specific innovation, applications, and morals. The innovation pivot includes blockchain agreement calculations, brilliant agreements, and disseminated calculations. The application pivot has blockchain's primary applications like cryptographic money and cultural applications. The morals hub includes morals concentrating on advancements that depend on conventional moral speculations. It has three levels. The full-scale level spotlights blockchain's institutional and cultural impacts. Meso-level spotlights on the ethical issues engaged with every one of blockchain's applications, like cryptographic forms of money. Miniature level spotlights the moral matters encountered with blockchain's innovation stack, like client security, exactness, property proprie-torship, availability, and equality. The structure has two tomahawks, specifically innovation and application. The elements related to any innovation are agreement, security, smart contract, interoperability, independence, straightforwardness, obligation, and strength. The applications associated with the merged advancements are AI-based legitimate administrations codified regulations, AI-based financial administrations, astute medical services checking and logging, and cooperative mechanized driving. The scene separates into three tomahawks. The first is the pivot of the moral, which remembers the honest establishments and conventional hypotheses for expansion to the morals of arising innovations. The subsequent pivot incorporates the applications associated with every one of AI, IoT, blockchain, and combined AI, IoT, and blockchain. The third pivot includes the points of interest of the advancements supporting collaborative AI, IoT, and blockchain. Fig. (**20**) depicts the same.

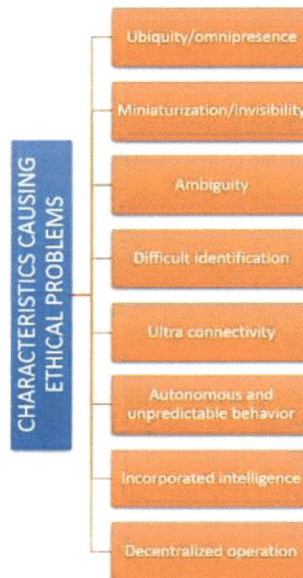

Fig. (19). Characteristics of IoT Causing Ethical Problems.

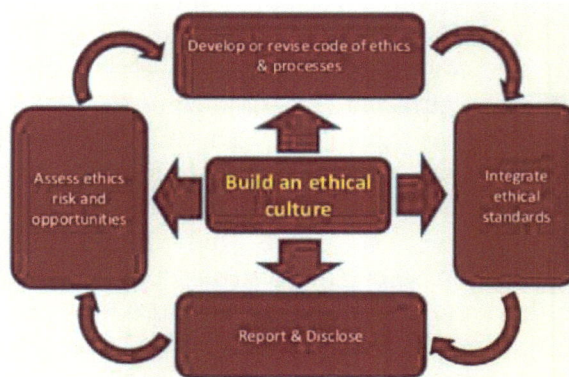

Fig. (20). Algorithm to Build Ethical Structure [82].

2.5. FUTURE DIRECTIONS OF IOT-AI

2.5.1. Assisted Intelligence

A type of intelligent computing [84] known as "ambient intelligence" is characterized by a wide range of always-available sensors and gadgets. The programs provide user-dependent services for aged and disabled individuals, such as regulating a person's movement, tracking or monitoring vital signs through analyzing perceived heterogeneous information, and spotting and responding to dangerous situations. They have to deal with various gadgets, from medium-capacity smartphones and tablets to essential resource-constrained sensors, actuators, consumer electronics, and wearable gadgets. Fig. (**21**) represents the Emergency monitoring system.

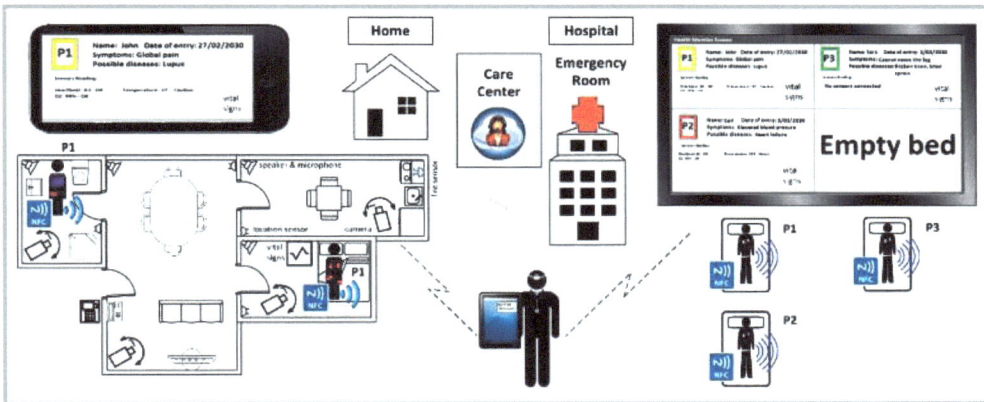

Fig. (21). Emergency monitoring system [83].

2.5.2. Augmented Intelligence

While improving information acquisition, comprehension, and display, augmented reality [86] doesn't take our attention away from the natural environment. Applications and industries can leverage these technologies to integrate domain-specific visualizations on a physical screen. Mobile augmented reality entails overlaying digital things over real-world ones on the screen to enhance and add value to interactions with reality. It is used in many plants for upkeep, repair, and training. Fig. (**22**) portrays the Architecture of augmented reality.

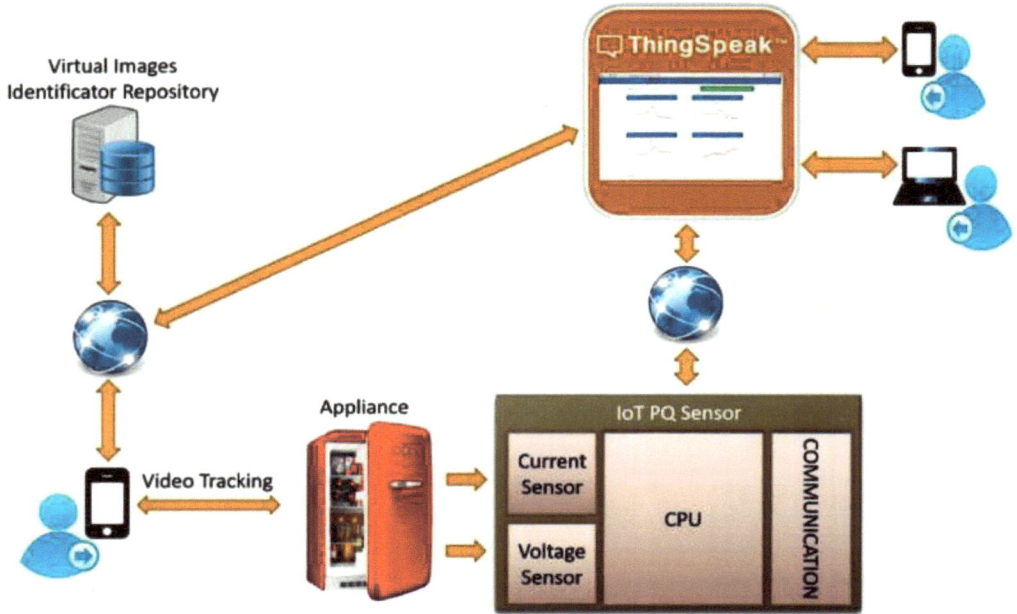

Fig. (22). Architecture of augmented reality [85].

2.5.3. Autonomous Intelligence

Robots and other intelligent machines used in manufacturing are physical systems that perform together in various dynamic physical environments. Such autonomous robots are vulnerable to many mechanical and operational issues because they are expected to function in multiple unanticipated circumstances. The defects that develop when such devices are in use must be promptly identified, diagnosed, and monitored to maintain operations and reduce unplanned downtime. Data-driven fault detection techniques in manufacturing contexts hold considerable promise due to developments in intelligent measuring technologies, hardware systems' computational power, and the field of deep learning. Anomalies in equipment functioning are identified using data-driven fault diagnosis techniques using features taken from measured sensor signals. Fig. (**23**) portrays system architecture.

Regarding a healthy baseline state, a diagnostic choice is made. Smart sensors that can perform sophisticated measurements can provide precise information about the machines' surroundings.

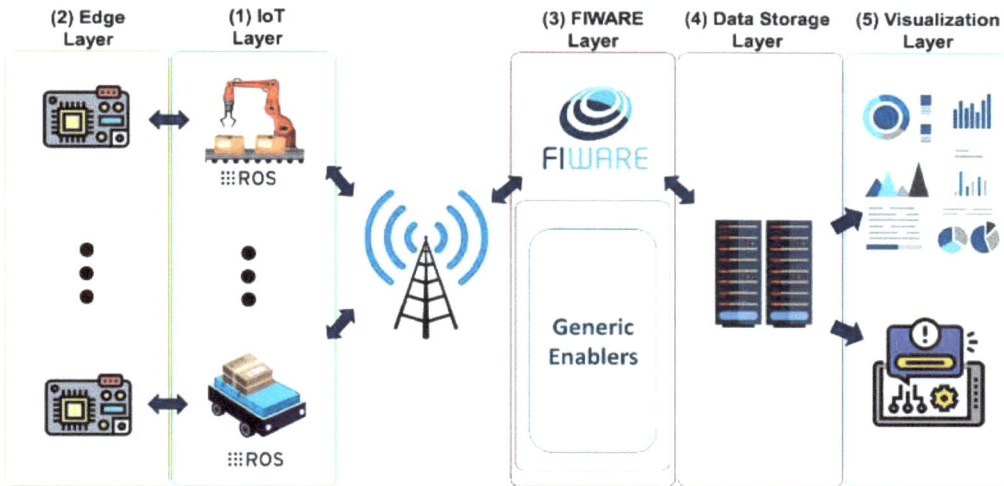

Fig. (23). System architecture [87].

CONCLUSION

The quality of human life, well-being, productivity, energy efficiency, and safety may be impacted by using intelligent technology in a home, building, or environment, including sensors, actuators, and artificial intelligence. The term "smart" is increasingly used to describe ways to improve the built environment, including homes, buildings, cities, transportation, and construction. Users of intelligent home assistance technologies and building automation mechanisms can enhance their quality of life while allowing AI to assess their behavior. The system can better anticipate user needs and make the best use of resources, including energy, by utilizing behavioral analysis.

REFERENCES

[1]   M. Mohamad Noor, and W.H. Hassan, "Current research on internet of things (IoT) security: A survey", *Comput. Netw.,* vol. 148, pp. 283-294, 2019.
[http://dx.doi.org/10.1016/j.comnet.2018.11.025]

[2]   A. Nagaraj, *Introduction to Sensors in IoT and Cloud Computing Applications.* Bentham Science Publishers: UAE, 2021.
[http://dx.doi.org/10.2174/97898114793591210101]

[3]   N. Ambika, Energy-perceptive authentication in virtual private networks using gps data.*Security, privacy and trust in the IoT environment.* Springer: Cham, 2019, pp. 25-38.
[http://dx.doi.org/10.1007/978-3-030-18075-1_2]

[4]   N. Ambika, Enhancing security in iot instruments using artificial intelligence.*in IoT and Cloud Computing for Societal Good, cham* EAI/Springer Innovations in Communication and Computing, 2022, pp. 259-276.
[http://dx.doi.org/10.1007/978-3-030-73885-3_16]

[5]   P.H. Winston, *Artificial intelligence.* Addison-Wesley Longman Publishing Co., Inc.: United States, 1992.

[6]   T. Dean, J. Allen, and Y. Aloimonos, *Artificial intelligence: theory and practice.* Benjamin-Cummings Publishing Co., Inc.: San Francisco, 1995.

[7]   K. Guo, Y. Lu, H. Gao, and R. Cao, "Artificial intelligence-based semantic internet of things in a user-centric smart city", *Sensors (Basel),* vol. 18, no. 5, p. 1341, 2018.
[http://dx.doi.org/10.3390/s18051341] [PMID: 29701679]

[8]   M.H. Devare, Cloud Computing and Innovations.*Applying integration techniques and methods in distributed systems and technologies.* IGI Global: US, 2019, pp. 1-33.
[http://dx.doi.org/10.4018/978-1-5225-8295-3.ch001]

[9]   S.K. Singh, S. Rathore, and J.H. Park, "Blockiotintelligence: A blockchain-enabled intelligent IoT architecture with artificial intelligence", *Future Gener. Comput. Syst.,* vol. 110, pp. 721-743, 2020.
[http://dx.doi.org/10.1016/j.future.2019.09.002]

[10]   O. Debauche, S. Mahmoudi, S.A. Mahmoudi, P. Manneback, and F. Lebeau, "A new edge architecture for ai-iot services deployment", *in The 17th International Conference on Mobile Systems and Pervasive Computing (MobiSPC),The 15th International Conference on Future Networks and Communications (FNC),The 10th International Conference on Sustainable Energy Information Technology,* 2020
[http://dx.doi.org/10.1016/j.procs.2020.07.006]

[11]   H. HaddadPajouh, R. Khayami, A. Dehghantanha, K-K.R. Choo, and R.M. Parizi, "AI4SAFE-IoT: an AI-powered secure architecture for edge layer of Internet of things", *Neural Comput. Appl.,* vol. 32, no. 20, pp. 16119-16133, 2020.
[http://dx.doi.org/10.1007/s00521-020-04772-3]

[12]   S.B. Calo, M. Touna, D.C. Verma, and A. Cullen, "Edge computing architecture for applying AI to IoT", *IEEE International Conference on Big Data,* 2017 Boston, MA, USA
[http://dx.doi.org/10.1109/BigData.2017.8258272]

[13]   E. Alreshidi, "Smart sustainable agriculture (SSA) solution underpinned by internet of things (IoT) and artificial intelligence (AI)", *Int. J. Adv. Comput. Sci. Appl.,* vol. 10, no. 5, pp. 93-102, 2019.
[http://dx.doi.org/10.14569/IJACSA.2019.0100513]

[14]   C. Iwendi, S.U. Rehman, A.R. Javed, S. Khan, and G. Srivastava, "Sustainable security for the internet of things using artificial intelligence architectures", *ACM Trans. Internet Technol.,* vol. 21, no. 3, pp. 1-22, 2021.
[http://dx.doi.org/10.1145/3448614]

[15]   Q. Liang, P. Shenoy, and D. Irwin, "Ai on the edge: Characterizing ai-based iot applications using specialized edge architectures", *IEEE International Symposium on Workload Characterization (IISWC),* 2020 Beijing, China
[http://dx.doi.org/10.1109/IISWC50251.2020.00023]

[16]   M. Song, K. Zhong, J. Zhang, Y. Hu, D. Liu, and W. Zhang, "In-situ ai: Towards autonomous and incremental deep learning for iot systems", *in IEEE International Symposium on High Performance Computer Architecture.,* 2018.(HPCA), Vienna, Austria

[17]   M. Kolhar, F. Al-Turjman, A. Alameen, and M.M. Abualhaj, "A three layered decentralized IoT biometric architecture for city lockdown during COVID-19 outbreak", *IEEE Access,* vol. 8, pp. 163608-163617, 2020.
[http://dx.doi.org/10.1109/ACCESS.2020.3021983] [PMID: 34812355]

[18]   H. Song, J. Bai, Y. Yi, J. Wu, and L. Liu, "Artificial intelligence enabled Internet of Things: Network architecture and spectrum access", *IEEE Comput. Intell. Mag.,* vol. 15, no. 1, pp. 44-51, 2020.
[http://dx.doi.org/10.1109/MCI.2019.2954643]

[19]   Y. Wu, "Cloud-edge orchestration for the Internet of Things: Architecture and AI-powered data

processing", *IEEE Internet Things J.,* vol. 8, no. 16, pp. 12792-12805, 2021.
[http://dx.doi.org/10.1109/JIOT.2020.3014845]

[20]   J. Park, M.M. Salim, J.H. Jo, J.C.S. Sicato, S. Rathore, and J.H. Park, "CIoT-Net: a scalable cognitive IoT based smart city network architecture", *Human-centric Computing and Information Sciences,* vol. 9, no. 1, p. 29, 2019.
[http://dx.doi.org/10.1186/s13673-019-0190-9]

[21]   R. Cárdenas, P. Arroba, and J.L. Risco Martín, "Bringing AI to the edge: A formal M&S specification to deploy effective IoT architectures", *J. Simul.,* pp. 1-18, 2021.

[22]   A.H. Sodhro, S. Pirbhulal, Z. Luo, K. Muhammad, and N.Z. Zahid, "Toward 6G architecture for energy-efficient communication in IoT-enabled smart automation systems", *IEEE Internet Things J.,* vol. 8, no. 7, pp. 5141-5148, 2021.
[http://dx.doi.org/10.1109/JIOT.2020.3024715]

[23]   N. Dhieb, H. Ghazzai, H. Besbes, and Y. Massoud, Scalable and secure architecture for distributed iot systems.*IEEE Technology & Engineering Management Conference.* TEMSCON: Novi, MI, USA, 2020.
[http://dx.doi.org/10.1109/TEMSCON47658.2020.9140108]

[24]   J. Mocnej, W.K.G. Seah, A. Pekar, and I. Zolotova, "Decentralised IoT architecture for efficient resources utilisation", *IFAC-PapersOnLine,* vol. 51, no. 6, pp. 168-173, 2018.
[http://dx.doi.org/10.1016/j.ifacol.2018.07.148]

[25]   N. Moustafa, "A new distributed architecture for evaluating AI-based security systems at the edge: Network TON_IoT datasets", *Sustain Cities Soc.,* vol. 72, p. 102994, 2021.
[http://dx.doi.org/10.1016/j.scs.2021.102994]

[26]   H.F. Azgomi, and M. Jamshidi, "A brief survey on smart community and smart transportation", *in IEEE 30th International Conference on Tools with Artificial Intelligence (ICTAI).,* 2018 Volos, Greece.

[27]   F. Zantalis, G. Koulouras, S. Karabetsos, and D. Kandris, "A review of machine learning and IoT in smart transportation", *Future Internet,* vol. 11, no. 4, p. 94, 2019.
[http://dx.doi.org/10.3390/fi11040094]

[28]   T. Liu, F. Sabrina, J. Jang-Jaccard, W. Xu, and Y. Wei, "Artificial intelligence-enabled ddos detection for blockchain-based smart transport systems", *Sensors (Basel),* vol. 22, no. 1, p. 32, 2021.
[http://dx.doi.org/10.3390/s22010032] [PMID: 35009574]

[29]   R.A. Gonzalez, R.E. Ferro, and D. Liberona, "Government and governance in intelligent cities, smart transportation study case in Bogotá Colombia", *Ain Shams Eng. J.,* vol. 11, no. 1, pp. 25-34, 2020.
[http://dx.doi.org/10.1016/j.asej.2019.05.002]

[30]   O. Alfarraj, "Internet of things with bio-inspired co-evolutionary deep-convolution neural-network approach for detecting road cracks in smart transportation", *Neural Comput. Appl.,* pp. 1-16, 2020.
[http://dx.doi.org/10.1007/s00521-020-05401-9]

[31]   S. Shukla, K. Balachandran, and V.S. Sumitha, "A framework for smart transportation using Big Data", *International Conference on ICT in Business Industry & Government (ICTBIG),* 2016 Indore, India
[http://dx.doi.org/10.1109/ICTBIG.2016.7892720]

[32]   J. Zhang, Y. Wang, S. Li, and S. Shi, "An architecture for IoT-enabled smart transportation security system: a geospatial approach", *IEEE Internet Things J.,* vol. 8, no. 8, pp. 6205-6213, 2021.
[http://dx.doi.org/10.1109/JIOT.2020.3041386]

[33]   C. Lin, G. Han, J. Du, T. Xu, L. Shu, and Z. Lv, "Spatiotemporal congestion-aware path planning toward intelligent transportation systems in software-defined smart city IoT", *IEEE Internet Things J.,* vol. 7, no. 9, pp. 8012-8024, 2020.
[http://dx.doi.org/10.1109/JIOT.2020.2994963]

[34]   R. Ke, Y. Zhuang, Z. Pu, and Y. Wang, "A smart, efficient, and reliable parking surveillance system with edge artificial intelligence on IoT devices", *IEEE Trans. Intell. Transp. Syst.,* vol. 22, no. 8, pp. 4962-4974, 2021.
[http://dx.doi.org/10.1109/TITS.2020.2984197]

[35]   S. Munirathinam, "Industry 4.0: Industrial internet of things (IIOT)", In: *Advances in computers* vol. 117. Elsevier, 2020, pp. 129-164.
[http://dx.doi.org/10.1016/bs.adcom.2019.10.010]

[36]   V.V. Popov, E.V. Kudryavtseva, N. Kumar Katiyar, A. Shishkin, S.I. Stepanov, and S. Goel, "Industry 4.0 and digitalisation in healthcare", *Materials (Basel),* vol. 15, no. 6, p. 2140, 2022.
[http://dx.doi.org/10.3390/ma15062140] [PMID: 35329592]

[37]   M. Javaid, A. Haleem, R. Vaishya, S. Bahl, R. Suman, and A. Vaish, "Industry 4.0 technologies and their applications in fighting COVID-19 pandemic", *Diabetes Metab. Syndr.,* vol. 14, no. 4, pp. 419-422, 2020.
[http://dx.doi.org/10.1016/j.dsx.2020.04.032] [PMID: 32344370]

[38]   P. Radanliev, D. De Roure, K. Page, J.R.C. Nurse, R. Mantilla Montalvo, O. Santos, L.T. Maddox, and P. Burnap, "Cyber risk at the edge: current and future trends on cyber risk analytics and artificial intelligence in the industrial internet of things and industry 4.0 supply chains", *Cybersecurity,* vol. 3, no. 1, p. 13, 2020.
[http://dx.doi.org/10.1186/s42400-020-00052-8]

[39]   B.B. Gupta, A. Tewari, I. Cvitić, D. Peraković, and X. Chang, "Artificial intelligence empowered emails classifier for Internet of Things based systems in industry 4.0", *Wirel. Netw.,* vol. 28, no. 1, pp. 493-503, 2022.
[http://dx.doi.org/10.1007/s11276-021-02619-w]

[40]   Y. Chen, Z. Han, K. Cao, X. Zheng, and X. Xu, "Manufacturing upgrading in industry 4.0 era", *Syst. Res. Behav. Sci.,* vol. 37, no. 4, pp. 766-771, 2020.
[http://dx.doi.org/10.1002/sres.2717]

[41]   E.G. Popkova, and B.S. Sergi, "Human capital and AI in industry 4.0. Convergence and divergence in social entrepreneurship in Russia", *J. Intellect. Cap.,* vol. 21, no. 4, pp. 565-581, 2020.
[http://dx.doi.org/10.1108/JIC-09-2019-0224]

[42]   P. Radanliev, D. De Roure, R. Nicolescu, M. Huth, and O. Santos, "Artificial intelligence and the internet of things in industry 4.0", *CCF Transactions on Pervasive Computing and Interaction,* vol. 3, no. 3, pp. 329-338, 2021.
[http://dx.doi.org/10.1007/s42486-021-00057-3]

[43]   P.W. Khan, Y.C. Byun, and N. Park, "IoT-blockchain enabled optimized provenance system for food industry 4.0 using advanced deep learning", *Sensors (Basel),* vol. 20, no. 10, p. 2990, 2020.
[http://dx.doi.org/10.3390/s20102990] [PMID: 32466209]

[44]   R.C. Santos, and J.L. Martinho, "An Industry 4.0 maturity model proposal", *J. Manuf. Tech. Manag.,* vol. 31, no. 5, pp. 1023-1043, 2019.
[http://dx.doi.org/10.1108/JMTM-09-2018-0284]

[45]   N. Ambika, Wearable sensors for smart societies: a survey.*Green Technological Innovation for Sustainable Smart Societies.* Springer: Cham, 2021, pp. 21-37.
[http://dx.doi.org/10.1007/978-3-030-73295-0_2]

[46]   L.K. Ramasamy, F. Khan, M. Shah, B.V.V.S. Prasad, C. Iwendi, and C. Biamba, "Secure smart wearable computing through artificial intelligence-enabled internet of things and cyber-physical systems for health monitoring", *Sensors (Basel),* vol. 22, no. 3, p. 1076, 2022.
[http://dx.doi.org/10.3390/s22031076] [PMID: 35161820]

[47]   B. Muthu, C.B. Sivaparthipan, G. Manogaran, R. Sundarasekar, S. Kadry, A. Shanthini, and A. Dasel, "IOT based wearable sensor for diseases prediction and symptom analysis in healthcare sector", *Peer-*

to-Peer Netw. Appl., vol. 13, no. 6, pp. 2123-2134, 2020.
[http://dx.doi.org/10.1007/s12083-019-00823-2]

[48] S. Kumar, R.D. Raut, and B.E. Narkhede, "A proposed collaborative framework by using artificial intelligence-internet of things (AI-IoT) in COVID-19 pandemic situation for healthcare workers", *Int. J. Healthc. Manag.,* vol. 13, no. 4, pp. 337-345, 2020.
[http://dx.doi.org/10.1080/20479700.2020.1810453]

[49] G. Xu, Y. Shi, X. Sun, and W. Shen, "Internet of things in marine environment monitoring: a review", *Sensors (Basel),* vol. 19, no. 7, p. 1711, 2019.
[http://dx.doi.org/10.3390/s19071711] [PMID: 30974791]

[50] D. Dobrilovic, V. Brtka, Z. Stojanov, G. Jotanovic, D. Perakovic, and G. Jausevac, "A model for working environment monitoring in smart manufacturing", *Appl. Sci. (Basel),* vol. 11, no. 6, p. 2850, 2021.
[http://dx.doi.org/10.3390/app11062850]

[51] S.L. Ullo, and G.R. Sinha, "Advances in smart environment monitoring systems using IoT and sensors", *Sensors (Basel),* vol. 20, no. 11, p. 3113, 2020.
[http://dx.doi.org/10.3390/s20113113] [PMID: 32486411]

[52] G. Gupta, R. Setia, A. Meena, and B. Jaint, "Environment monitoring system for agricultural application using IoT and predicting crop yield using various data mining techniques", *5th International Conference on Communication and Electronics Systems (ICCES),* 2020 Coimbatore, India
[http://dx.doi.org/10.1109/ICCES48766.2020.9138032]

[53] R. Arridha, *Classification extension based on IoT-big data analytic for smart environment monitoring and analytic in real-time system.,* vol. 7, no. 2, pp. 82-93, 2017.*International journal of space-based and situated computing.,* vol. 7, no. 2, pp. 82-93, 2017.
[http://dx.doi.org/10.1504/IJSSC.2017.086821]

[54] M. Nargotra, and M.J. Khurjekar, "Green house based on IoT and AI for societal benefit", *International Conference on Emerging Smart Computing and Informatics (ESCI),* 2020 Pune, India
[http://dx.doi.org/10.1109/ESCI48226.2020.9167637]

[55] T. Brito, B. Azevedo, A. Valente, A. Pereira, J. Lima, and P. Costa, Environment monitoring modules with fire detection capability based on IoT Methodology*Science and Technologies for Smart Cities,* 2021, pp. 211-227.
[http://dx.doi.org/10.1007/978-3-030-76063-2_16]

[56] V. R, "Smart and secure IoT and AI integration framework for hospital environment", *Journal of ISMAC,* vol. 1, no. 3, pp. 172-179, 2019.
[http://dx.doi.org/10.36548/jismac.2019.3.004]

[57] Q. Zhou, M. Xiao, L. Lu, J. Zeng, W. He, and C. Li, "A data-secured intelligent iot system for agricultural environment monitoring", *Wireless Communications and Mobile Computing.,* pp. 1-12, 2022.

[58] S.L. Ullo, and G.R. Sinha, "Advances in iot and smart sensors for remote sensing and agriculture applications", *Remote Sens. (Basel),* vol. 13, no. 13, p. 2585, 2021.
[http://dx.doi.org/10.3390/rs13132585]

[59] D.R. Vincent, N. Deepa, D. Elavarasan, K. Srinivasan, S.H. Chauhdary, and C. Iwendi, "Sensors driven ai-based agriculture recommendation model for assessing land suitability", *Sensors (Basel),* vol. 19, no. 17, p. 3667, 2019.
[http://dx.doi.org/10.3390/s19173667] [PMID: 31450772]

[60] H. Li, S. Li, J. Yu, Y. Han, and A. Dong, "AIoT Platform design based on front and rear end separation architecture for smart agricultural", *4th Asia Pacific Information Technology Conference,* 2022pp. 208-214 Virtual Event Thailand
[http://dx.doi.org/10.1145/3512353.3512384]

[61]   N. Gupta, M. Khosravy, N. Patel, N. Dey, S. Gupta, H. Darbari, and R.G. Crespo, "Economic data analytic AI technique on IoT edge devices for health monitoring of agriculture machines", *Appl. Intell.,* vol. 50, no. 11, pp. 3990-4016, 2020.
[http://dx.doi.org/10.1007/s10489-020-01744-x]

[62]   T. Anand, S. Sinha, M. Mandal, V. Chamola, and F.R. Yu, "AgriSegNet: Deep aerial semantic segmentation framework for IoT-assisted precision agriculture", *IEEE Sens. J.,* vol. 21, no. 16, pp. 17581-17590, 2021.
[http://dx.doi.org/10.1109/JSEN.2021.3071290]

[63]   B. Ragavi, L. Pavithra, P. Sandhiyadevi, G.K. Mohanapriya, and S. Harikirubha, "Smart agriculture with AI sensor by using Agrobot", *Fourth International Conference on Computing Methodologies and Communication (ICCMC),* 2020 Erode, India
[http://dx.doi.org/10.1109/ICCMC48092.2020.ICCMC-00078]

[64]   M. Dholu, and K.A. Ghodinde, "Internet of things (iot) for precision agriculture application", *2nd International conference on trends in electronics and informatics (ICOEI),* 2018 Tirunelveli, India
[http://dx.doi.org/10.1109/ICOEI.2018.8553720]

[65]   A. Chehri, I. Fofana, and X. Yang, "Security risk modeling in smart grid critical infrastructures in the era of big data and artificial intelligence", *Sustainability (Basel),* vol. 13, no. 6, p. 3196, 2021.
[http://dx.doi.org/10.3390/su13063196]

[66]   S.S. Ali, and B.J. Choi, "State-of-the-art artificial intelligence techniques for distributed smart grids: a review", *Electronics (Basel),* vol. 9, no. 6, p. 1030, 2020.
[http://dx.doi.org/10.3390/electronics9061030]

[67]   D. Wang, H. Wang, and Y. Fu, "Blockchain-based IoT device identification and management in 5G smart grid", *EURASIP J. Wirel. Commun. Netw.,* vol. 2021, no. 1, p. 125, 2021.
[http://dx.doi.org/10.1186/s13638-021-01966-8]

[68]   M. Fouad, R. Mali, A. Lmouatassime, and M. Bousmah, "Machine learning and iot for smart grid", *Int. Arch. Photogramm. Remote Sens. Spat. Inf. Sci,* vol. XLIV-4/W3-2020, pp. 233-240, 2020.
[http://dx.doi.org/10.5194/isprs-archives-XLIV-4-W3-2020-233-2020]

[69]   G. Efstathopoulos, P. Grammatikis, P. Sarigiannidis, V. Argyriou, A. Sarigiannidis, K. Stamatakis, M. Angelopoulos, and S. Athanasopoulos, "Operational data based intrusion detection system for smart grid", *24th International Workshop on Computer Aided Modeling and Design of Communication Links and Networks (CAMAD),* 2019 Limassol, Cyprus
[http://dx.doi.org/10.1109/CAMAD.2019.8858503]

[70]   V. Odelu, A.K. Das, M. Wazid, and M. Conti, "Provably secure authenticated key agreement scheme for smart grid", *IEEE Trans. Smart Grid,* vol. 9, no. 3, p. 1, 2016.
[http://dx.doi.org/10.1109/TSG.2016.2602282]

[71]   S.C. Dharmadhikari, V. Gampala, C.M. Rao, S. Khasim, S. Jain, and R. Bhaskaran, "A smart grid incorporated with ML and IoT for a secure management system", *Microprocess. Microsyst.,* vol. 83, p. 103954, 2021.
[http://dx.doi.org/10.1016/j.micpro.2021.103954]

[72]   K. Razzaq Malik, M. Habib, S. Khalid, F. Ullah, M. Umar, T. Sajjad, and A. Ahmad, "Data compatibility to enhance sustainable capabilities for autonomous analytics in IoT", *Sustainability (Basel),* vol. 9, no. 6, p. 877, 2017.
[http://dx.doi.org/10.3390/su9060877]

[73]   A. Jabbari, and J.B. Mohasefi, "A secure and LoRaWAN compatible user authentication protocol for critical applications in the IoT environment", *IEEE Trans. Industr. Inform.,* vol. 18, no. 1, pp. 56-65, 2022.
[http://dx.doi.org/10.1109/TII.2021.3075440]

[74]   A. Faid, M. Sadik, and E. Sabir, "An Agile ai and IOT-augmented smart farming: a cost-effective

cognitive weather station", *Agriculture,* vol. 12, no. 1, p. 35, 2021.
[http://dx.doi.org/10.3390/agriculture12010035]

[75] P. Lynggaard, and K. Skouby, "Complex iot systems as enablers for smart homes in a smart city vision", *Sensors (Basel),* vol. 16, no. 11, p. 1840, 2016.
[http://dx.doi.org/10.3390/s16111840] [PMID: 27827851]

[76] M. Abu-Tair, S. Djahel, P. Perry, B. Scotney, U. Zia, J.M. Carracedo, and A. Sajjad, "Towards secure and privacy-preserving iot enabled smart home: architecture and experimental study", *Sensors (Basel),* vol. 20, no. 21, p. 6131, 2020.
[http://dx.doi.org/10.3390/s20216131] [PMID: 33126629]

[77] J. Zhang, and M. Wu, "Blockchain use in IoT for privacy-preserving anti-pandemic home quarantine", *Electronics (Basel),* vol. 9, no. 10, p. 1746, 2020.
[http://dx.doi.org/10.3390/electronics9101746]

[78] B.D. Deebak, F.H. Memon, K. Dev, S.A. Khowaja, and N.M.F. Qureshi, "AI-enabled privacy-preservation phrase with multi-keyword ranked searching for sustainable edge-cloud networks in the era of industrial IoT", *Ad Hoc Netw.,* vol. 125, p. 102740, 2022.
[http://dx.doi.org/10.1016/j.adhoc.2021.102740]

[79] P. Fraga-Lamas, S.I. Lopes, and T.M. Fernández-Caramés, "Green iot and edge ai as key technological enablers for a sustainable digital transition towards a smart circular economy: an industry 5.0 use case", *Sensors (Basel),* vol. 21, no. 17, p. 5745, 2021.
[http://dx.doi.org/10.3390/s21175745] [PMID: 34502637]

[80] S. Venkatraman, A. Overmars, and M. Thong, "Smart home automation—use cases of a secure and integrated voice-control system", *Systems,* vol. 9, no. 4, p. 77, 2021.
[http://dx.doi.org/10.3390/systems9040077]

[81] I. Rodríguez-Rodríguez, J.V. Rodríguez, N. Shirvanizadeh, A. Ortiz, and D.J. Pardo-Quiles, "Applications of artificial intelligence, machine learning, big data and the internet of things to the covid-19 pandemic: a scientometric review using text mining", *Int. J. Environ. Res. Public Health,* vol. 18, no. 16, p. 8578, 2021.
[http://dx.doi.org/10.3390/ijerph18168578] [PMID: 34444327]

[82] S. Tzafestas, "Ethics and law in the internet of things world", *Smart Cities,* vol. 1, no. 1, pp. 98-120, 2018.
[http://dx.doi.org/10.3390/smartcities1010006]

[83] J. Cubo, A. Nieto, and E. Pimentel, "A cloud-based Internet of Things platform for ambient assisted living", *Sensors (Basel),* vol. 14, no. 8, pp. 14070-14105, 2014.
[http://dx.doi.org/10.3390/s140814070] [PMID: 25093343]

[84] P. Manickam, S.A. Mariappan, S.M. Murugesan, S. Hansda, A. Kaushik, R. Shinde, and S.P. Thipperudraswamy, "Artificial intelligence (AI) and internet of medical things (IoMT) assisted biomedical systems for intelligent healthcare", *Biosensors (Basel),* vol. 12, no. 8, p. 562, 2022.
[http://dx.doi.org/10.3390/bios12080562] [PMID: 35892459]

[85] M. Alonso-Rosa, A. Gil-de-Castro, A. Moreno-Munoz, J. Garrido-Zafra, E. Gutierrez-Ballesteros, and E. Cañete-Carmona, "An IoT Based Mobile Augmented Reality Application for Energy Visualization in Buildings Environments", *Appl. Sci. (Basel),* vol. 10, no. 2, p. 600, 2020.
[http://dx.doi.org/10.3390/app10020600]

[86] N. Ambika, An augmented edge architecture for ai-iot services deployment in the modern era.*Handbook of Research on Technical, Privacy, and Security Challenges in a Modern World.* IGI Global: US, 2022, pp. 286-302.

[87] Ö. Gültekin, E. Cinar, K. Özkan, and A. Yazıcı, "Real-time fault detection and condition monitoring for industrial autonomous transfer vehicles utilizing edge artificial intelligence", *Sensors (Basel),* vol. 22, no. 9, p. 3208, 2022.
[http://dx.doi.org/10.3390/s22093208] [PMID: 35590898]

[88]   H. Ramalingam, and V.P. Venkatesan, "Conceptual analysis of Internet of Things use cases in Banking domain", *TENCON 2019-2019 IEEE Region 10 Conference.,* 2019 Kochi, India [http://dx.doi.org/10.1109/TENCON.2019.8929473]

CHAPTER 3

Cloud with AI

Abstract: Distributed computing is essential in our present-day lives as it empowers a scope of utilizations from framework to virtual entertainment. Such framework should adapt to changing burdens and developing use mirroring social orders' communication and reliance on robotized figuring frameworks while fulfilling the nature of administration requirements. Empowering these frameworks is a companion of practical innovations orchestrated to satisfy the need to develop registering applications. There is a need to distinguish fundamental advances in licensing future applications. Cloud suppliers, for example, Facebook, Google and Amazon, use an enormous scope of Cloud Server farms to arrange heterogeneous nature administration requirements. Cloud registering stages can give a bound-together connection point over heterogeneous assets found in the Web of Things-based applications, which work on the dependability of cloud administrations. This chapter discusses cloud-AI architecture, applications, challenges and future directions.

Keywords: Applications of cloud-AI, Artificial intelligence, Cloud-AI architecture, Cloud computing, Distributed computing, Edge computing.

3.1. INTRODUCTION

Distributed computing has, as of late, emerged as another system for working with and conveying administrations over the Web [1, 2]. The standard monetary limitations and becoming computational expense, require capacity, investigation, and showing of information that has forced fundamental changes for the current cloud model. It is the on-request openness of end-client assets, particularly data capacity and handling power, without an immediate exceptional association by the client. Distributed computing is the on-request availability of organization assets, particularly information capacity and handling power, without outstanding and direct administration by the clients. Imitation learning is the examination of terminal calculations that usually work through the experience. It empowers systems to take in and improve without being explicitly redone regularly. It centers around the headway of programs that can find a reasonable speed and use it to find out on their own. Fig. (**1**) depicts the Cloud computing model.

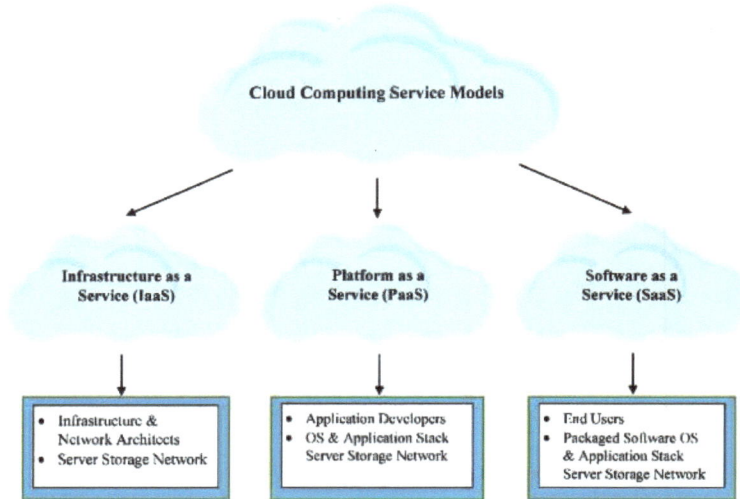

Fig. (1). Cloud computing model [3].

3.2. AI CLOUD INFRASTRUCTURE

The service composer has several related modules in a multiple cloud base environment. These modules are the cloud [5] combiner, the composition convertor, the composition planner, service ontologies, and numerous cloud base environments. Deep learning-based edge artificial intelligence typically relies on sufficient data samples to train deep neural networks to extract features or attributes. Mobile and Internet of Things (IoT) devices at the network's edge with limited communication and computation capabilities, such as smart watches, intelligent robots, and so on, frequently generate these data samples. Fig. (**2**) represents cloud computing architecture.

The suggestion [6] is to research an asset designation methodology in light of a Long Short Term Memory calculation. The preparation activity depends on minimizing a cost capability that diversely gauges the positive and negative forecast blunders and the comparing over-provisioning and under-provisioning costs. It is an expectation procedure. Traffic can't be precisely anticipated, and attempts to misjudge or misjudge traffic corresponds to the upsides of over-provisioning and under-provisioning costs. A reconfiguration calculation utilizes the anticipated traffic values to reconfigure transmission capacity and cloud assets. A traffic forecast calculation uses LSTM-based progressed expectation instruments to foresee the traffic values. The Operation Support System/Business Support System might get the deliberate genuine traffic values from the checked organization gadgets; then, at that point, it might play out the forecast calculation to decide the anticipated traffic values. The Network Function Virtualization

Orchestrator gets the expected traffic values. By applying the reconfiguration, the analysis can settle on redistributing data transfer capacity and cloud assets or potentially relocating Virtual Network Function Instances. Virtual Manager Infrastructures and organization regulators are utilized to activate the reconfigurations concluded by the Network Function Virtualization Orchestrator. Fig. (**3**) represents the same.

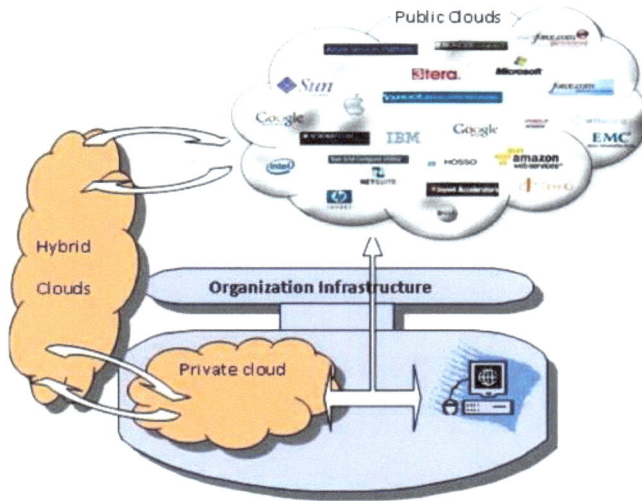

Fig. (2). Cloud computing architecture [4]

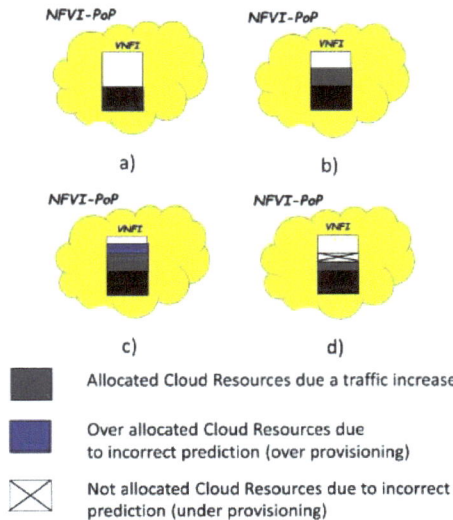

Fig. (3). Cloud Resource infrastructure [6].

Different significance testing filters are modified with an AI-based convolution brain network classifier [7]. The picture succession has been achieved from the single monocular camera progressively. It handles and acknowledges the item to be put away in the cloud server farm for not-so-distant future exchange. A variety histogram is finished to ascertain the dispersion of shade of pixels in a picture. The result will be a measurable diagram type of conveyance of variety, which is utilized to find the moment variety in the development of the body parts. The member's face and arms are sufficient to comprehend the way of behaving of a specific individual. Generally, the goal is towards the human head and arms checking when chest area parts are concerned. It observes interior organs after head configuration. The foundation district of the picture proceeds as the first stage in the hair variety identification strategy.

The work [8] is a cooperation understanding between the Italian Association of Medical Physicists and the National Institute for Nuclear Physics. It is a robust figuring framework, preparing AI models, outfitted with secure capacity frameworks, consistent with information assurance guidelines, which will speed up the turn of events and broad approval of AI-based arrangements in the Medical Imaging field of research. It examines the chance of beating the flow obstructions that forestall the turn of events, colossal scope approval, and dependability evaluation of AI-put-together DSS depending with respect to complex multimodal heterogeneous patients' data. The work is the collaboration between the Medical and High-Energy Physics research fields as an effective procedure to accomplish proficient pragmatic answers for conquering the momentum to prompt a critical stage towards the solid, quality-guaranteed, and effective execution of AI-based arrangements in the clinical field. The improvement and approval of AI-based strategies for Medical Physics applications, from finding to enhancing assets and therapeutics, share the requirement for non-trifling processing infrastructures. It has a mind-boggling registering foundation, with assets of more than 200 Petabytes of capacity and registering offices with a sum of more than 100,000 figuring centers. INFN-Cloud offers capacity and figure capacities to make and run versatile applications in a unique climate, adapting to the necessities of a gigantic assortment of purpose cases.

ABCI Cloud Storage and ABCI Public Datasets permit clients to store info and result in information on tasks to be run on the ABCI figure hubs and to impart them to ABCI clients as well as non-ABCI clients. The plan [9] coordinates the S3-based object capacity into the AI, and HPC merged framework and is a utilization instance of ABCI. Storage administration permits clients to utilize existing information and move and share programming in different mists. The work implements the way information encryption between client hubs and the stockpiling and gives a choice to empower very still information encryption on the capacity. It incorporated the record of the executives of the capacity administration into ABCI's principal board framework for records and gatherings.

3.3. APPLICATIONS OF CLOUD-AI

With the ongoing promotion of the Web and the all-inclusive presence of sensors, the rise of important information prompts another developmental stage: computer-based intelligence 2.0. The quick turn of events and combination of new computer-based intelligence innovations with Web advances is a fundamental piece of this new period. It will empower the game-changing change of models, means, and environments concerning their application to the public economy, prosperity, and public security. The development of new advancements likewise empowers another period of simulated intelligence. The primary highlights of computer-based intelligence 2.0 incorporate the story of information-driven natural discernment capacity for concentrated profound learning, Web-based swarm insight, innovation situated human-machine expanded knowledge, as well as the ascent of cross-media thinking.

3.3.1. Banking

Banks cannot deal with carelessness. They need to rethink their upper hands considering significant changes driven by progress in data innovation and severe strain from companies. A long-haul direction of relationship banking smoothes out motivating forces and supports bank customers' drawn-out needs. The artificial insight will strengthen the banking and monetary organizations to reclassify their capability, establish heavy items and administrations, and, most conspicuously, brunt client experience obstructions. In the machine age period, banks will wind up testing with the assistance of fintech organizations. It utilizes refined advancements that enhance or re-establish human laborers with tasteful algorithms. Artificial intelligence suppresses human experts in business exercises since human determination is expensive. Synthetic intelligence uses machine learning and learns things throughout some undefined time frame. Subsequently, it guarantees the most noteworthy exactness in the computation and looks at the tremendous measure of information.

The work [10] uses blockchain innovation and smart contracts as a reasonable answer for conquering the respectability issue due to its standard and decentralized record. Shrewd agreements mechanize strategy authorization, monitor information uprightness, and forestall information phony. Engineering-based works by building a design to keep the enemy from entering the framework. There is a client on the client-side, brilliant agreements in the blockchain network, and the cloud stage. Clients will cooperate with the cloud stage, for example, transferring ML datasets from their got climate, preparing the ML framework on the cloud stage, and calling the cloud's API to utilize AI administrations. To guarantee no information uprightness infringement all through the ML lifecycle in the cloud climate, we propose a design in light of the NIST online protection system by fostering a few modules that will team up with the blockchain network. There are five modules, Identity Management and Access Contro, API Gateway, Integrity Module, Logging Monitoring, and Storage Management. It has six conventions for our initial three modules, IDMA, API entryway, and Integrity Module. The IDMA module is answerable for dealing with the client enlistment and login process. Every client restricts their exercise and forestalls an inconsistent way of behaving. The IDMA module will furnish the client with a qualification that will be a token for authentication. API Gateway handles API demands from clients needing to utilize cloud administrations. Trustworthiness Module plans to protect the uprightness of ML preparing information and model by utilizing blockchain. Logging and Monitoring mean recording information streams and client exercises. Capacity Management tries to keep up with the framework's reinforcement information process routinely. The information will be put away in a scrambled structure to keep secrecy.

Fig. (**4**) represents the same.

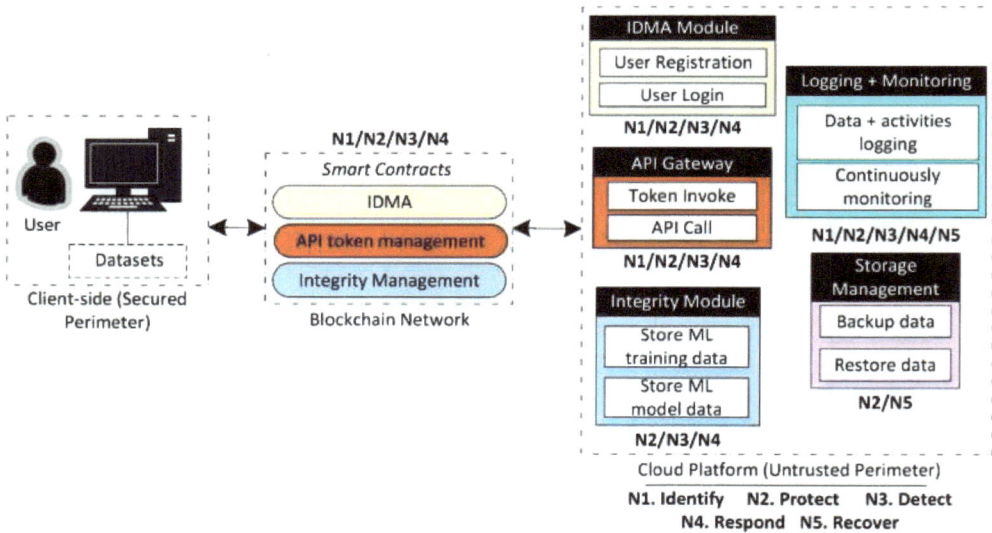

Fig. (4). Proposed architecture [10].

The review [11] utilized compact and instructive investigation techniques, as it is principally a quantitative report. Furthermore, these strategies help to accumulate quantitative information to acquire a more profound knowledge of the connection between various examination variables. The research configuration is exploratory and graphic. The kind of examination attempted is exploratory as it contains top-to-bottom reviews notwithstanding subjective and quantitative investigation. It is a detailed exploration and logical examination of the current situation with artificial consciousness utilizing current realities and data collected. The way to deal with this study is depended on an example used to gather critical quantitative information from respondents. The review strategy gathered information by studying 112 clients from chosen banks. The exploration instrument utilized here to assemble quantitative information was a formal and shut poll. The information collected is Primary and Secondary information, quantitative and subjective information, examined to reach determinations and suggestions. It accumulates primary data through an overview of people's consciousness about using artificial brainpower in financial areas. The work drafts a poll for the study and completes irregular examines. It asserts optional information through the web, including web, e-magazines, research papers, digital books, papers, *etc*.

The work [12] centers fundamentally around the exploration issue of dynamic cycle support and its improvement utilizing essential elements of AI techniques, for example, regulated, unaided, and semi-administered learning. It also presents critical advantages coming about because of the referenced arrangements used during the time spent in business association management. It examines five contextual analyses led in March 2021 in large financial establishments with more than 250 staff. The financial business uses ML/AI arrangements. The exploration system depends on a subjective methodology for planning contextual investigations having eight open inquiries. The respondents included directors of huge financial organizations that consistently apply ML/AI arrangements. The examination results showed that AI arrangements significantly affect the speed increase of the dynamic interaction and its adequacy and effectiveness increment.

Jamovi [13] led an objective examination of the review questions and reliant and autonomous variables to approve the connection between the factors. Fifteen banks and ten respondents in the bank offices were chosen and given over a nearby finished poll for essential information assortment. Mathematical scale from 1-10. The two finishes of the continuum address the two limits of the estimating peculiarities. The corroborative component is causal connections among idle and recognizable factors in deduced characterized, hypothesis-determined models. Corroborative Factor Analysis might give supportive data to the examiner about the information's fit to a specific. Theory inferred estimating model.

3.3.2. E-Commerce

Computerized reasoning [14] has assisted in the vital preparation, consolidations, acquisitions, and promotion of items with designing. Crucial arranging is a hierarchical administration action utilized to define boundaries, center assets, reinforce tasks, and evaluate and change bearings on a case-by-case basis. It is a multi-specialist framework that expands the comprehension of people or gatherings in navigation. The frameworks empower a human-specialist group to perform mental undertakings better than human or programming specialists alone, particularly in high-stakes choice-making. The framework permits gatherings of leaders to effectively connect with a lot of data utilizing discourse, signal, and information perception procedures to help the most common way of assessing choices for consolidations and acquisitions.

Every element [15], the client, vendor, client banks, and trader banks, registers with the installment door to make its mystery key with the entryway. Secret vital components are essential to getting correspondence. Moreover, the client and vendor likewise make a private key between themselves. The client analyzes the vendor and solicitations for the item, with their brief character on the dealer site. The trader sends the solicitation to the installment passage. The client can interface their impermanent nature to the trader site to make a request. After making the request, RSA encryption conceals client card data to get ciphertext. The dealer side-tracks to the installment door for the encryption and unscrambling processes. The client bank and the client utilize the RSA mark to execute an electronic signature on the archive using the secret key. A declaration authority has authorized the public key set. The installment passage executes some check steps (encryption, unscrambling, and approval) and advances esteem deduction solicitations to the backer and a few encoded messages to the acquirer. The primary role of this framework is to make public and confidential keys for brokers and banks. It stores keys in the vital data set for clients after the critical age process. In the unscrambling system, RSA gathers the client's card subtleties after receipt of the ciphertext from the client and decodes the ciphertext. The installment entryway approves the approval for the installment stage after the client's card subtleties decode. The ciphertext is made and interpreted by RSA unscrambling to get the client's card data from the bank's site after it gets the ciphertext from the installment door. After decoding the client's card subtleties, the bank will approve the installment exchange, given the client's affirmation. Following the business, the bank will illuminate the client and the dealer regarding the installment confirmation. The client starts the exchange by mailing their passing personality to the server. In the whole exchange process, the client promptly contacts the shipper. Fig. (**5**) depicts the same.

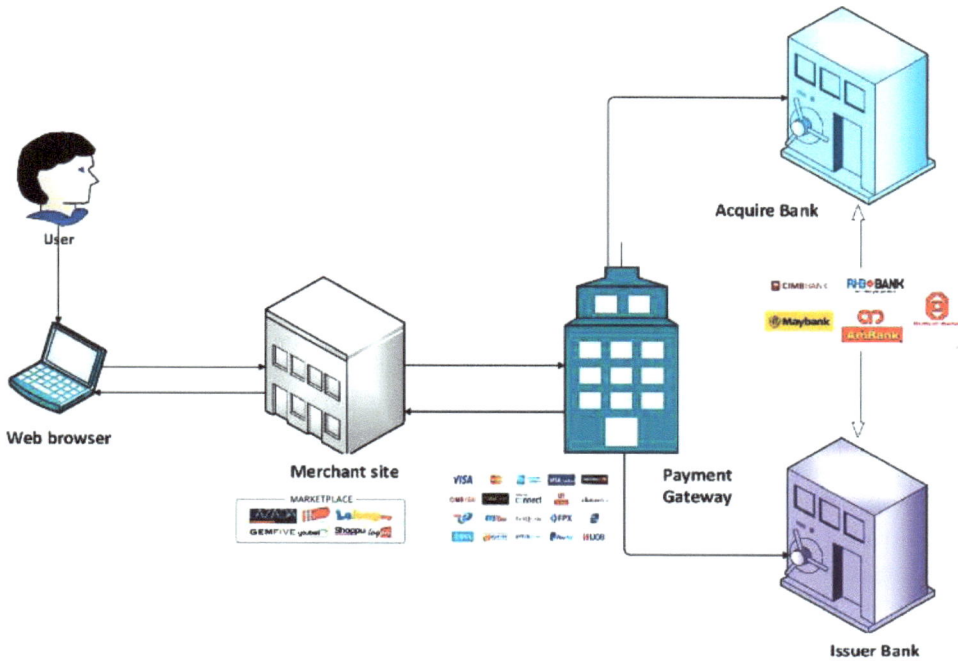

Fig. (5). Proposed E-payment system [15].

There are numerous portable distributed computing frameworks for various uses, including medical services applications. The conventional frameworks include a set of cloud assets. The clients of various sorts of gadgets utilized through the Internet have gotten to from a distance. The enormous spread of portable applications has immense measures of information that should be handled and broken down proficiently, significantly quicker, and with power complexity. In this MCC model [16], the cloudlets are set close to the medical clinic and cover a region that can be gotten to approved individuals who can get to the patient's data and follow their status from a distance.

The whole information investigation engineering [17] comprises four phases: gathering, putting away, handling, and consuming. Each stage will have an alternate cloud administration explicitly dealing with explicit undertakings. These administrations can cooperate to smooth out the whole cycle, to be specific organization. Organized information is profoundly standardized by broad patterns and put away in social data sets, supporting conditional business application lines. The information design and diagram in the Data Warehouse improve SQL question execution. The outcomes are functional announcing and investigation through a few business insight devices. Cleaned, altered, and put away data set table information. Information handling incorporates purifying, changing, arranging, and conglomerating information. The work includes ML innovations in the information investigation processes and suggests a more specific example for the E-Commerce industry.

A cloud-edge administration [18] addresses triple-input boundaries, yield parameters, and a sequential succession of QoS values. The help work process is a theoretical portrayal of the business cycle. A help work process frames as practical assignments and control undertakings. Among them, useful errands are answerable for satisfying applicable prerequisites, and control assignments are liable for controlling the construction of the work process to guarantee smooth participation between valuable appointments. An administration work process design incorporates four sorts: succession, decision, equal, and cycle. For various help work process structures, the estimation recipes for the worth and cost credits of help are different. A cloud-edge administration summon a proper cloud-edge administration to execute a sub-task in a help work process. A help work process usually comprises numerous subtasks. In this way, the execution of a help work process generally requires a bunch of administration summons.

3.3.3. Smart City

Automatic reasoning calculations give capacities to handle a lot of information and to identify examples and elements that would stay undetected utilizing conventional methodologies. The reason for associating parts of urban life in shrewd urban communities works around contemporary and arising advances, for example, distributed computing, the Web of Things, and existing digital frameworks addressing the most recent chain in current unrest alluded to as Industry 4.0. The intelligent framework is of specific significance for structural designing and establishes critical parts of savvy urban communities. Fig. (**6**) depicts the smart city scenario.

Savvy urban areas and networks [20] are an arising research field that covers numerous points and advances by significant advances in innovation, changes in business activities, and general ecological challenges. The undertakings can comprehensively have three levels, *i.e.*, vital, strategic, and functional. The essential capabilities contain undeniable level (and longer-term) arranging choices, for example, course decisions, traffic stream control, and fuel quotes. Conversely, functional errands incorporate low-level (present moment) and consistent routine undertakings, for example, parallel power in light of quick ecological info and in-vehicle data sources, for example, driver checking. The strategic performances fall in the two and are mid-level, medium-term errands, including, yet not restricted to, turning, overwhelming, hole change, and consolidating, given neighborhood mindfulness around the vehicle.

Fig. (6). Smart city Scenario [19].

The work [21] is a reasoning-based semantic IoT crossover administration design to incorporate heterogeneous IoT gadgets to help astute administrations. It empowers adaptable associations among heterogeneous devices. It has three layers. The foundation layer deals with a wide range of intelligent gadgets. The gadget is the premise of developing the IoT. The brilliant gadget has three unique sorts- sensors, actuators, and a mixture of gadgets. Sensors are fundamentally utilized for detecting the climate and can be named temperature, dampness, light, cameras, savvy groups, RFID perusers, and so on. The help the board layer is principally answerable for gadget the executives, information investigation and administration arrangement. It is conveyed in the Cloud and the assistance region. It connects the client with the Cloud.AI point of interaction is developed to interface the IoT stage and the artificial intelligence module. All locations can use the simulated intelligence connection point to access the manufactured intelligence module for information examination.

The proposed design [22] has four distinct stages. The proposed model comprises four practical steps. The first stage, gadget sending, includes different shrewd gadgets with synthetic intelligence and blockchain execution. In this stage, a colossal measure of information is created and communicated to the edge knowledge stage. The subsequent step, edge knowledge, involved a computerized reasoning-focused base station associated with blockchain at the organization's edge. Each haze hub with blockchain innovation in the mist stage comprises an automated reasoning-empowered base station. The stream of data includes six layers of activity. The top layer is an even layer that relates to the gadget-sending stage for the assortment of information continuously. The correspondence and control layer are answerable for edge processing. The help and overseeing layer relates to the mist registering, and the application layer compares to cloud computing. The gathered data conveys to the correspondence level that goes about as a moderate for imparting information starting with one hub and then onto the next. The reconciliation of manufactured reasoning and blockchain for IoT applications uses an agreement calculation to accomplish security and versatility.

The proposal [23] recommends a four-layer model which joins and connection points of these components by sending innovations. It involves an assortment of smart homes with IoT. They offer administrations to their clients. The singular shrewd home has an AAI framework, which controls and cycles its intelligent home administrations. By consolidating these AAI frameworks, utilizing 5G to access the Web and the Bed benefits, the ICT reason for a smart city with Incorporated Brilliant Home and Savvy City. The IoT implanted in the shrewd homes produces context-oriented data, which is insightfully handled by the brilliant homes.

3.3.4. Healthcare

The Surrounding Insight worldview [24] addresses the future vision of smart registering where conditions support individuals possessing them. It guarantees a practical understanding of the abundance of logical data acquired from such inserted sensors. It will adjust the foundation to the client's necessities straightforwardly and expectantly. The frameworks can be delicate, responsive, versatile, and pervasive. While encompassing insight draws from artificial intelligence, it isn't inseparable from computer-based intelligence. The frameworks can upgrade the medical care space emphatically. For instance, encompassing insight innovation can be utilized to screen the well-being status of more established grown-ups or individuals with constant infections and give assistive consideration to people with physical or mental limits. It very well may be utilized for creating enticing administrations to inspire individuals to lead better ways of life. It can change restoration settings or overall upgrade people's prosperity. At last, it can uphold medical care experts by giving inventive correspondence and checking devices. These frameworks will provide well-being checking straightforwardly and unpretentiously. Fig. (7) depicts the same.

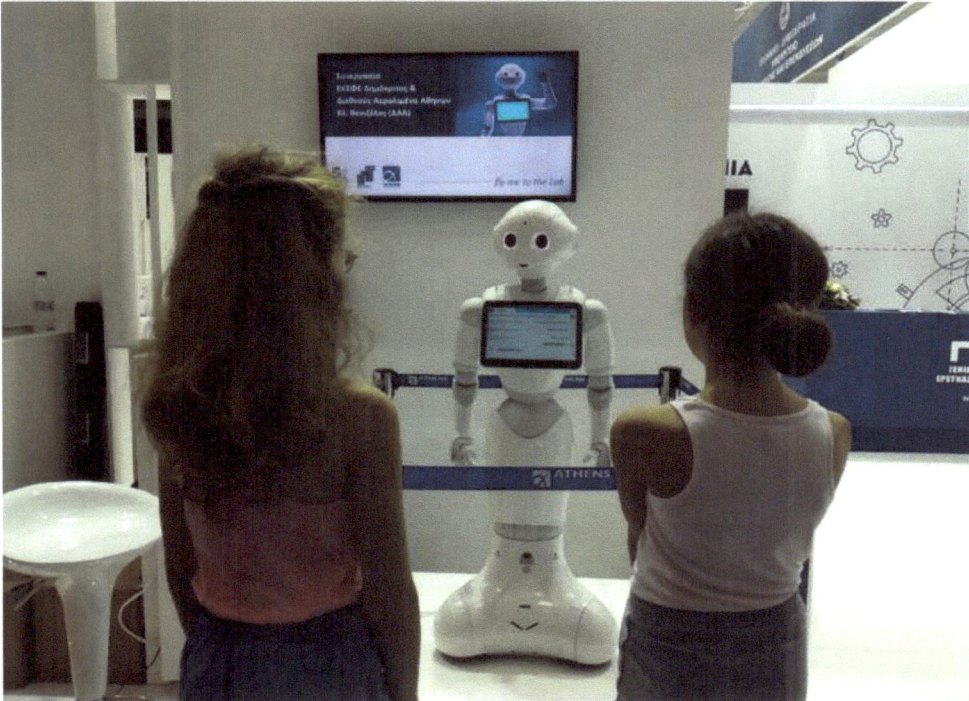

Fig. (7). Pepper Robot [24].

The work [25] is a simulated intelligence-based practical and productive medical care application. Simulated intelligence based distributed computing stages synchronize the cycles of heterogenous stages by creating economical, solid, united, and interoperable organizations. The information separating, looking at and checking procedures from sensors and actuators in the whole clinical scene are worked with by cloud-empowered advances for engrossing and tolerating the whole arising wave of revolution. The calculation is a smart and dynamic calculation for amplifying the CPS-based medical care activity time with high unwavering quality, interoperability, and convergence. It gathers the ECG information to inspect the wellbeing status of old or ongoing patients with the IoT-based digital actual framework. It is a shrewd and self-versatile dynamic way to deal with focus on crisis and basic patients in relationship with the chose boundaries for further developing medical care quality at sensible expenses. Fig. (**8**) depicts the same.

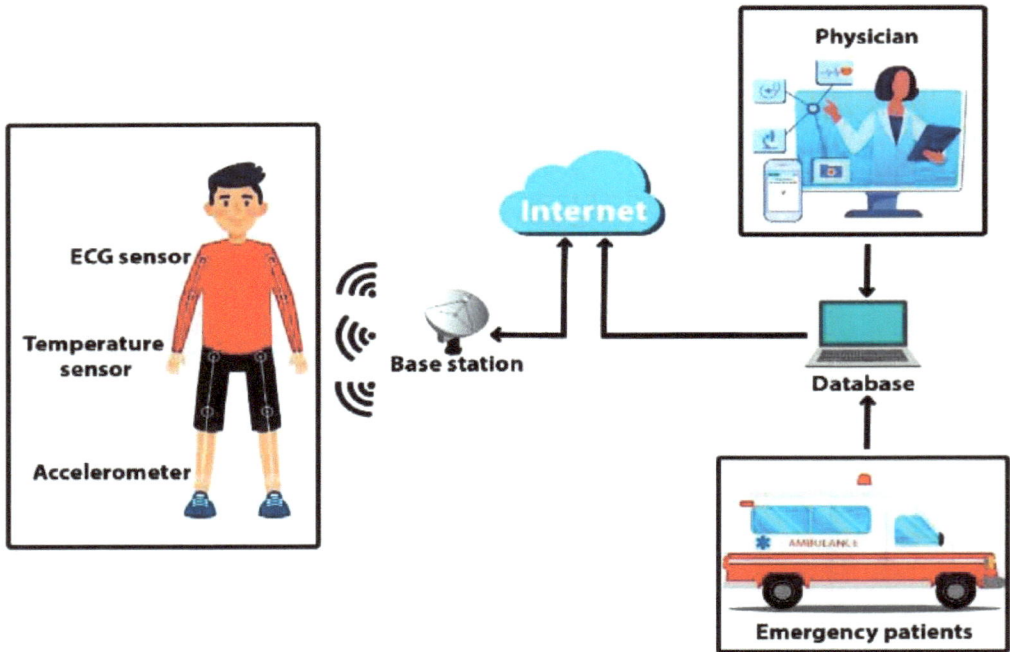

Fig. (8). System Architecture [25].

The versatile organization [26] advances the clients' administration solicitation to the cloud server after approving that they are genuine users. The cloud supplier processes the solicitation and offers the expected support. The proposed model comprises disseminated cloudlets associated with one another through WiFi and an expert CloudLet, which is liable to the executives and is associated with the virtual cloud server. Suppose the versatile client is moving endlessly and not cloudlet range. In that case, the portable client must associate straightforwardly with the venture cloud to play out a task utilizing remote correspondence technology. But, on the off chance that the versatile client is still in the/cloudlet or master cloudlet range, then it can interface straightforwardly to those cloudlets utilizing WiFi to do the expected positions.

The survey [27] explores the attainability and prerequisites of the future medical care framework for Saudi Arabia. The work looks at Lord Faisal Expert Clinic and Exploration Focus. It is one of the most outstanding Saudi medical clinics in Organ Transplantation, Oncology, Hereditary Infections, and Cardiovascular Sicknesses. It comprises 25 clinical divisions. The RC contains various resea-rchers who are upheld with trend-setting innovations to do explores cell science, Human Malignant growth Genomic, Sub-atomic Biomedicine and 13 other divisions and programs. The Half breed cloudlet MCC model could be applied to different emergency clinics in various Saudi urban areas like Al-Noor expert medical clinic in Makkah and Ruler Fahad Expert Emergency clinic in Dammam.

Cloudlet innovation [28] is accessible to examine patient records and remove suggested highlights from the patient data set. It is a transport burden and limits sharing. The medical care frameworks in brilliant city satisfy needs by adjusting distributed computing. The medical care association relies upon cloud climate for handling and stockpiling of immense measure of information. The portable client offloads undertakings to the cloudlets associated with the expert cloudlet through the small organization. The expert cloudlet processes the errand and sends it to the end client. The application requires access to vast information from associations inside and beyond the limits. The information design is regularly robust. It is backings granularity interaction. The prerequisites of the medical care framework are distinguished and broken down given the consequence of the cycle regarding throughput. This stage recognizes the computational and communicational necessities of medical care framework application.

The work [29] utilizes the Crow Inquiry Improvement calculation based Flowed Long Transient Memory model for sickness conclusion. The implanted sensors continue with comprehensive analyses to gauge and recognize ordinary and unusual pulses. The subjects are with shrewd gadgets. Cell phones process the data and sort it as either solid or unfortunate. The android stage performs the expectation of diabetes and effective pulse. Pre-handling involves steps like information change, design transformations, and class naming. iForest strategy dispose of exceptions that exist in quiet information. CSO-CLSTM model characterizes the information into reality and the non-presence of the illness.

The work [30] proposes an ad-libbed model of arranging versatile e-medical services in the board framework to help the Google Cloud Medical Services Programming interface, including HL7.FHIR and DICOM. RIA approves the clients to collaborate by the framework. RIA is made of content language codes to execute areas of strength for a showcase for Web clients. These applications can interface with the cloud too. The cloud server deals with the information base through Amazon's database. REST establishes the connection or point of interaction between RIA clients and cloud servers. The application part works with the client and server that can execute basics for the whole system. This layer proceeds to a few operational guidelines, for example, data security, Web capabilities, trade information, and application inquiry. The public authority service will deal with the administration of this layer from the upper level with its specific point of interaction. The outcasts connected with clinical administrations like assurance and drugs are, in like manner, added with the cloud using this layer.

The individual well-being records will have information about a patient's thoughts. Specialists are to permit patients to perform their clinical procedures, approve them, and store them in their accounts. Patients choose to keep up the data in their PHR accounts.

The suggestion [31] explores whether sending distributed computing can help lessen operating costs in medical services places. We utilized board information from 2008 to 2019 for 156 medical services places. The work uses Decent Impact and Arbitrary Impact models. The outcomes recommend that the organization of distributed computing helps lessen operating costs in medical care places. This exploration uses board information procedures to accomplish the examination objective. If approaching a board of information, there are critical benefits to completely utilizing this rich construction. The board information empowers us to address a more extensive scope of subjects and tackle more complex issues than is reachable with unadulterated time series or cross-sectional data alone. Table **3.1** Represents the implementation details of various contributions.

Table 3.1. Represents the implementation details of various contributions.

Contribution	Implementation Details
[7]	• The datasets comprise images of 0–9 bits which can be grouped into a training set of a larger volume of images. • CNN training the datasets that involve the processes such as uploading datasets along with layers of input, Convolutional, Pooling, Convolution and Pooling, Dense and legit. • It uses a cloud-based MMIS algorithm.
[8]	• INFN-Cloud is a multi-site, multi-organization federated Cloud infrastructure that is used.
[9]	• Amazon S3 compatible interface is used for storage • RING version 7.4 used has 24 nodes cluster. • 13 PB storage space is provided.
[10]	• It uses Windows 10 host machine with Intel Core i5-7200U @2.50 GHz CPU and 4 GB memory.
[17]	• It uses Data Lake and Amazon SageMaker.
[21]	• It uses Alljoyn, an open-source software framework originally developed by Qualcomm and the Alljoyn platform.
[25]	• The work uses a single-chip wearable electrocardiogram (ECG) with the support of an analog front-end (AFE) chip model (*i.e.*, ADS1292R).
[26]	• The work uses Mobile Cloud Simulator (MCCSIM) tool.
[29]	• The work uses a PC with specifications such as Motherboard - MSI Z370 A-Pro, Processor - i5-8600k, Graphics Card - GeForce 1050Ti 4GB, RAM - 16GB and File Storage - 1TB HDD.

3.3.5. Robotics

Advanced mechanics [32, 33] have seen huge improvements throughout the last many years bringing about its expanded applications to a few genuine issues, including computerized fabricating, extra-earthly tasks, automated search and salvage, calamity mechanical technology, self-driving vehicles, socially assistive robots, and medical services and clinical robots. The robots utilized in many of these applications are single robots restricted by their installed equipment and computational imperatives. Cloud advanced mechanics is a collaborative innovation between distributed computing and administration advanced mechanics empowered through progress in remote systems administration, enormous scope stockpiling and correspondence advancements, and the ubiquitous presence of Web assets over late years. Distributed computing engages robots by offering them quicker and more impressive computational abilities through enormously equal calculation and higher information storerooms. It likewise gives admittance to open-source, large datasets and programming, agreeable learning capacities through information sharing, and human information through publicly supporting. Fig. (**9**) depicts the cloud Robotics Framework.

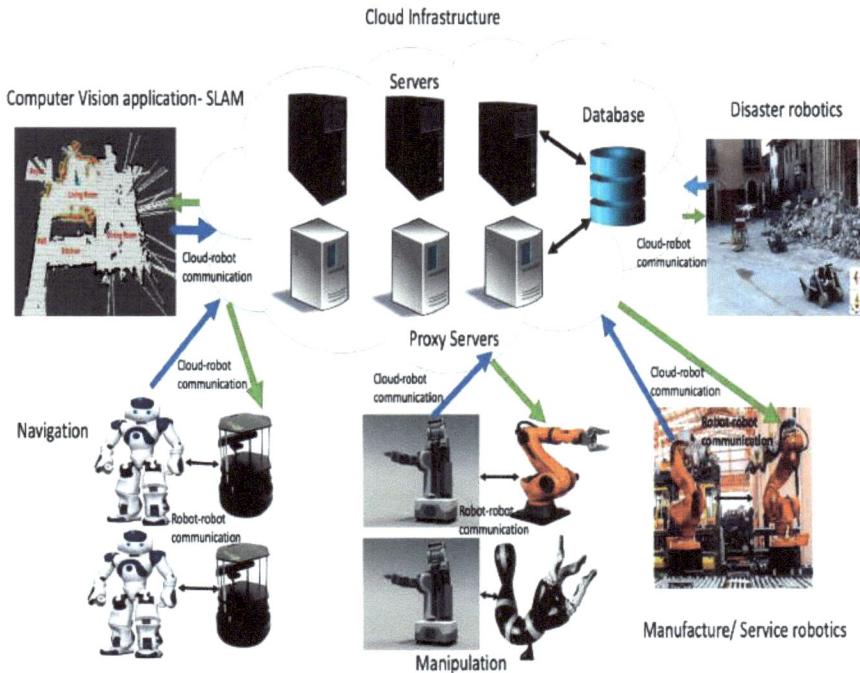

Fig. (9). Cloud Robotics Framework [32].

RGB-D SLAM calculation [34] has two sections. The assignment of the front-cut-off is to separate the spatial friendship between various perceptions. The undertaking of the back-end is to upgrade the posture data of the camera in the posture diagram utilizing a non-straight blunder capability. The front-finish of the RGB-D Hammer calculation, highlight focuses identification and descriptor extraction is performed on each RGB picture input by the camera, and element focuses descriptors of two adjoining outlines. The system obtains profundity data from the related profundity picture. It gets a bunch of 3D point correspondences between two neighboring casings. The comparing connection assesses the 6D movement change, and afterward, the movement change is enhanced to get the upgraded 6D movement change. In the back finish of the RGB-D Hammer calculation, a chart-based present streamlining technique introduces the posture map utilizing the 6D movement change relationship from the front end. Fig. (**10**) depicts the same.

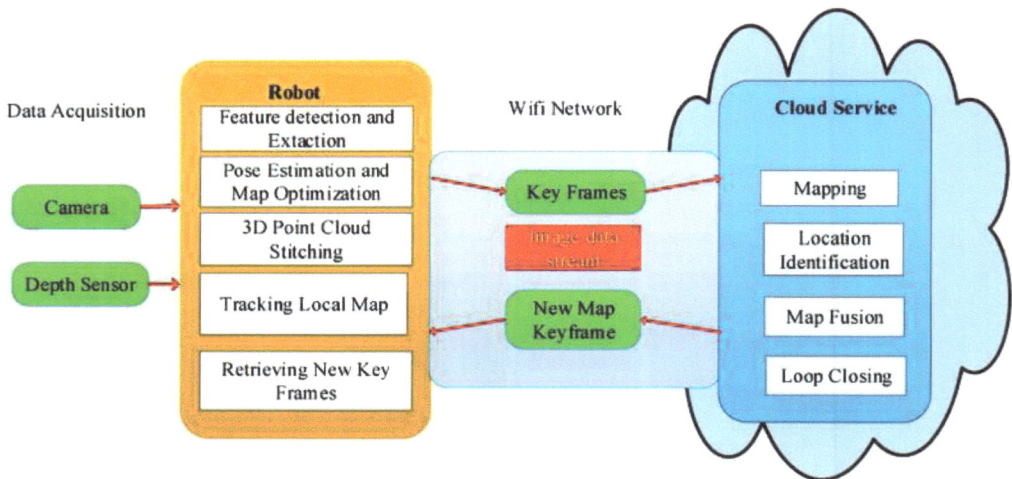

Fig. (10). RGB-D SLAM with cloud robot [34].

The hybrid cloud mechanical technology [35] calculation model proposes the C2RO cloud automated technology stage as a handling model utilizing both edge and distributed computing advancements in robotics. The gadget layer runs a light calculation on the gadgets. It remembers a speedy control response of the robots for a climate through a shut control circle. The edge layer moves to the brink of the organization, where edge hubs facilitate the framework. The cloud foundation layer is for escalated handling or collective information stockpiling communicated to the cloud.

The work [36] gives interfaces that are much simpler to utilize yet still help the majority of the usefulness of these computer-based intelligence administrations. It establishes another programming climate for youngsters. The Programming interface expresses the given text pitch, rate, volume, language, and voice control. The primary form of the talk takes a text contention and a discretionary capability. Its nonconcurrent idea of acknowledgment administrations powers a dependence upon continuations. The block utilizes the 'listen' block that upholds occasion broadcasting and a worldwide variable. It communicated when something was heard and perused a worldwide variable containing the last thing spoken. A block arranges the camera. The picture acknowledgment block has a boundary indicating which cloud supplier, a continuation that will get a depiction of the picture. The trial has 25 college understudies and six kids.

The robot knowledge [37] is modified using the IBM Watson computer-based intelligence Cloud administration. The mechanical stage utilized for building a model of CATHI and running our examinations is the humanoid "Pepper". It had the organization of a MoCA-like psychometric test. It gives directions and gathers information through its multimodal interfaces for the resulting handling and mechanized scoring by the IBM Watson AI. The whole organization meeting is sound recorded by the robot's mouthpieces. The robot additionally takes photos of the client's drawings for the visuospatial/leader abilities. The automated mental test estimates similar regions of the MoCAs. The subtests have identical names. The robot utilized non-verbal correspondence signals to help a more normal Human-Robot Interaction. IBM Watson is a subset of the IBM Cloud benefits that emphasize giving improved manufactured brainpower arrangements, which IBM alludes to as a mental capacity that can insert into innovation applications. Watson Collaborator arranges the test work process, Watson Text to Discourse for creating the robot's voice during the organization, Watson Discourse to Text to perform discourse acknowledgment, and Watson Visual Acknowledgment to examine the hand-drawn pictures. NaoQi structure's Python SDK composed Python scripts that ran on the robot and took care of its way of behaving during the organization. The correspondence with the IBM Cloud was executed as HTTP POST demands, created by the Watson Designer Cloud module for Python.

3.4. CHALLENGES OF CLOUD-AI

3.4.1. Resource Management

For hosting and delivering software solutions for many industrial applications, cloud computing has established itself as a dependable, affordable, and scalable computing service. The widespread demand for hosting application services on the cloud has been fueled by the deployment of cloud data centers across the globe. Most cloud providers offer a wide range of deployment options that help users tailor resources to their needs. However, Industry 4.0's adoption of AI and IoT applications has raised the overall demand for cloud resources. These cloud data centers need a lot of energy to operate effectively. To reduce energy usage, costs, and carbon footprints, it must manage cloud resources efficiently. Supplying comprehensive resource management for long-term cloud computing is a challenge.

The work [38] is a Petri net-based framework for resource preservation with custom cloud and edge computing for Emergency department systems. The proposed framework describes and has proven effective in modeling non-consumable resources. Key performance indicators like the patient length of stay, resource utilization rate, and average patient waiting time are modeled and optimized in a real-world scenario using a resource preservation net. Task assignments and completed process notifications transmit from the edge nodes to the cloud, where the databases and workflow software are stored. Every resource has an edge node-working smart device, like a smartphone or tablet. The edge node notifies the cloud that a particular resource is available in the pool and ready to be re-assigned when the help completes the assigned task. Fig. (**11**) portrays the same.

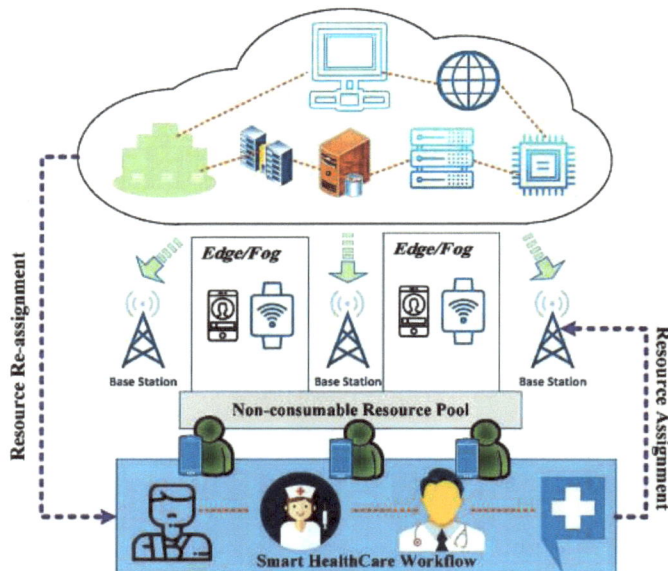

Fig. (11). Edge-based smart healthcare framework [38].

The work [4] ensures that technology is cost-effectively available for women's education. Top-to-bottom and bottom-to-top approaches are dual-sided interactive architecture. It keeps its capability and flexibility, appealing to both the provider and the customer. This architecture functions as an organization that enrolls users of various types and abilities in the bottom-to-top approach. Services are indexed for proper handling even though the top-to-bottom approach delivers them to registered providers and consumers. The architecture's environment is its most crucial component. Members of the distributed cloud—consumers, providers, and hybrids—are subject to centralized control. The enrolment module distinguishes between the kind of membership and the member's identity. There are also various cloud types, including personal, public, and hybrid ones. In the setting, each cloud is fully equipped and offers services. In the proposed architecture, each cloud stands out on its own. The members are indexed and located by the centrally controlled module, particularly hybrid handling, which grants and denies access to services and provides resources. Fig. (**12**) depicts the same.

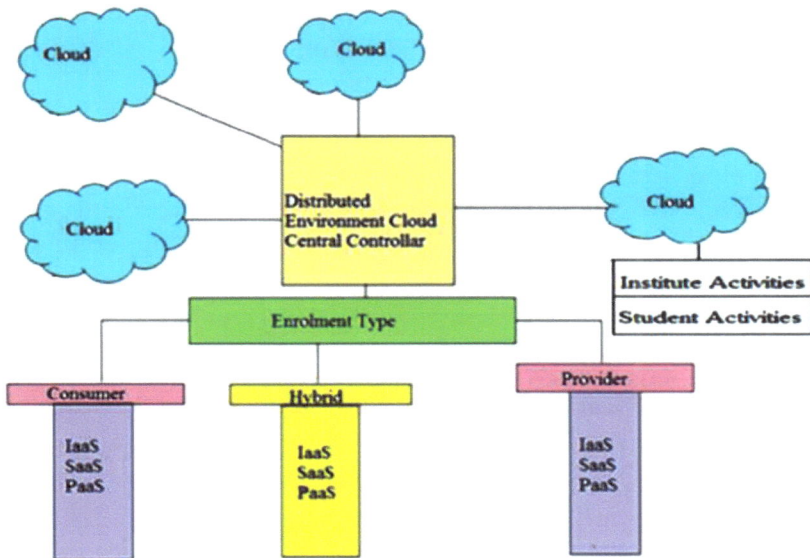

Fig. (12). Proposed architecture [4].

The recommendation is HUNTER [39], a holistic resource management strategy for sustainable cloud computing based on artificial intelligence. The goal of maximizing data center energy efficiency formulates as a multi-objective scheduling problem in the proposed model. It has three significant models, including thermal, energy, and cooling. HUNTER generates optimal scheduling decisions by utilizing a Gated Graph Convolution Network as a substitute model to approximate the Quality of Service for a system state. The physical cloud testbed and CloudSim toolkit simulate the work. Users assign jobs to the cloud data centers by sharing workloads. IoT sensors collect the data, which is then sent to the centers through gateway devices like smartphones and tablets. A graphical user interface for cloud users to use to interact with the system and submit their workloads, service level agreements, and details about the quality of service. The central cloud server assigns jobs to different compute resources.

3.4.2. Fault Tolerance

The primary component of cloud systems is sharing computer resources among various users. Platforms for software, hardware, and applications are shared resources. Infrastructure as a Service, Platform as a Service, and Software as a Service are the three main layers of cloud architecture. Although faults can occur at any of these layers, the software is where most strategies for systems to recover from errors are developed and put into practice. Depending on the fault's nature, system engineers may need to intervene manually to recover the system properly.

Cluster-based, fault-tolerant mechanisms [40] address the work strategy's data-intensive nature of scientific workflow tasks. Resource management acquires and manages cloud resources through infrastructure as a service. Workflow Admission receives the scientific data and transforms them into abstract scientific workflows before passing them on to the following component. Workflow Mapper transforms abstract scientific workflows into executable scientific workflows, which transfer to Workflow Scheduler. The work process Scheduler changes over the executable logical work processes into occupations and afterward appoints them to the expected assets. Workflow Engine is in charge of the execution procedure. Using a cluster-based, fault-tolerant mechanism, the Workflow Engine executes the jobs assigned to each workflow as the Workflow Scheduler receives. The application interface returns the outcome of each workflow to the appropriate user following its execution by Workflow Engine as jobs. WorkflowSim is used to perform the simulation. Fig. (**13**) depicts the same.

SDN nodes [41] on fog nodes are how the proposed model receives vehicle messages. Software-defined network controllers prioritize messages two ways after receiving them from nearby units. A software-defined network innovative gateway processes vehicle messages following embedded rules, forward them to other vehicles when necessary, and sends them to the Cloud or fog for storage and processing. The intelligent gateways are near the roadside in fog nodes. The controller periodically updates the routing tables based on the information received by connecting to the nearby SDN nodes. The controller is in edge fog nodes. VANET Vehicles' messages and information are processed and stored nearby by fog nodes. When VANET data demands it, heavy computation and permanent storage in the Cloud. CloudSIm and iFogSim are used to implement the proposed model. Fig. (**14**) depicts the same.

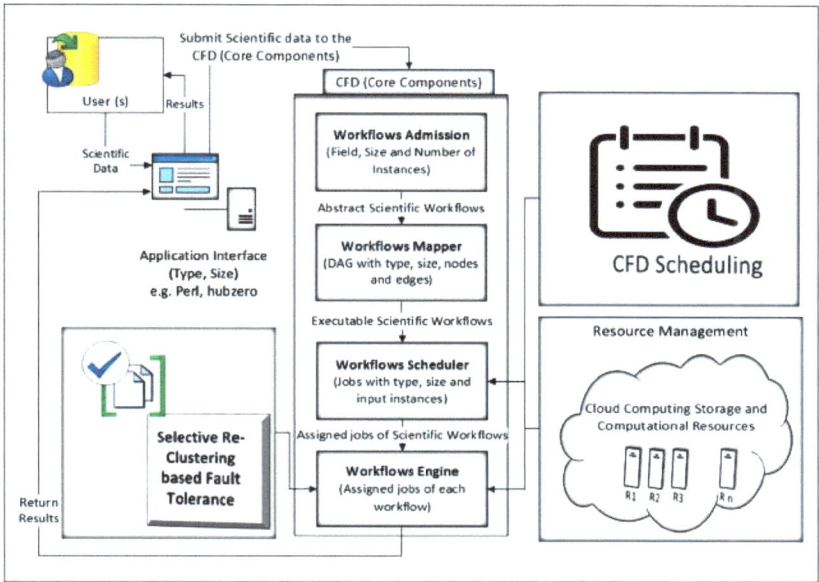

Fig. (13). cluster-based, fault-tolerant and data-intensive strategy [40].

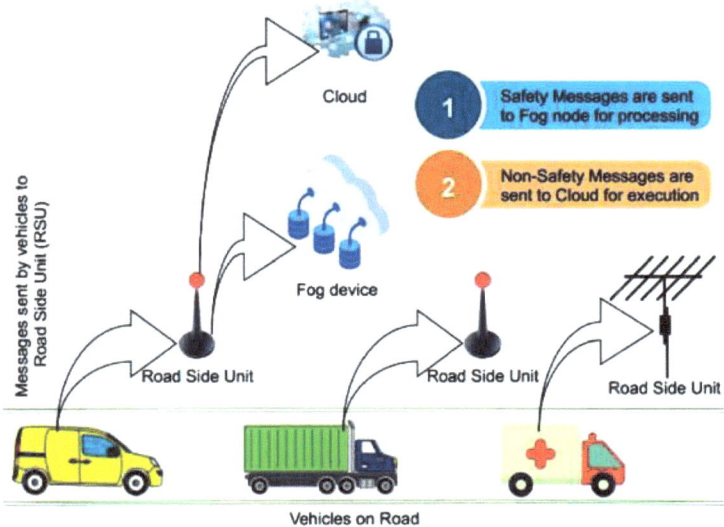

Fig. (14). System Architecture [41].

This work [42] focuses on a novel AI-driven proactive fault-tolerant scheduling scheme for cloud data centers. There are two stages to the Prediction-based Energy-aware Fault-tolerant Scheduling plan. Based on this probability, it predicts the likelihood of a task failing. A failure-prone and non-failure task queue organizes failure-prone and failure-prone tasks, respectively. The scheduling method is used for each type of function separately. There are three parts to the schedule plan. A DNN classifies tasks into failure-prone and non-failure-prone categories. The replication-oriented elegant vector reconstruction method developed for a fault-tolerant mechanism creates super jobs from failure-prone tasks. The super and non-failure-prone duties are assigned to appropriate hosts using vector bin packing. In the failure-prone task queue, failure-prone lessons are in the earliest-deadline-first order. The three failure-prone tasks are selected from the line and divided into three copies of each job. After that, the purpose of the vector reconstruction approach is to reconstruct super tasks from replicate copies. The three dimensions of the requirement for CPU, RAM, and storage sort all items, which are then sequentially placed in the first bin with sufficient capacity. The simulation uses a computer with an Intel(R) Core (TM) i5-3230M processor running at 2.60 GHz, 8.0 GB of RAM, 750 GB of disk storage, the Windows 10 operating system, NetBeans IDE 8.2, and JDK 8.0. Using the data set, a DNN is implemented using TensorFlow. CloudSim is used for the simulation.

The HPC cluster [43] has a lot of nodes. Hosting this cluster on a machine with high computing performance will be necessary. Virtualization software is installed on the virtualization cluster nodes, allowing a single node to function as multiple nodes. Amazon's Elastic Compute Cloud service provides elastic cloud computing.VMs from one or more physical clusters are placed on dispersed servers. The fault tolerance, and disaster recovery, virtual machines replicate across multiple servers. The administrator must record or describe the sources of configuration information. Customers can manage user accounts while using EC2 and build virtual machines. Using VDI's built-in remote desktop protocol, the cloud forensic investigator connects to a virtual machine located far away. It supports two different protocols for VMware Horizon View VDI - PCoIP and Microsoft's RDP. The virus-resistant and stringently mandated APEX server offload card can protect and guarantee a consistent user experience regardless of task or activity level. The PCM makes communication easier for the view connection server and endpoints. If the PCM is used in a firewalled environment, the PCoIP Security Gateway needs to be configured.

3.4.3. Security and Privacy

Big data is a vast collection of structured, semi-structured, and unstructured information typically annotated with implicit information and gathered from various gadgets, including cellphones, laptops, traffic cameras, and sensors. Although these technological advancements are lovely, they also highlight additional issues that are solved, such as big data processing and storage, user privacy protection, and the security of sensitive data.

An AI-enabled IoT-CPS [44] that doctors can use to detect diseases in patients based on artificial intelligence. It identifies conditions like diabetes, heart disease, and gait problems. Patients and the elderly suffer from various symptoms of each disease. The dataset is retrieved from the Kaggle repository. The AI-enabled IoT-CPS Algorithm identifies diseases for classification. The training dataset creates some classification rules and classifies patients' illnesses from the training dataset. It takes every instance from the disease training dataset for the patient. It takes all of the values for the target attribute from each specimen. It uses the importance of all target attributes to determine the global disorder amount. The Classification Rule Generation Method uses Classification rules based on GDA, OA, and R. This algorithm returns all the Highest Priority Attribute and their values along with the target attribute value as classification rules after locating the highest target attribute value. The Disease Prediction Algorithm uses classification rules to predict the diseases of patients. It uses classification rules and Patient Disease Testing Data from wearable devices worn by patients or older adults as input. It decides what action to take by comparing attribute values to classification rules. Fig. (**15**) represents the same.

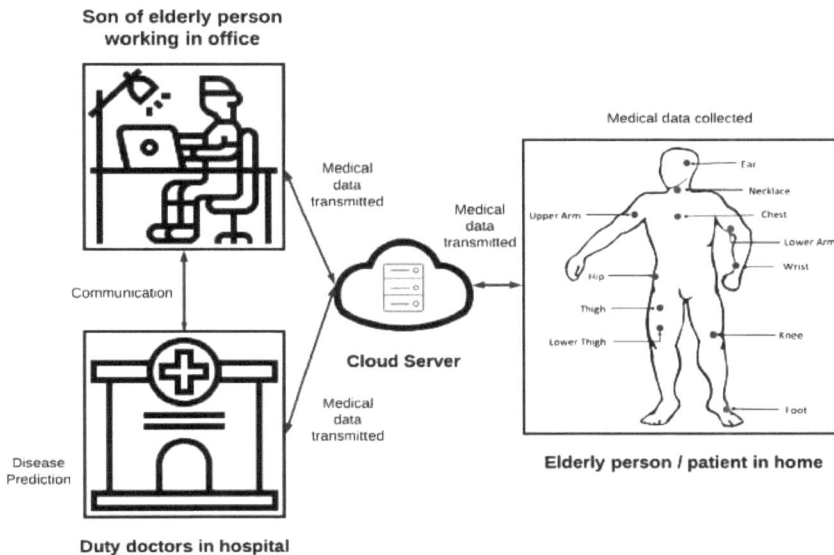

Fig. (15). Artificial intelligence with IoT-CPS [44].

The work [45] has large amounts of clinical data as inputs for accurate confirmation and coding. A quantum channel connects QKD pairs individually. The Sender and the Receiver use the secure quantum communication link to exchange cubits, and an open communication link employing a traditional cryptographic strategy is used to exchange crucial information. Blockchain is also a valuable method for retrieving cloud user data. The current operational patient monitory facility is an automated electrical user's clinical database that plays a significant role in preserving and monitoring the user's information. The primary issue concerns the breach of confidential patient personal files. The planned system is well-organized, able to handle a lot of cloud data, and it produces the best resolution for controlling the framework through the various layers. After the bi-linear cyclical cluster and two basic and polarizing cubits, both the source user and destination user require chaotic random producers. There are three approaches to the offered prototype framework: encrypting, QKRD, and computing consumer integrity metrics to decipher cloud users' private data processes. After implementing enciphering and decoding algorithms, the input accepts the cloud consumer attribute values to compute user integrity. After that, each user's weight can forward to the secure blockchain-based quantum essential production. The following steps are CP-ABE-based individual session key generation and chaotic integrity metric-based quantum production process in cloud consumer attributes. The chaotic quantum key and computed user integrity metrics utilized in the initial setup, random essential creation, enciphering, and deciphering processes make up the final step. The quantum, public, private, and master keys are utilized on cloud consumer input attributes. The control structure policy has access to the decision tree in the cloud customer's ciphered message, so these attributes can only decipher the encrypted text. It makes use of S3 and Amazon Elastic Compute Cloud. Fig. (**16**) depicts the same.

3.4.4. Serverless Computing

An appealing paradigm for deploying cloud applications has developed with serverless computing, specifically functions-as-a-service. It is partly because enterprise application architectures have recently shifted to containers and microservices. With the subsequent development of cloud computing architectures, serverless platforms present new capabilities that will make creating scalable microservices more straightforward and affordable. A more extensive range of applications has been supported by its use. From the standpoint of a cloud user, serverless platforms offer programmers a streamlined programming model for their applications. It reduces costs by billing for execution time rather than resource allocation; and enables quickly deploying small chunks of cloud-native event handlers. Serverless computing offers a cloud provider the chance to manage the complete development stack, cut operational costs through effective resource management and optimization, and promote the use of an ecosystem of other cloud provider services.

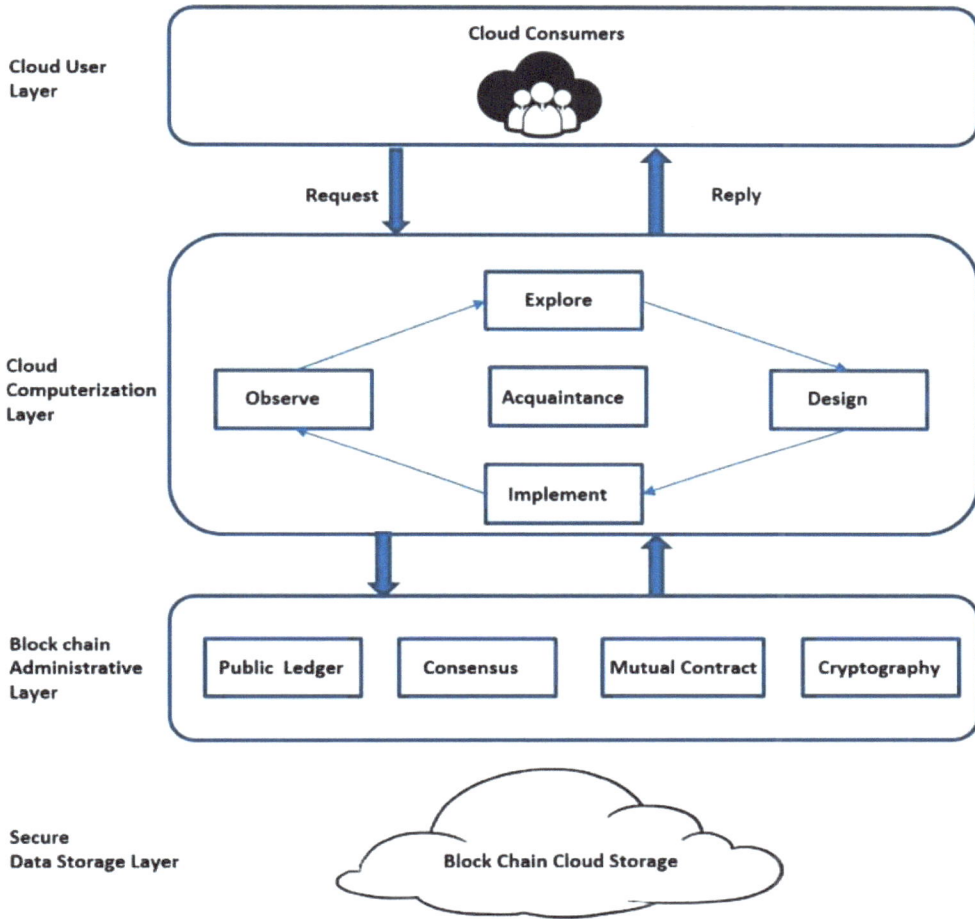

Fig. (16). QCPABE framework [45].

The intelligent grid design [46] was proposed by the Iraqi Ministry of Electricity and evaluated using the conventional computing design. Multiple meetings, workshops, and field visits to various Iraqi MOELC departments, including the Planning Department, Operation Department, and Control Department, were used to gather data. It connects to four major government distribution companies (zone 2) in Baghdad, the Middle East, the South, and the North of Iraq. Zone 3, where smaller branches or sub-regions represent the various Iraqi provinces geographically closer to a zone-2 area, is dominated by each significant distribution company. In an emergency or natural disaster, optical fiber and microwave links connect all distribution companies in zone 2 to the ministry headquarters in zone 1. There are many parts to it. It uses resource sharing through specific application components based on business logic. The application tier is responsible for resolving critical issues and enhancing productivity. In shared resources, the data tier interacts with data in permanent storage or various database schemes. By mapping the value of data with analytics information like power consumption forecasting, the analytics tier is in charge of providing operational flexibility in the generation and distribution of energy. An essential tool for controlling and monitoring connected devices is the API gateway. Fig. (**17**) represents the same.

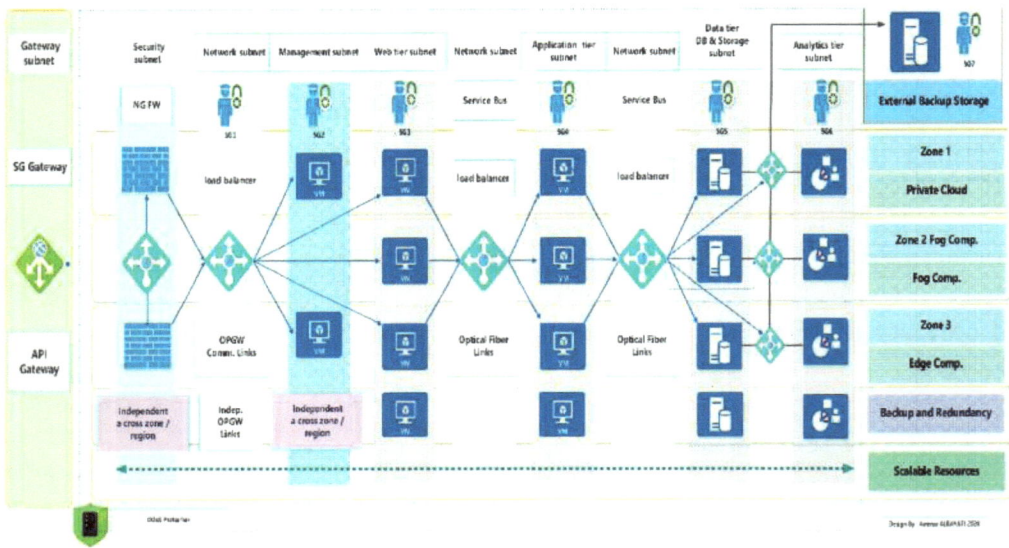

Fig. (17). proposed architecture [46].

The work [47] makes use of two distinct IBM Cloud Kubernetes Service Kubernetes clusters. The sample service used in the experiments is on the service cluster. Each of the nine nodes in the collection has a 64 GB memory and 16 vCPU, making it possible to host all Knative components without compromising performance. One node in the client cluster has 16 vCPUs and 64 GB of memory. It is in charge of sending requests to the service cluster to generate load. As an IKS user, the agent coordinates the experiment's process flow and manages the activities of both groups, including updating the sample service's configuration based on collected metrics. On the service cluster, the Knative resources are installed. Auto-scaling additional pods on demand and controlling the state of the deployed sample service is possible. We update the service's concurrency configuration with each iteration in the second experiment by employing RL's trial-and-error approach.

Applications are delivered by recommendation [48] *via* AI platforms hosted in the cloud. Through biosensors, cognitive mobile personal assistants continuously monitor health data and can anticipate and issue alerts in critical situations, such as critically low blood sugar levels. A representative, anonymized sample of the entire population serves as the basis for the service provider's base model's training. Each patient requires individual model adjustments and fine-tuning. Transfer learning methods and data gathered during runtime at the edge refine the base model before sending it to the edge device. While using AI-enhanced mobile devices, faulty parts are identified, diagnosis paths can be suggested, and the technician's actions can be recorded and verified. When instantaneous information is relevant, a device with AI accelerators uses video stream analytics. Setting mindful strategies can assist with a confided-in simulated intelligence work process. It uses several NVIDIA Jetson TX2 modules and clusters of Raspberry Pi 3 Model B+ with artificial intelligence accelerators.

The project is the architecture and prototype of a serverless platform-based chatbot in which developers combine stateless functions to carry out practical tasks. There are four levels of serverless actions and a microservice endpoint in the basic architecture. Audio I/O is the first level of processing, converting user audio input into text and vice versa. This architecture component is optional and only utilized when you cannot enter text. Text I/O is the second processing level and is in charge of getting user input to the right set of serverless actions for domain-specific processing. Domain-specific chatbot capabilities are the focus of the third level of processing. At the time of deployment, the work binds parameter values with OpenWhisk.

The work [49] runs on any cloud provider that supports serverless and microservice components and fully supports multi-cloud deployments. A generic, multi-cloud, hybrid application provisioning method's requirements serve as its foundation. The MELODIC platform with the Functionizer extension supports the multi-cloud hybrid application provisioning method. Model-driven engineering automates various steps in the multi-cloud, hybrid application management lifecycle. It also lets you run as many instances as possible within a particular cloud provider and use all of the available resources. Serverless, which uses highly light component types, enables significant cost reduction. The components are modeled in CAMEL and implemented *via* the Melodic platform.

The AIBLOCK Framework [50] has three parts. The framework's first layer is the Internet of Things layer. IoT devices can use communication protocols like

Zigbee, Bluetooth, WiFi, and Bluetooth Low Energy to receive and transmit data from sensors. The TLS protocol sends the data to the server over a secure communication channel. The Hardware Gateway Node sits in the middle of the serverless platform and the IoT layer. The IoT layer sensor sends data to the gateway node, which then sends the data to the serverless Datacenter. Data integration blockchain transactions are carried out. Software Gateway Node is in charge of sending the raw data to the serverless platform and receiving the results from the serverless platform after the calculation. The serverless processes the gateway node's data when it receives a request and employs the ML model to generate the COVID-19 results.

3.4.5. Data Processing

The Internet of Things has significantly impacted various crucial industries, including smart factories, water, transportation, and smart cities. Cloud computing has rapidly grown in popularity for processing and storage resources for numerous applications, including IoT applications. The orchestration and collaboration between the cloud and the edge provide an essential computing architecture for the Internet of Things applications. Intelligent orchestration in this architecture is made possible by artificial intelligence, which is a potent tool. Due to the excellent transmission distance, traditional centralized cloud computing, far from IoT devices, generates significant latency overheads. Additionally, it significantly increases the bandwidth needed for communication networks between IoT devices and the cloud. Many delay-sensitive IoT applications cannot accept the increase in delay.

The study [51] looks at four distinct Central China areas with high population densities and dense vegetation containing various types of Chu tombs. A unique segment-by-segment LiDAR processing and analysis strategy is based on LiDAR data to extract and identify archaeological remains beneath the Earth's surface. There are five components to the proposed system - LiDAR data collection, ground point filtering and classification, point cloud pattern analysis of Chu tombs, feature transformation and extraction, and visible remote sensing verification are all included. After the popular LiDAR point cloud filtering and classification software, Terrasolid removes the trees, vegetation, and buildings. LiDAR point cloud processing for tomb classification and identification begins with a ground point cloud. Terrasolid offers both automatic and manual variety and filtering options. Some famous Chu tombs are subjected to pattern analysis to discover the precise patterns of Chu tombs. Fig. (**18**) represents the same.

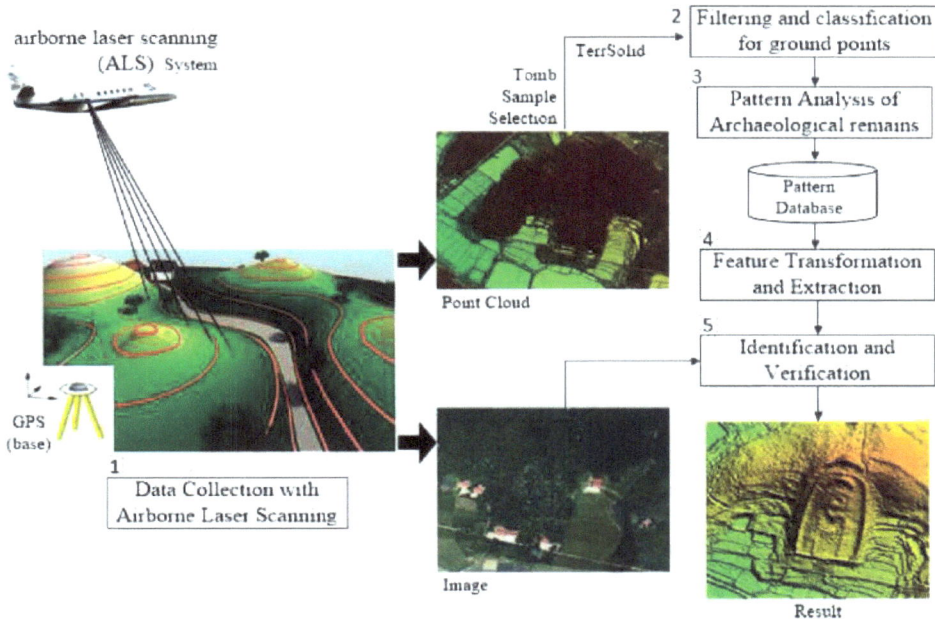

Fig. (18). Framework of proposed architecture [51].

The mobile edge computing layer [52] has IoT devices that perform data collection and pre-processing functions. Since IoT devices have different owners and edge servers may belong to various service providers, incentive mechanisms are necessary for collaboration. The three layers make up the proposed architecture. Industrial cloud computing platforms support a variety of IIoT applications. The industrial edge gateway is in charge of balancing networking, computing, and storage resources and managing data collection processes from edge servers. Edge servers make up the base layer. A model is trained with a small amount of data and labels to enable the model's initial intelligence. The pre-trained model labels the unlabeled data. The training dataset is updated with a selection of the newly labeled data. The mutual verification of multimodal data obtains the recently added data. The freshly added labeled data are used to train the model.

The power meter [53] considers advanced AI in DSM for intelligent homes. A cloud analytics-assisted electrical EMS architecture, designed and implemented as edge analytics in the architecture described and developed toward a next-generation smart sensing infrastructure for smart homes, is the environment in which the prototype in this work operates. The work used a push notification service for DSM in intelligent dwellings in conjunction with the AI-enabled and Arduino MCU-based innovative power meter prototype, the bright AIoT edge analytics-empowered power meter prototype, and the cloud analytics-assisted electrical EMS architecture. A central energy management controller is installed in an innovative home environment and communicated. It uses the internet with a cloud, providing user-centric IoT applications for homeowners and home appliances. Based on market pricing, it monitors remotely and reacts with DR signals for highly efficient electricity generation by the utility from bulk generation. It has a power company-owned smart meter (instead of a power company-owned traditional wattmeter). It has a central energy management controller installed in The utility's electricity pricing signals, and demand response signals are received by the smart meter, which serves as a communication gateway between the bright home environment and the utility. These signals include market prices for DSM in an SG. It connects to EMC data on electrical energy consumption sent to the utility *via* AMI for other data science analytics.ZigBee can be used as the communication protocol for smart plugs. In addition to serving as an in-home display, It can use an EMC for remote load control and data visualization in a home environment. Time synchronization is used by all distributed and deployed smart AIoT edge analytics power meters in an SG for DSM. Each of the local intelligent AIoT edge analytics power meters collects and analyzes small amounts of data, which is then sent to cloud storage and merged into cloud analytics. Macro insights are returned to IoT sources and end users by AI trained in cloud analytics and deployed on-site on each local smart AIoT edge analytics power meter. Using PHP, the MySQL relational database, and the Apache HTTP server, developers can create web applications in the Windows web development environment known as WampServer. Php My Admin, on the other hand, makes it simple for developers to manage their databases. For cloud analytics-trained data science analytics/AI, a mashup of JavaTM, R, and Python is ideal. The FCM clustering RBF-ANN was deployed as edge analytics on the AI-enabled and Arduino MCU-based innovative power meter prototype and trained in cloud analytics on the data science analytics engine. An MCU board called Arduino MEGA 2560 is based on the 8-bit ATmega2560 MCU from Atmel®. It has four Universal Asynchronous receivers/Transmitters, 54 Digital Input/Output (I/O) pins, 16 analog inputs, and so on. Fig. (**19**) represents the same.

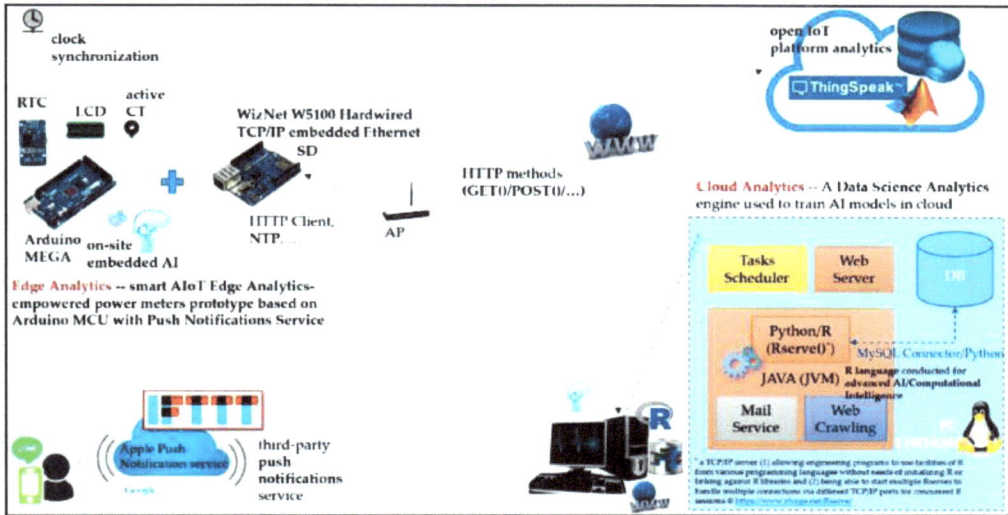

Fig. (19). Cloud analytics Architecture [53].

Developers [54] will be able to concentrate on domain-specific details without worrying about distributed training and inference thanks to DAIaaS, which will help systemize the mass production of technologies for more innovative environments. The simulations use a variety of parameters to represent the devices at each layer, each of which has its distinct resource capabilities. Uplink and downlink bandwidth simulate the communication capabilities. Each machine has unique power consumption characteristics in both idle and busy states. The modules are arranged in a directed graph, with edges separating them to signify the flow of data or work between them. Camera, Motion Detector, Object Detector, Object Tracker, Camera Control, and User Interface are the application's six modules. Camera Ctrl contains the pan-tilt-zoom actuator, the part that adjusts the zoom based on the PTZ parameters, while the Camera includes the sensor. The Obj Detector module sends two workloads to the Motion Detector, which is always in position -the location of the object in the Obj Tracker and the thing detected in the User Interface. The motion video stream is sent to the Obj Detector module when motion is detected. The cloud houses the Obj Detector module. In the IoE-6G scenario, the Obj Tracker module is in the cloud, while in the IoE-Fog-6G scenario, it is in the fog node. After receiving the tracked objects' coordinates, it calculates the PTZ configuration using the workload and camera control. The Obj Detector sends a video stream of the tracked objects to the User Interface, which is always in the cloud. Each application has one or more application loops, which are modules that measure the end-to-end delay between the beginning and end of the loop. The tuple of modules is the only control loop in the Smart Surveillance application. The figure is the layout of the simulated airport, which includes the system's main components. A gateway router that serves as a fog device covers the smaller areas that make up the entire airport landscape. All edge devices in that region can connect to this router. Simulated edge devices fall into three categories. Each intelligent Camera, barcode reader, and the counter device is connected to a particular kind of sensor or actuator. Fig. (**20**) represents the same.

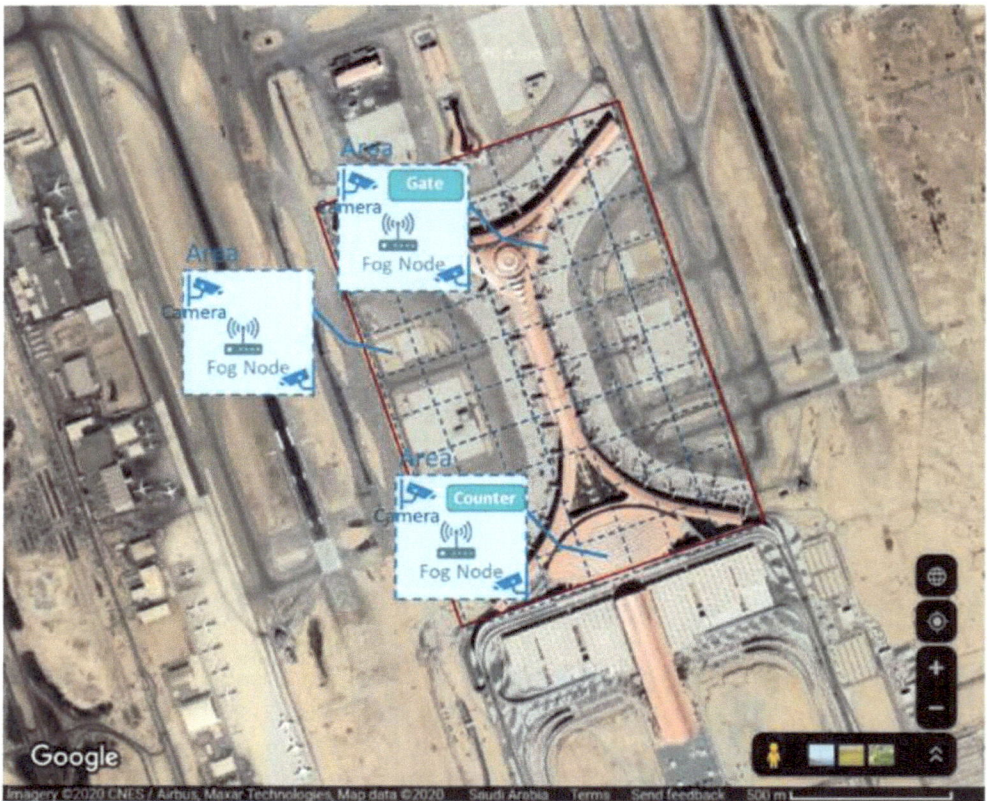

Fig. (20). King Abdul Aziz International Airport (Smart Airport Layout) [54].

The placement of Deep Neural network inference models [55], abstracted as a network embedding problem in a Cloud Fog Network architecture where power savings are introduced through trade-offs between processing and networking, is formulated in the review of Mixed Integer Linear Programming. Virtual service request, made up of three virtual machines, is embedded in the network, which only uses IoT devices. Multiple virtual machines are connected *via* virtual links in the request. It must embed an input virtual machine for each service request in the IoT layer.

Point and range queries and typical multi-dimensional queries can be processed quickly using this method [56]. There are two types of machine nodes in the cluster. The only difference between controller and agent nodes is that if a machine acts as the primary node, it will store some metadata about the entire system in addition to the usual data that secondary nodes must also store. For efficiency and security, agent nodes keep data records and their replicas. Although a Cloud platform differs from Client-Server architecture-based systems in that it does not require central servers, it still requires a set of machines to maintain metadata about the system, making many operations more efficient. Client requests frequently target the controller nodes in the cloud platform. After that, the client will directly communicate with the future secondary nodes relevant to the request after the controller nodes select those agent nodes. The cloud platform divides query processing into two phases -processing the request on selected secondary nodes and locating relative nodes. The work creates a global platform index by creating local indices on each machine.

Executing the query on local indices and combining the results could be used to respond to requests to the virtual global index. During the relative node locating phase, the system selects all cluster nodes as query candidates. The bandwidth for communication was 1Gps. Each machine had a 320G disk, 4GB of main memory, and a 2.33GHz Intel Core2 Quad CPU. The system used Ubuntu 9.04 Server OS on the machines. The authors ran ten simulation experiments with 100 to 1000 nodes. One device controls distribution, stores metadata, and serves as a controller node. The remaining five machines each represent between 100 and 1000 secondary nodes.

3.5. FUTURE DIRECTIONS OF CLOUD-AI

3.5.1. Edge Computing

Smart devices, sensors, and actuators are all part of the Internet of Things and interact and communicate with one another and end users. Edge devices, which are at the network's edge and are controlled centrally from the cloud, are in charge of managing and protecting IoT devices. IoT data is continuously transported from apps to a central storage unit, often found in a cloud data center. Some IoT applications need real-time processing and low latency time. It is not appropriate to use cloud computing to handle such requirements. Therefore, edge computing, which deploys cloud-computing-like capabilities at the network's edge, is essential for meeting these criteria. A new distributed IT architecture known as edge computing [57] pushes some or all of the data storage, services, and computing applications away from the central nodes and toward the end user. Real-time applications benefit from edge computing by having lower latency and reaction times. Edge computing expands the capabilities of cloud computing to the edge of the network. Fig. (**21**) represents Edge computing architecture.

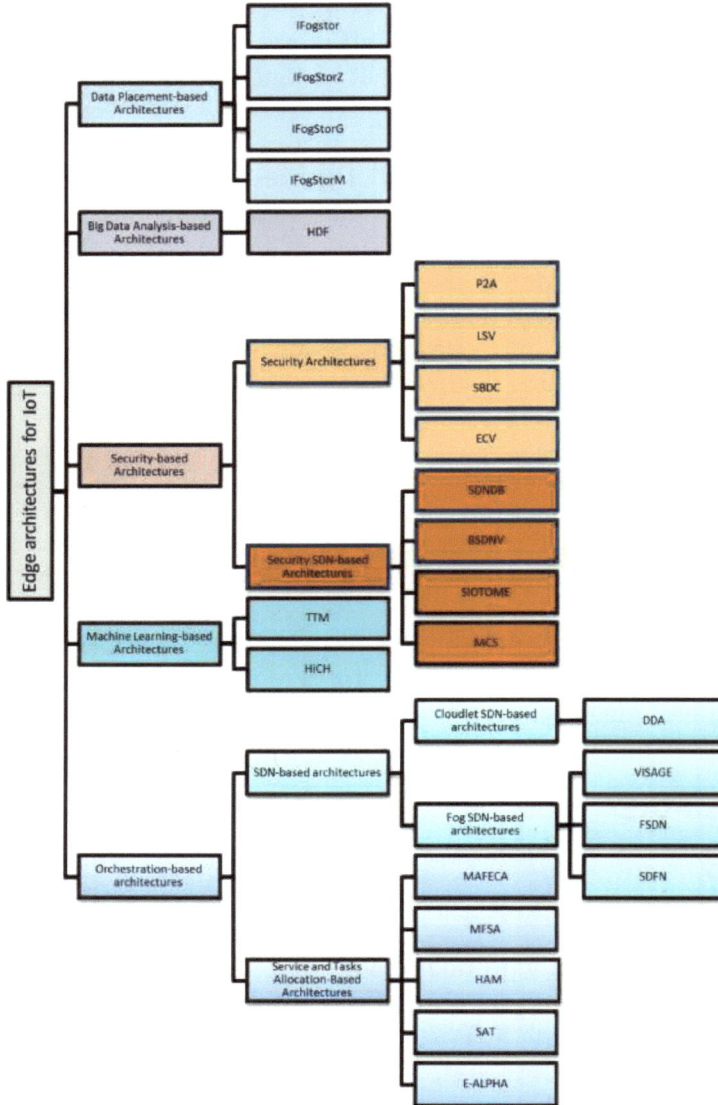

Fig. (21). Edge computing architecture [58].

3.5.2. Distributed Ledger

Data travels in both directions from suppliers, manufacturers, distributors, retailers, and customers *via* numerous steps of supply chains that span multiple geographies, means of transportation, and industries. Data flow is required to enable essential business choices that could affect product cost and market share. The distribution phase of cargo cannot be tracked in validated, pseudo-real time by current information systems. Other parties are occasionally informed of this information by a single source, the carrier. In the distribution phase, this study [59] introduces a framework that provides online shipment tracking data to all stakeholders. There are two types of distributed ledgers: private ledgers and public ledgers, which facilitate information interchange and flow. Each shipment has a unique personal register only the trading partners participating in the payload may access. This design decision appears to go against the stated transparency ideal. Fig. (**22**) depicts Interactions among the participants.

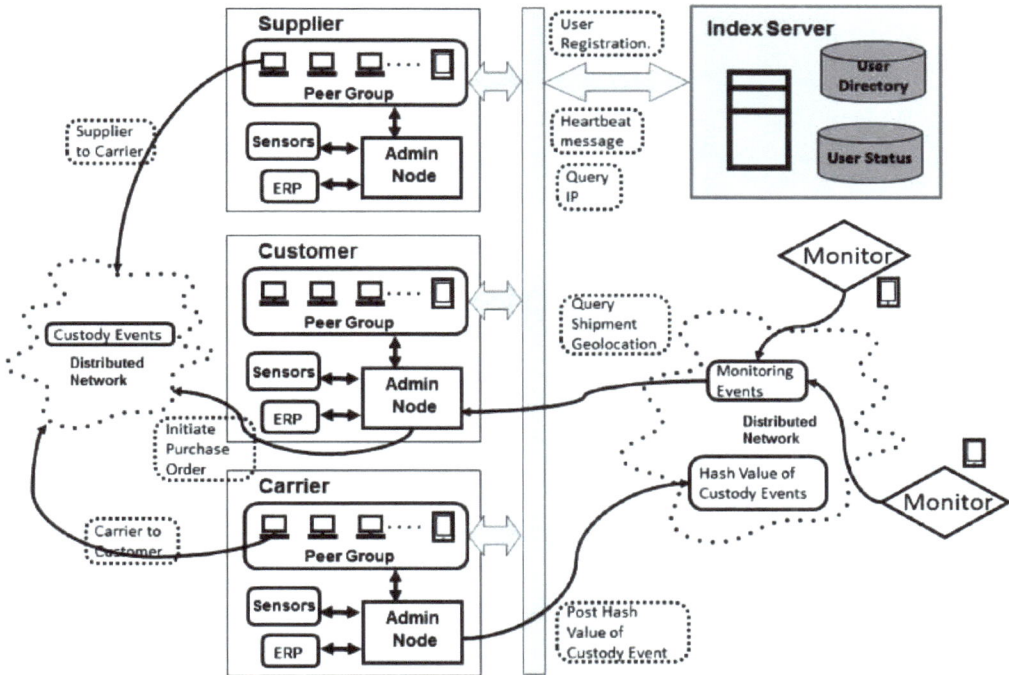

Fig. (22). Interactions among the participants [59].

3.5.3. Cryptocurrency

Digital currencies use cryptography to guarantee security and anonymity. They are a particular kind of digital currency designed to offer safety and anonymity using encryption so that transactions are directly authenticated or confirmed by users throughout a decentralized peer-to-peer system rather than by intermediaries like central banks. Fig. (**23**) portrays the same.

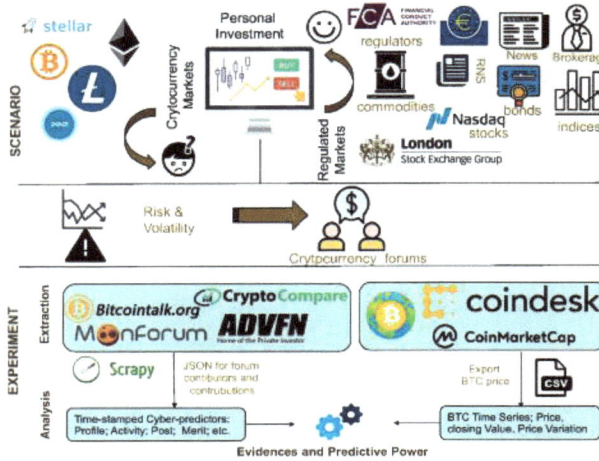

Fig. (23). Overview of the work [60].

3.5.4. Supporting Analytics

Fig. (**24**) describes the system framework.

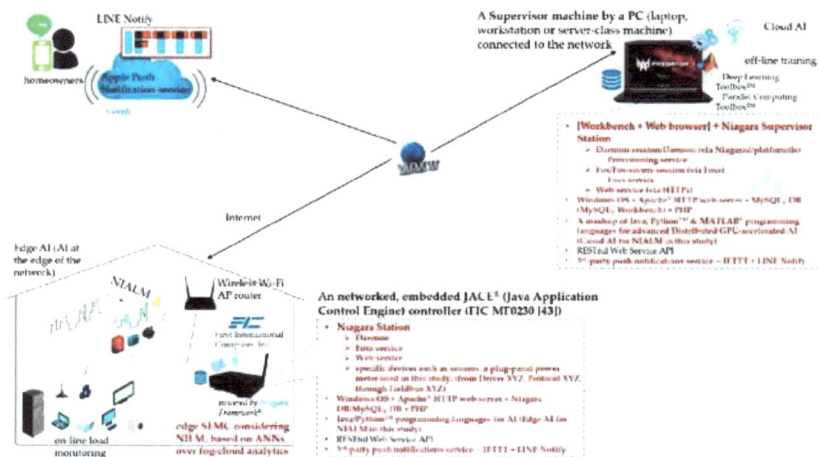

Fig. (24). System framework [61].

CONCLUSION

Machines that have been taught to think and act like humans use artificial intelligence to mimic human intelligence. Problem-solving is a function of both human intellect and artificial intelligence. Artificial intelligence technologies have become essential to advancing cloud application functionality. Instead of being hosted on a local computer or server, cloud apps are used in a cloud environment. Future cloud application performance, marketing tactics, organizational work-flow, and consumer behavior are all likely to change due to artificial intelligence. Organizations can streamline cloud computing applications required in organization servers and computers using artificial intelligence.

REFERENCES

[1] T. Alam, "Cloud-based iot applications and their roles in smart cities", *Smart Cities,* vol. 4, no. 3, pp. 1196-1219, 2021.
[http://dx.doi.org/10.3390/smartcities4030064]

[2] N. Ambika, Aiding IoT and Cloud to Control COVID-19: A Systematic Approach.*Pervasive Healthcare.* Springer: Cham, 2022, pp. 349-365.
[http://dx.doi.org/10.1007/978-3-030-77746-3_21]

[3] U.A. Butt, M. Mehmood, S.B.H. Shah, R. Amin, M.W. Shaukat, S.M. Raza, D.Y. Suh, and M.J. Piran, "A review of machine learning algorithms for cloud computing security", *Electronics (Basel),* vol. 9, no. 9, p. 1379, 2020.
[http://dx.doi.org/10.3390/electronics9091379]

[4] R. Nasim, H. Ullah, S.S. Rizvi, A. Abbasi, S. Khan, R. Riaz, and A. Paul, "A cloud-based enterprise resource planning architecture for women's education in remote areas", *Electronics (Basel),* vol. 9, no. 11, p. 1758, 2020.
[http://dx.doi.org/10.3390/electronics9111758]

[5] M.H. Devare, Challenges and Opportunities in High Performance Cloud Computing.*Research Anthology on Architectures, Frameworks, and Integration Strategies for Distributed and Cloud Computing.* IGI Global: US, 2021, pp. 1989-2018.
[http://dx.doi.org/10.4018/978-1-7998-5339-8.ch096]

[6] V. Eramo, F.G. Lavacca, T. Catena, and P.J. Perez Salazar, "Proposal and Investigation of an Artificial Intelligence (AI)-Based Cloud Resource Allocation Algorithm in Network Function Virtualization Architectures", *Future Internet,* vol. 12, no. 11, p. 196, 2020.
[http://dx.doi.org/10.3390/fi12110196]

[7] R. Dhaya, and R. Kanthavel, "Cloud—based multiple importance sampling algorithm with AI based CNN classifier for secure infrastructure", *Autom. Softw. Eng.,* vol. 28, no. 2, p. 16, 2021.
[http://dx.doi.org/10.1007/s10515-021-00293-y]

[8] A. Retico, M. Avanzo, T. Boccali, D. Bonacorsi, F. Botta, G. Cuttone, B. Martelli, D. Salomoni, D. Spiga, A. Trianni, M. Stasi, M. Iori, and C. Talamonti, "Enhancing the impact of artificial intelligence in medicine: a joint aifm-infn italian initiative for a dedicated cloud-based computing infrastructure", *Phys. Med.,* vol. 91, pp. 140-150, 2021.
[http://dx.doi.org/10.1016/j.ejmp.2021.10.005] [PMID: 34801873]

[9] Y. Tanimura, S. Takizawa, and H. Ogawa, "Building and evaluation of cloud storage and datasets services on AI and HPC converged infrastructure", *2020 IEEE International Conference on Big Data (Big Data).,* 2020 Atlanta GA, USA
[http://dx.doi.org/10.1109/BigData50022.2020.9377729]

[10]   E.N. Witanto, Y.E. Oktian, and S.G. Lee, "Toward data integrity architecture for cloud-based ai systems", *Symmetry (Basel)*, vol. 14, no. 2, p. 273, 2022.
[http://dx.doi.org/10.3390/sym14020273]

[11]   N. Kaur, S.L. Sahdev, M. Sharma, and L. Siddiqui, "Banking 4.0:'The influence of artificial intelligence on the banking industry & how AI is changing the face of modern day banks", *Int. J. Manag.*, vol. 11, no. 6, pp. 578-585, 2020.
[http://dx.doi.org/10.34218/IJM.11.6.2020.049]

[12]   L. Ziora, Machine-learning solutions in the management of a contemporary business organisation: a case study approach in a banking sector.*Rational Decisions in Organisations.* Auerbach Publications, 2022, pp. 189-201.
[http://dx.doi.org/10.1201/9781003030966-14]

[13]   S. Tiwari, S. Bharadwaj, and S. Joshi, "A study of impact of cloud computing and artificial intelligence on banking services, profitability and operational benefits", *Journal of Computer and Mathematics Education,* vol. 12, no. 6, pp. 1617-1627, 2021.

[14]   P.H. Winston, *Artificial intelligence.* Addison-Wesley Longman Publishing Co., Inc.: United States, 1992.

[15]   M.A. Hassan, Z. Shukur, and M.K. Hasan, "An efficient secure electronic payment system for e-commerce", *Computers,* vol. 9, no. 3, p. 66, 2020.
[http://dx.doi.org/10.3390/computers9030066]

[16]   L.A. Tawalbeh, R. Mehmood, E. Benkhlifa, and H. Song, "Mobile cloud computing model and big data analysis for healthcare applications", *IEEE Access,* vol. 4, pp. 6171-6180, 2016.
[http://dx.doi.org/10.1109/ACCESS.2016.2613278]

[17]   J. Yeung, S. Wong, and A. Tam, "Data analytics architectures for e-commerce platforms in cloud", *International Journal for Applied Information Management,* vol. 1, no. 1, pp. 1-5, 2021.
[http://dx.doi.org/10.47738/ijaim.v1i1.3]

[18]   H. Gao, W. Huang, and Y. Duan, "The cloud-edge-based dynamic reconfiguration to service workflow for mobile ecommerce environments: a QoS prediction perspective", *ACM Trans. Internet Technol.,* vol. 21, no. 1, pp. 1-23, 2021.
[http://dx.doi.org/10.1145/3391198]

[19]   C. Englund, E.E. Aksoy, F. Alonso-Fernandez, M.D. Cooney, S. Pashami, and B. Åstrand, "AI perspectives in smart cities and communities to enable road vehicle automation and smart traffic Control", *Smart Cities,* vol. 4, no. 2, pp. 783-802, 2021.
[http://dx.doi.org/10.3390/smartcities4020040]

[20]   P. Cardullo, C. Di Feliciantonio, and R. Kitchin, *The right to the smart city.* Emerald Group Publishing, 2019.
[http://dx.doi.org/10.1108/9781787691391]

[21]   K. Guo, Y. Lu, H. Gao, and R. Cao, "Artificial intelligence-based semantic internet of things in a user-centric smart city", *Sensors (Basel),* vol. 18, no. 5, p. 1341, 2018.
[http://dx.doi.org/10.3390/s18051341] [PMID: 29701679]

[22]   A. Sharma, E. Podoplelova, G. Shapovalov, A. Tselykh, and A. Tselykh, "Sustainable smart cities: convergence of artificial intelligence and blockchain", *Sustainability (Basel),* vol. 13, no. 23, p. 13076, 2021.
[http://dx.doi.org/10.3390/su132313076]

[23]   K.E. Skouby, and P. Lynggaard, "Smart home and smart city solutions enabled by 5G, IoT, AAI and CoT services", *International Conference on Contemporary Computing and Informatics (IC3I),* 2014 Mysore, India
[http://dx.doi.org/10.1109/IC3I.2014.7019822]

[24]   M. Kyrarini, F. Lygerakis, A. Rajavenkatanarayanan, C. Sevastopoulos, H.R. Nambiappan, K.K.

Chaitanya, A.R. Babu, J. Mathew, and F. Makedon, "A Survey of robots in healthcare", *Technologies (Basel),* vol. 9, no. 1, p. 8, 2021.
[http://dx.doi.org/10.3390/technologies9010008]

[25]   A.H. Sodhro, and N. Zahid, "AI-enabled framework for fog computing driven e-healthcare applications", *Sensors (Basel),* vol. 21, no. 23, p. 8039, 2021.
[http://dx.doi.org/10.3390/s21238039] [PMID: 34884048]

[26]   A.T. Lo'ai, W. Bakhader, R. Mehmood, and H. Song, "Cloudlet-based mobile cloud computing for healthcare applications", *IEEE Global Communications Conference.,* 2016 Washington, DC, USA

[27]   A.T. Lo'ai, and S. Habeeb, "An integrated cloud based healthcare system", *Fifth International Conference on Internet of Things: Systems, Management and Security,* 2018 Valencia Spain
[http://dx.doi.org/10.1109/IoTSMS.2018.8554648]

[28]   R. Somula, C. Anilkumar, B. Venkatesh, A. Karrothu, P. Kumar, and R. Sasikala, "Cloudlet services for healthcare applications in mobile cloud computing", *in 2nd international conference on data engineering and communication technology,* 2019 Pune, Maharashtra, India
[http://dx.doi.org/10.1007/978-981-13-1610-4_54]

[29]   R.F. Mansour, A.E. Amraoui, I. Nouaouri, V.G. Díaz, D. Gupta, and S. Kumar, "Artificial intelligence and internet of things enabled disease diagnosis model for smart healthcare systems", *IEEE Access,* vol. 9, pp. 45137-45146, 2021.
[http://dx.doi.org/10.1109/ACCESS.2021.3066365]

[30]   R. Kohli, A. Garg, S. Phutela, Y. Kumar, and S. Jain, An improvised model for securing cloud-based e-healthcare systems.*IoT in healthcare and ambient assisted living.* Springer: Singapore, 2021, pp. 293-310.
[http://dx.doi.org/10.1007/978-981-15-9897-5_14]

[31]   A. AlTwaijiry, "Impact of cloud deployment on operational expenses of healthcare centers", *Empirical Quests for Management Essences,* vol. 1, no. 1, pp. 1-9, 2020.

[32]   O. Saha, and P. Dasgupta, "A comprehensive survey of recent trends in cloud robotics architectures and applications", *Robotics,* vol. 7, no. 3, p. 47, 2018.
[http://dx.doi.org/10.3390/robotics7030047]

[33]   M. Corrales, M. Fenwick, and N. Forgó, *Robotics, AI and the Future of Law.* Springer: Singapore, 2018.
[http://dx.doi.org/10.1007/978-981-13-2874-9]

[34]   Y. Liu, H. Zhang, and C. Huang, "A novel rgb-d slam algorithm based on cloud robotics", *Sensors (Basel),* vol. 19, no. 23, p. 5288, 2019.
[http://dx.doi.org/10.3390/s19235288] [PMID: 31805628]

[35]   N.K. Beigi, B. Partov, and S. Farokhi, "Real-time cloud robotics in practical smart city applications", *28th Annual International Symposium on Personal, Indoor, and Mobile Radio Communications (PIMRC),* 2017 Montreal, QC, Canada
[http://dx.doi.org/10.1109/PIMRC.2017.8292655]

[36]   K. Kahn, "Child-friendly programming interfaces to AI cloud services", *in European Conference on Technology Enhanced Learning,* 2017 Tallinn, Estonia

[37]   A. V. S. L. A. C. D. M. J. & S. A. Di Nuovo, "Assessment of cognitive skills *via* human-robot interaction and cloud computing", *Journal of bionic engineering,* vol. 16, no. 3, pp. 526-539, 2019.
[http://dx.doi.org/10.1007/s42235-019-0043-2]

[38]   S. Oueida, Y. Kotb, M. Aloqaily, Y. Jararweh, and T. Baker, "An Edge Computing Based Smart Healthcare Framework for Resource Management", *Sensors (Basel),* vol. 18, no. 12, p. 4307, 2018.
[http://dx.doi.org/10.3390/s18124307] [PMID: 30563267]

[39]   S. Tuli, S.S. Gill, M. Xu, P. Garraghan, R. Bahsoon, S. Dustdar, R. Sakellariou, O. Rana, R. Buyya, G. Casale, and N.R. Jennings, "HUNTER: AI based holistic resource management for sustainable cloud

computing", *J. Syst. Softw.,* vol. 184, p. 111124, 2022.
[http://dx.doi.org/10.1016/j.jss.2021.111124]

[40]   Z. Ahmad, A.I. Jehangiri, M.A. Ala'anzy, M. Othman, and A.I. Umar, "Fault-tolerant and data-intensive resource scheduling and management for scientific applications in cloud computing", *Sensors (Basel),* vol. 21, no. 21, p. 7238, 2021.
[http://dx.doi.org/10.3390/s21217238] [PMID: 34770545]

[41]   S.A. Syed, M. Rashid, S. Hussain, F. Azim, H. Zahid, A. Umer, A. Waheed, M. Zareei, and C. Vargas-Rosales, "QoS aware and fault tolerance based software-defined vehicular networks using cloud-fog computing", *Sensors (Basel),* vol. 22, no. 1, p. 401, 2022.
[http://dx.doi.org/10.3390/s22010401] [PMID: 35009941]

[42]   A. Marahatta, Q. Xin, C. Chi, F. Zhang, and Z. Liu, "PEFS: AI-driven prediction based energy-aware fault-tolerant scheduling scheme for cloud data center", *IEEE Trans. Sustain. Comput.,* vol. 6, no. 4, pp. 655-666, 2021.
[http://dx.doi.org/10.1109/TSUSC.2020.3015559]

[43]   S.R. Gundu, P. Charanarur, K.K. Chandelkar, D. Samanta, R.C. Poonia, and P. Chakraborty, "Sixth-generation (6g) mobile cloud security and privacy risks for ai system using high-performance computing implementation", *Wirel. Commun. Mob. Comput.,* vol. 2022, pp. 1-14, 2022.
[http://dx.doi.org/10.1155/2022/4397610]

[44]   L.K. Ramasamy, F. Khan, M. Shah, B.V.V.S. Prasad, C. Iwendi, and C. Biamba, "Secure smart wearable computing through artificial intelligence-enabled internet of things and cyber-physical systems for health monitoring", *Sensors (Basel),* vol. 22, no. 3, p. 1076, 2022.
[http://dx.doi.org/10.3390/s22031076] [PMID: 35161820]

[45]   K.K. Singamaneni, K. Ramana, G. Dhiman, S. Singh, and B. Yoon, "A novel blockchain and bi-linear polynomial-based qcp-abe framework for privacy and security over the complex cloud data", *Sensors (Basel),* vol. 21, no. 21, p. 7300, 2021.
[http://dx.doi.org/10.3390/s21217300] [PMID: 34770606]

[46]   A. Albayati, N.F. Abdullah, A. Abu-Samah, A.H. Mutlag, and R. Nordin, "A Serverless Advanced Metering Infrastructure Based on Fog-Edge Computing for a Smart Grid: A Comparison Study for Energy Sector in Iraq", *Energies,* vol. 13, no. 20, p. 5460, 2020.
[http://dx.doi.org/10.3390/en13205460]

[47]   L. Schuler, S. Jamil, and N. Kühl, "AI-based resource allocation: Reinforcement learning for adaptive auto-scaling in serverless environments", *IEEE/ACM 21st international symposium on cluster, cloud and internet computing (CCGRID),* 2021 Melbourne, Australia
[http://dx.doi.org/10.1109/CCGrid51090.2021.00098]

[48]   T. Rausch, W. Hummer, V. Muthusamy, A. Rashed, and S. Dustdar, "Towards a serverless platform for edge {AI}", *2nd USENIX Workshop on Hot Topics in Edge Computing (HotEdge 19),* 2019 Washington, USA

[49]   K. Kritikos, and P. Skrzypek, "Simulation-as-a-service with serverless computing", *IEEE World Congress on Services (SERVICES),* 2019 Milan, Italy
[http://dx.doi.org/10.1109/SERVICES.2019.00056]

[50]   M. Golec, D. Chowdhury, S. Jaglan, S.S. Gill, and S. Uhlig, "AIBLOCK: Blockchain based Lightweight Framework for Serverless Computing using AI", *22nd IEEE International Symposium on Cluster, Cloud and Internet Computing (CCGrid),* 2022 Taormina, Italy
[http://dx.doi.org/10.1109/CCGrid54584.2022.00106]

[51]   S. Wang, Q. Hu, F. Wang, M. Ai, and R. Zhong, "A Microtopographic feature analysis-based lidar data processing approach for the identification of chu tombs", *Remote Sens. (Basel),* vol. 9, no. 9, p. 880, 2017.
[http://dx.doi.org/10.3390/rs9090880]

[52]   Y. Wu, "Cloud-edge orchestration for the Internet of Things: Architecture and AI-powered data

processing", *IEEE Internet Things J.,* vol. 8, no. 16, pp. 12792-12805, 2021.
[http://dx.doi.org/10.1109/JIOT.2020.3014845]

[53]   Y.Y. Chen, Y.H. Lin, C.C. Kung, M.H. Chung, and I.H. Yen, "Design and implementation of cloud analytics-assisted smart power meters considering advanced artificial intelligence as edge analytics in demand-side management for smart homes", *Sensors (Basel),* vol. 19, no. 9, p. 2047, 2019.
[http://dx.doi.org/10.3390/s19092047] [PMID: 31052502]

[54]   N. Janbi, I. Katib, A. Albeshri, and R. Mehmood, "Distributed artificial intelligence-as-a-service (daiaas) for smarter ioe and 6g environments", *Sensors (Basel),* vol. 20, no. 20, p. 5796, 2020.
[http://dx.doi.org/10.3390/s20205796] [PMID: 33066295]

[55]   B.A. Yosuf, S.H. Mohamed, M.M. Alenazi, T.E. El-Gorashi, and J.M. Elmirghani, "Energy-Efficient AI over a Virtualized Cloud Fog Network", *Twelfth ACM International Conference on Future Energy Systems,* 2021 Italy
[http://dx.doi.org/10.1145/3447555.3465378]

[56]   X. Zhang, J. Ai, Z. Wang, J. Lu, and X. Meng, "An efficient multi-dimensional index for cloud data management", *in first international workshop on Cloud data management,* 2009 Hong Kong China
[http://dx.doi.org/10.1145/1651263.1651267]

[57]   S. Chen, Q. Li, M. Zhou, and A. Abusorrah, "Recent advances in collaborative scheduling of computing tasks in an edge computing paradigm", *Sensors (Basel),* vol. 21, no. 3, p. 779, 2021.
[http://dx.doi.org/10.3390/s21030779] [PMID: 33498910]

[58]   S. Hamdan, M. Ayyash, and S. Almajali, "Edge-computing architectures for internet of things applications: a survey", *Sensors (Basel),* vol. 20, no. 22, p. 6441, 2020.
[http://dx.doi.org/10.3390/s20226441] [PMID: 33187267]

[59]   H. Wu, Z. Li, B. King, Z. Ben Miled, J. Wassick, and J. Tazelaar, "A Distributed ledger for supply chain physical distribution visibility", *Information (Basel),* vol. 8, no. 4, p. 137, 2017.
[http://dx.doi.org/10.3390/info8040137]

[60]   A. Fernández Vilas, R.P. Díaz Redondo, D. Couto Cancela, and A. Torrado Pazos, "Interplay between cryptocurrency transactions and online financial forums", *Mathematics,* vol. 9, no. 4, p. 411, 2021.
[http://dx.doi.org/10.3390/math9040411]

[61]   Y.Y. Chen, M.H. Chen, C.M. Chang, F.S. Chang, and Y.H. Lin, "A smart home energy management system using two-stage non-intrusive appliance load monitoring over fog-cloud analytics based on tridium's niagara framework for residential demand-side management", *Sensors (Basel),* vol. 21, no. 8, p. 2883, 2021.
[http://dx.doi.org/10.3390/s21082883] [PMID: 33924090]

[62]   M. Junaid, A. Shaikh, M.U. Hassan, A. Alghamdi, K. Rajab, M.S. Al Reshan, and M. Alkinani, "Smart agriculture cloud using ai based techniques", *Energies,* vol. 14, no. 16, p. 5129, 2021.
[http://dx.doi.org/10.3390/en14165129]

CHAPTER 4

Integration of AI and IoT-cloud

Abstract: Cyber objects, stockpiles, datasets and synthetic intellect are avant-garde methodologies. They surround the knowledge and transmission methods. It includes different types of community procedures, including teaching, recreation, habitat, finance, healthcare, enterprise, administration and production. IoT links the globe to cyberspace and virtual planet using cyber, and yields a portion of information. The repository calibration atmosphere promotes the approach of knowledge, and constructs conclusions using dataset investigation and apparatus education. This chapter talks about its characteristics, applications, challenges and future scope.

Keywords: Artificial intelligence, Applications of cloud-IoT, Cloud-IoT integration, Cloud-IoT architecture, Integration of cloud-IoT, Machine learning.

4.1. INTRODUCTION

Most software packages nowadays help with seamless data acquisition and archiving, which include the Internet of Things and cloud computing as critical components. It offers the end user accessible conveniences like home automation, storage of enormous data streams, and flexibility for changing the data volume. Artificial intelligence is widely used in various industries.

4.2. CHARACTERISTICS OF INTEGRATION

Cloud fabricating is a brilliant, organized assembling model that embraces distributed computing, targeting developing needs for higher item individua- lization, more extensive worldwide collaboration, information-concentrated advan- cement, and expanded market-reaction spryness [1, 2]. In cloud fabricating, clients can helpfully get on-request benefits, supporting the whole life pattern of an item through network admittance to a shared pool where it has dispersed virtualized assembling assets and bound together administration in a configurable and upgraded way. Cloud production intermingles distributed computing, IoT [3, 4], administration computing, Artificial Intelligence, and assembling informatization innovations. Cloud fabricating considers changing the assembling industry to support arranged gathering, adding to forming a digital society for future digital actual assembling.

The Internet of Things is an organization of items implanted with sensors and networks so that they can trade data with other associated gadgets. Modest sensors worked on a remote network, and adaptability through distributed computing have all made it conceivable to cost-really gather and interact loads of information, dissect it, and follow up on it quickly. IoT combined with AI can frame the establishment and, sometimes, even conceptualize new items and administrations. Various applications that pair IoT with AI assist organizations with better figuring out chances and setting them up for fast reactions, better overseeing laborer security and digital dangers. Fig. (**1**) is the representation of the infrastructure of Cloud-IoT.

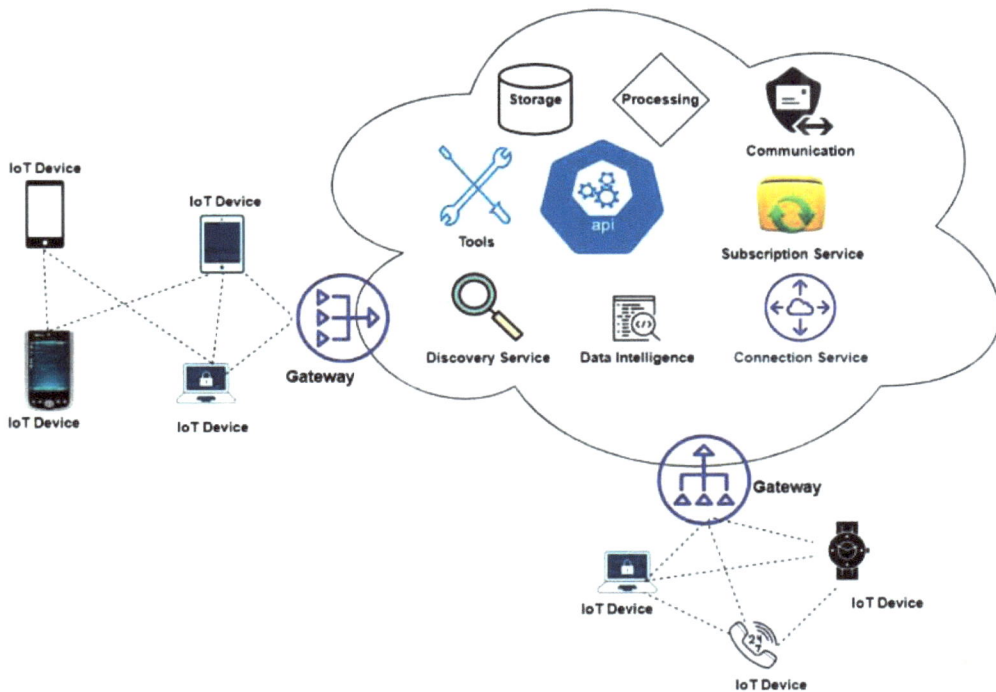

Fig. (1). Cloud-IoT infrastructure [5].

4.2.1. Ubiquitous Sensing

Anything can be hosted on the Internet and made available for usage, as needed, to create and provide increasingly complex services in the cloud. Today's IoT world requires the cloud functionalities indicated in the first paragraph. The on-demand and elasticity aspects are essential for adequate and scalable service supply, and resource pooling improves the efficiency and reliability of service delivery.

Each agrarian subsystem [6] of the device can be associated with and handled utilizing USN and IoT, ideal models. The gadgets are between operable and the environment in an omnipresent sensor network that uses IoT standards to convey and make cloud administrations. An action, administration, or cycle is shaped by things and handling modules that work by exploiting the correspondence facilities. Edge registering gives the unwavering quality of reaction in control processes. Web Cloud gives availabilities, stockpiling, and scientific assets that clients, things, or other services can take advantage of. The edge layer provides interoperability and time reaction. Cloud administrations give web administrations, information capacity, and examination. The programming stage has information obtaining, control-correspondence processes, cloud administrations, and apparatuses for agronomists. The same is depicted in Fig. (2).

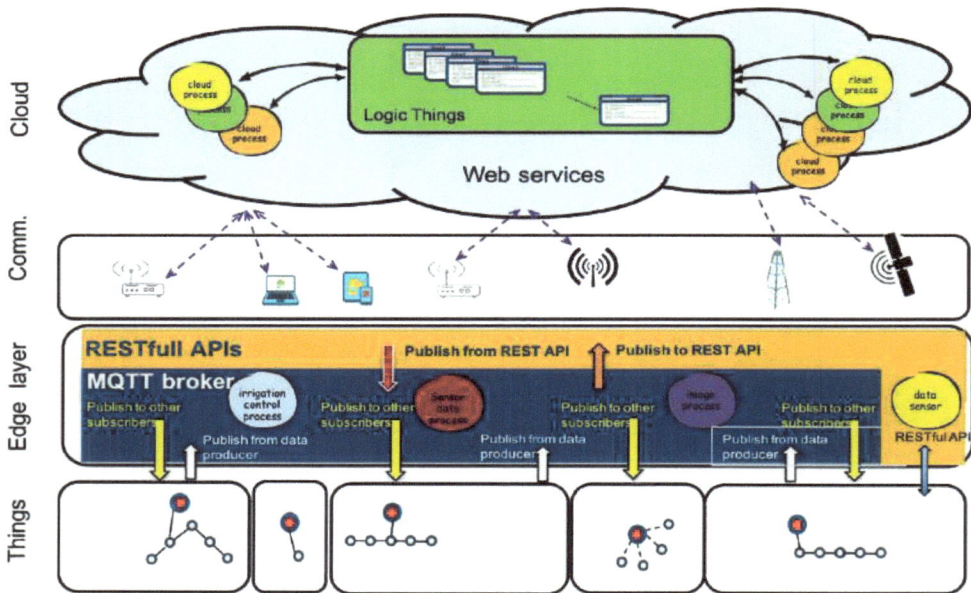

Fig. (2). Proposed architecture [6].

The Stack4Things structure [7] targets executing a new methodology for administering brilliant IoT hubs. It follows an on-request, administration-situated provisioning model. The Stack4Things lightning-pole runs under the gadget's local climate accessible for engineers and communicates with the OS apparatuses and administrations accessible on the gadget detecting and activation assets through UNIX-style filesystem-based reflections of the virtual interfaces, either GPIO for inserted sheets or, regularly, API-intervened for mobiles. It addresses the resource with the Cloud framework permitting the end clients to oversee hub-facilitated assets in any event when corners are behind a NAT or a strict firewall. A set of order line-based clients, among which the Stack4Things Iotronic order line client, and utilizing a Web program through a bunch of REST APIs, are given by the center OpenStack administrations and the Stack4Things IoTronic itself. Keystone runs as a bunch of supervisors in a WSGI-fit Web server along with its APIs. Authentication tokens are put away in a Memcached instance. To approve an approaching solicitation, Keystone adopts a bunch of qualifications provided by the responsible client. The client's name, a secret phrase, a client name, and an API key address the certification. Keystone oversees ventures, gatherings, and roles. Roles concede to clients or meetings as for projects. It adds clients, eliminating clients from a community for an undertaking separately awards or repudiates. Every token given by Keystone remembers a rundown of jobs for the client for the project. It carries out the RBAC model at the degree of API calls, appointments and undertakings.

4.2.2. Virtual Maintenance

The Internet of Things is regarded as one of the disruptive technologies of the future and has received a lot of recent study interest. IoT devices are tinier sensors or actuating components attached to everyday items that may send and receive orders. Cloud computing technology offers enormous computation and storage capacity over the Internet to circumvent the constrained resources of IoT devices. The idea of virtualization is introduced, which provides a flexible interface to manipulate and interact with actual IoT devices to make it easier to access and operate IoT devices in the cyber world. IoT devices allow flexible connectivity between sensors and actuators in the virtual world through virtual objects. Virtualization's seamless duplication and sharing of resources across many domains is another benefit. The entire system is called a Cyber-Physical System built for physical world observation and control through the virtual world in IoT scenarios. The virtual world is also known as the cyber world.

The subsequent virtual organization administrations [8] offer extraordinary adaptability and cost benefits to them. Network Function Virtualization and organization execution are the key innovations close to the Internet of Things. Involving these virtual organization capabilities as the structure blocks for making Virtual Network Services, carriers can alter how the organization administrations are provided. They are ready to bear the agonies of rolling out this significant improvement to receive the rewards of the decreased expense of sending, nimbleness in presenting new administrations, simplicity of scaling, freedom from restrictive hardware, and seller security. The virtual assets for the building are from the in-house data center, and the transporter cloud is possessed *via* transporters or public mists maintained by Cloud Service Providers. Virtual networks are out of virtual organization capabilities acknowledged as VNF1 to VNF8. Administration Function Chains comprise an arranged arrangement of interconnected VNFs, which perform the pre-customized procedure on the traffic directed through them.

The Imtidad reference engineering [9] is a system for decoupling applications, smoothing out the plan, and sending disseminated AI administrations over the cloud, fog, and edge layers. The design records generally expected administrations to make new DAIaaS administrations from the determination of the application to support creation and operations. The administration improvement and organization process start with choosing an application space for this situation. A dataset chosen application, so the planned model might be prepared and approved. The dataset procurement process incorporates dataset approval and pre-handling in anticipation of preparation. Profound Learning models are designed, crafted, enhanced, and supported. The TensorFlow model is a streamlined rendition. Outer assessment does validation. Validation should be possible by clients, administration fashioners, suppliers, or an outsider, for example, auditors. Use cases are recognized considering potential situations and plans of action for provisioning disseminated AI administrations and skin sickness-finding administrations over the cloud, fog, and edge layers. These plan various administrations that suit different circumstances and necessities. Administrations are recorded in an administrations index for the client to choose one of them and use it to analyze a sore picture. Fig. (**3**) portrays the same.

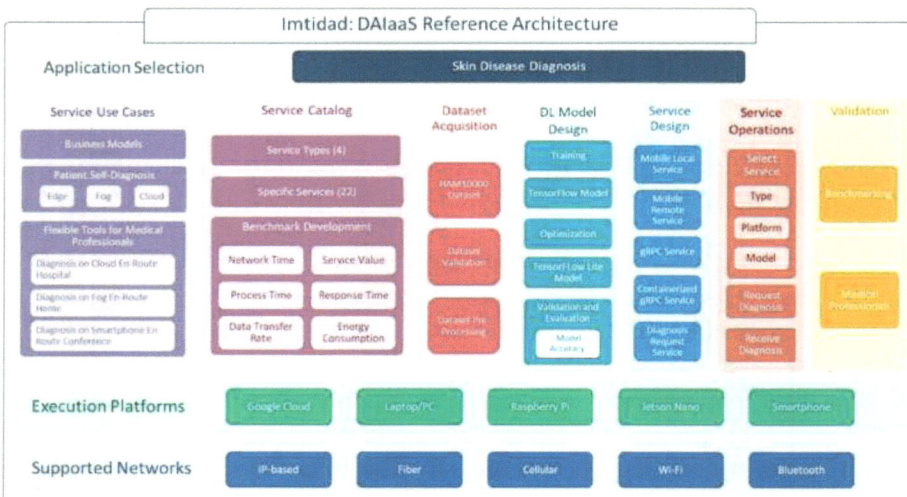

Fig. (**3**). Imidad Reference model [9].

An FP issue and execution of the board in the cloud-based VNS [10] must be a cooperative cycle among the components comprising the VNS and the administration frameworks engaged with making and dealing with the assistance. Some of these necessities incorporate huge high-layered, multi-source, and diverse data mining volumes. The information created by a functional framework is enormous and high-layered. It has a half-and-half structure comprising a mix of shallow and profound learning models that use for location, restriction of FP issues, and foreseeing high-level levels of looming shortcomings with high precision. The work presented markers as pointers are delivered by a functional organization and estimations taken by the tasks staff. An enormous number of markers are straightforwardly or in a roundabout way connected with the event of an FP issue. These markers become significant highlights in the datasets. Occasions that produce these markers connect with correspondence, QoS, handling, gear, and environment. The measurements utilized *via* transporters to quantify the organization's well-being give essential data about the FP issues at the large-scale level. ETSI reports on help accessibility and assistance quality notice measurements that should be gathered and examined. The ETSI bunch detail on help quality measurements perceives that it is essential to have level-headed and quantitative measurements to help recognize issues when they emerge and support the customers greatly. The work assigns models with a solitary layer of nonlinearity. The structure has three principal sub-frameworks. Information pre-handling includes grouping and standardization of the dataset to eliminate inclinations. The pre-handling strategy may likewise include decreasing highlights given some measure like relationship with the names. In the preparation mode, the accessible dataset splits into preparing and test datasets, which design and test every one of the models. During the activity, the marker information is gone through the system to recognize and confine issues. The two levels utilize shallow AI models in the two-stage execution for identifications. The prepared model can then take markers coming about because of new occasions as contributions to choose from a Level I, whether the combination of features is a shortcoming.

4.2.3. Service-oriented Provision

In the framework of IoT [11], dynamic collaboration platforms, intelligent device interconnection, and self-configurable gadgets are seen as attractive development tools for home services and commercial processes. These qualities support many innovative services, including intelligent homes, smart mobility, e-healthcare, and smart cities.

Due to the IoT's resource limitations and growing user expectations, it must provide adequate services without sacrificing service quality or cost. Combining IoT and computing technologies like cloud, edge, and fog computing has become necessary. To eliminate the IoT's limited resources, the IoT can employ cloud computing as a virtual resource usage infrastructure by providing an on-demand utility pricing model. On the other hand, convergence technology has emerged to inspire IoT to produce a collection of composite services based on the quality-of-service approach to meet users' requirements.

SmartWater [12] joins the state-of-the-art advances in sensor mists, profound learning, information thinking, and information handling and examination. The information charts are taken advantage of to display the water network in a semantic and multi-social way. Gradual organizations learn rich portrayals of water substances, specifically the impacted water zones. The choice system produces water on the board plan contingent upon the water zones' flow states. The proposed structure has four layers. The intelligent sensors layer depends on sensor-cloud engineering that changes the water climate into brilliant, self-checked water zones. This layer uses notable figuring ideal models, for example, autonomic processing, sensor organizations, and support learning. This review has utilized a real-world dataset to tentatively approve the significant highlights of the proposed brilliant water-checking framework. The executive layer addresses the information handling, and the board offices permit acknowledging different procedures on the water information, which were recently gathered and yielded by sensors. The waterwork processes layer fills in as a vault of conceptual water the board plans. The water examination layer assists in the choice with support and suggestions regarding the condition of water zones. After changing the water zones' data into an information chart structure, the checking stage begins at each watering zone. The information gathered by water quality sensors is then, at that point, sifted and utilized to refresh the water knowledge graph. Fig. (**4**) depicts the same.

The proposal [13] presents a robust QoS provisioning structure for administration-situated IoT utilizing a backtracking inquiry enhancement calculation. The QoPF system boosts the composite help quality in the IoT application layer by creating harmony between administration dependability and satisfactory expense of the computational time. The planning stage has an immediate association with detecting administration requests. The activity in this stage is worried about gathering the help demanded by the information gatherer and putting away every one of them in a line. All gathered solicitations ship off at the following stage for additional handling and analysis. The calculation stage chooses the ideal help piece through the assistance states separation, which incorporates three help classes: finished assistance, available help, and flexible service to recognize the approaching solicitations. The decision support process sends the choice made about the competitor administrations to the approval stage as per the request wherein they benefit from planning. The approval stage is devoted to estimating the assistance quality.

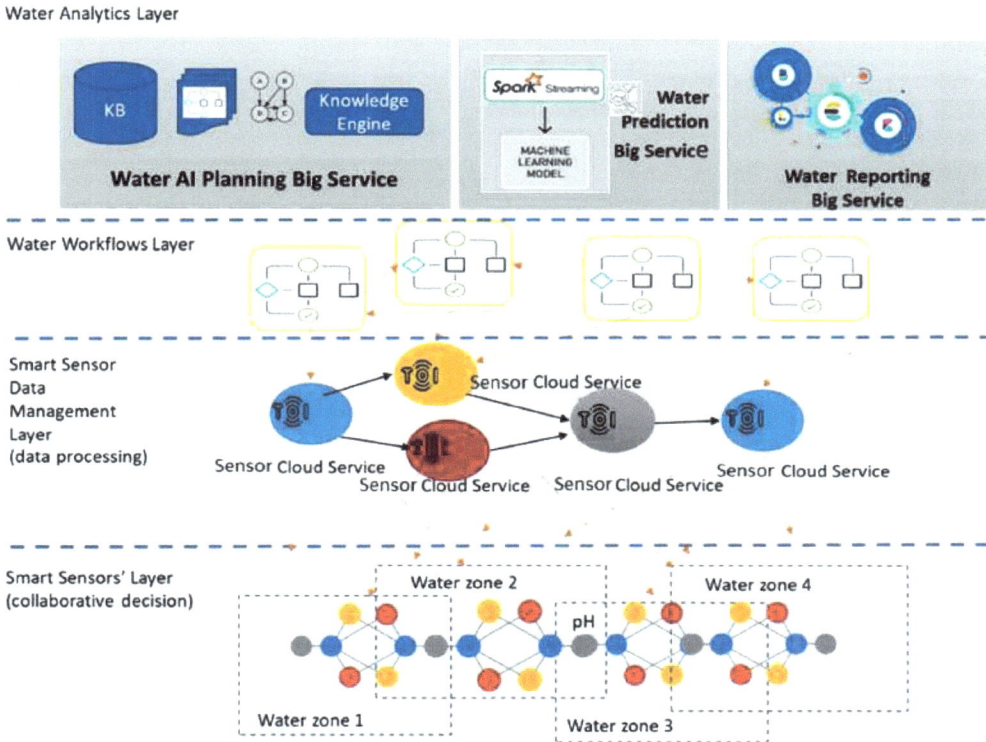

Fig. (4). Smart water monitoring framework [12].

The suggestion is Service-Oriented QOS-Assured distributed computing engineering [14]. It incorporates an actual gadget and virtual asset layer, cloud administration arrangement layer, cloud administration of the executives and multi-specialist layer to help QOS-Assured cloud administration arrangement and solicitation. The tangible assets change into different assets, like figuring, stockpiling, and network assets, by virtualization innovation. They can be associated together to shape an adaptable, bound together assets pool to progressively designate various applications and administration necessities, along these lines, further develop assets usage rate. These exercises are taken into consideration by Physical Device and Virtual Resource Layer. Cloud administration arrangement layer can give a few types of administrations by capabilities creation offered by actual gadget and virtual asset layer. The Cloud administration director and multi-specialist layer deal with various administrations given by the cloud administration arrangement layer and find QOS-guaranteed cloud administration in help repertory per the client's cloud administration are a necessity.

4.2.4. Efficient Collaboration and Seamless Integration

Distributed computing offers an on-request administration stage that apportions consistent admittance to the limitless stockroom of the unavoidable and conveyed framework, which incorporates computational power, a humongous information base, programming, and business information examination. CloudIoT structure grants consistent application organization and delivery utilizing Cloud administration-based models. A portion of the essential attributes of CloudIoT execution incorporates, for all intents and purposes, limitless extra room and computational power for IoT hubs, unavoidable and omnipresent help model for clients, cross-stage support for applications, and productive asset on the board, and start-t--finish quality. The variation of the Cloud stage for IoT leans toward various reasons, which include being financially achievable, dependable and execution, quick flexibility, adaptability, and strong security.

The framework [15] is both to help the patients and to help clinical experts in the consistent well-being observation of countless patients and information at run-time. The framework has sensors and gadgets associated with the patient to identify and forestall any crisis circumstance in the emergency clinic and at home. The door changes the messages got from the different sensors to DPWS-consistent administrations to give a conventional method for recovering sensor information inside a nearby organization. The organization correspondence is accountable for speaking with the entirety of the heterogeneous gadgets. The cloud stage gathers pushed data from the organization's correspondence utilizing a REST-based API. Its fundamental capability is to facilitate the far-off administration of the detected information at run-time, permitting improved client access and taking care of interest flexibility, responding to specific circumstances as indicated by the checking results. The same is depicted in Fig. (**5**).

It is a theoretical building structure [16] for medical services checking framework that considers the scope of viewpoints, including information assortment, transmission, handling, and distributed storage. The information procurement/ detecting layer frames the organization of sensors, including wearable gadgets that gather and record the well-being information of patients. The sensors screen fundamental signs, such as internal heat level, heartbeat rate, and blood strain, and record the information in clinical data sets. The design's information transmission/sending layer gives the connection point to impart and share the information. The sensing layer is liable for safely moving patient data to a healthcare organization's far-off server farm. Cloud gives information investigation that utilizes sensor information notwithstanding e-wellbeing records to determine better and forecast wellbeing-related diseases. The biosensors are on the human body as little implantations on the skin. Every sensor is freely fit for detecting, checking, handling basic information, and sending it remotely to a remote cloud framework. The sensor hubs are likewise provided for following patient areas and precisely deciding the actual state and movement of the patient, *i.e.*, strolling, running, or sitting inactive at one spot. The physiological information transfers into the cloud through an EHR framework. A separate clinical profile is within the cloud for each patient. This patient information is imparted to clinical experts and clinical medical care frameworks for their examination and assessment. Clinical experts, for example, doctors and specialists, can administer fast tolerant consideration by getting to the clinical information on the cloud and giving well-qualified sentiments. Clinical specialists can suggest lifesaving medications and prescriptions that should be accessible in drug store stores. The drug specialist can look at patients' clinical profiles and hypersensitive responses before offering drugs.

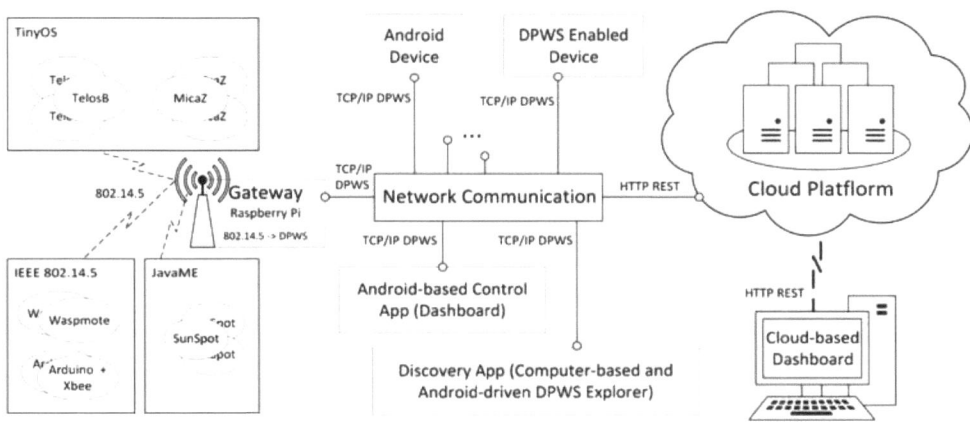

Fig. (5). Architecture of the system [15].

4.2.5. Knowledge-intensive Approach

Knowledge-Based Engineering is suggested as an appropriate solution to increase designers' productivity and free time for innovation and creativity at the expense of the repetitive and non-added-value operations that significantly impede the entire design process. These design ideas could be distinct iterations of the same concept or new product configurations. As a result, the design process moves into its convergence phase, where the best solutions are chosen to go to the following stages of design refinement. Many alternative models need to be (re)generated and distributed across many discipline specialists, who are frequently not geographically collocated, for analysis and assessment during this diverging/ converging process. It is usual for the outputs produced by one analysis tool to require additional processing before they can be used as inputs by another.

In the proposed model [17], IoT-cloud gives detecting administrations on request founded on the interest and area of portable users. It plans a detecting information report of sensors in light of good and room of versatile clients. When mobile clients have no-solicitation, the static transmission mode is set to sensors to save energy. When there is a universal client demand from a particular region, just sensors in the space having a place with the client's locale of interest enacts to give detecting administrations. The explicit necessities of utilizations and clients set off. The model endeavors the cloud's ability to set off detection in sensor hubs on request. We expect that in portable registering applications. The cloud can follow clients' areas and knows when a client needs to detect information and in which region. The cloud is a facilitator to control the planning of actual sensor hubs on request. Specifically, given the necessities of utilization and the current area of a versatile client, the cloud makes a booking solicitation to a sensor network close to the client to serve. The cloud gathers homogeneous virtual sensors from a similar geographic district with comparable detecting designs into one bunch. The IoT cloud generally tracks versatile clients who are right now involving detecting administrations in a geological locale. Fig. (**6**) represents the same.

It is a versatile and extensible IoT-Enabled Process Data Analytics Pipeline [18] to empower examiners to ingest information from IoT gadgets, remove information from this information, and connect them to handle information. CoreDB is a Data Lake as a Service to recognize information sources and ingest the enormous cycle of information in the Information Lake. It deals with various data set innovations, offers an implicit plan for security and following, and gives a solitary REST API to sort out, record, and question the information and metadata in the Data Lake. Information Lake provides the establishment with enormous information examination *via* naturally organizing the crude information in the Data Lake and setting them up for determining bits of knowledge. The Data Curation APIs in the Knowledge Lake give curation undertakings like extraction, connecting, synopsis, comment, advancement, and order. The style process will segregate the interaction investigator from the course of unequivocally dissecting various aspects like time, area, movement, and entertainer, and that's only the tip of the iceberg. The framework will want to utilize intuitive synopsis age to choose and group stories powerfully. Process Analytics empowers investigators to connect with the accounts and control the goals of rundowns.

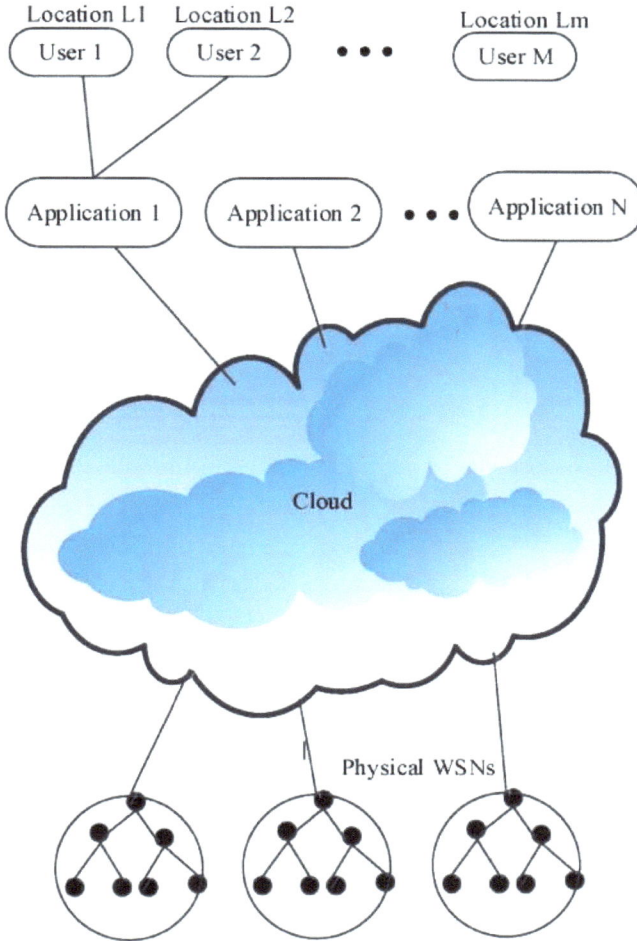

Fig. (6). Location-based Cloud IoT Integration [17].

4.3. APPLICATIONS OF AI AND IOT-CLOUD

Modern technologies like the Internet of Things (IoT), cloud computing, big data processing, and artificial intelligence have revolutionized society. These technologies complement one another and give rise to several interdisciplinary and cross-disciplinary fields of study. IoT uses multiple protocols and the Internet to link physical and virtual worlds for devices. The devices produce large amounts of data containing necessary facts about the physical world. Cloud computing platforms facilitate big data processing, using machine learning and extensive data analysis to make wise decisions. This section details the various domains of the field. Fig. (7) portrays the different applications using the technology.

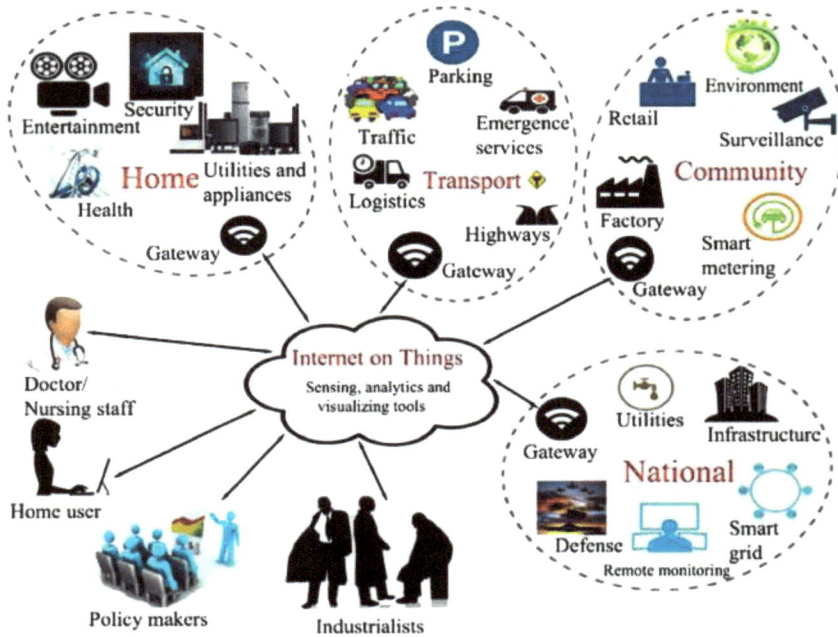

Fig. (7). Domains of IoT [19].

4.3.1. Smart Meters

Smart cities result from the extensive use of artificial intelligence and Internet of Things technology. In today's modern society, the technical fusion of IoT and AI technologies provides new insights into home automation, home healthcare, home security, and home energy management in smart homes. The conventional power grid/electrical power system, intended to monitor and manage electrical appliances in electrical energy management properly, cannot meet the difficulties of the current world, which the intelligent grid addresses.

The repository investigation-assisted electrical EMS framework [20] cooperates with the intelligence-enabled and Arduino MCU-based intelligent energy meter paradigm. It combines clever artificial intelligence. The devices have edge examination-empowered, with push message assistance for demand-side management in intelligence houses. A residence energy management system has a bi-directional transmission medium between surroundings. It replies to response alerts based on-demand assessment and electric usefulness that watches commands. It studies assembled electrical fuel spending information from shrewd dwellings. The wise edge investigating energy gauges dispersed and organized in the grid are period-synchronized. Microdata collected and explored by regional intelligent edge examination energy indicators are shipped to the repository and congregated in stockpiles. Macro understandings by AI qualified in warehouse examination and then embedded on-site on provincial-wise examination gauges are shipped to devise origins. Fig. (**8**) depicts the same.

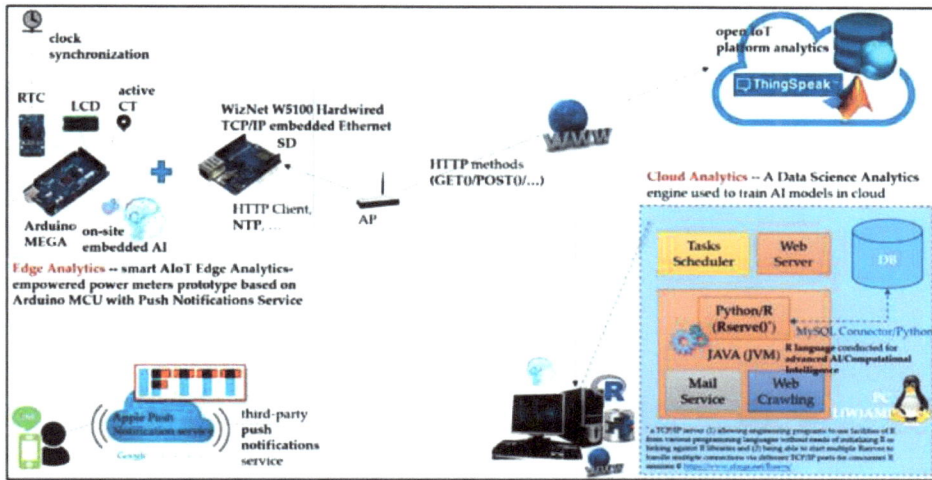

Fig. (8). Cloud analytics-assisted EMS architecture [20].

The work [21] expects to foster a savvy power usage IoT stage with a profound conviction network for power use, including display. It contains remote and programmed activity, power utilization investigation, and information perception capabilities. The savvy checking and control module is a climate control system with an entryway that interfaces and controls the machines through an implanted ZigBee arrangement. A programmable shrewd IoT door interface is an IoT cloud server of brilliant power used through the Internet and reports the functional boundaries and working states. The cloud stage deals with arranging elements of the energy-saving systems in light of the power utilization highlights investigated by a profound conviction network calculation, which empowers the programmed order of the power usage circumstance.

The work is an ideal Internet-of-Things-based Energy Management structure [22] for general dispersion networks in Smart Cities of shiftable burdens. The conveyance network incorporates a few feeders comprising various obligations, energy capacity, wind turbines, and a few Microgrids. The Microgrids come with Photovoltaic exhibits, and the level of their heaps outfitted with brilliant meters can move their utilization regarding the market energy costs. The circulation network has a progressive structure to exchange energy and data from the discount energy market to consumers. The Microgrids meet their energy balance regarding the energy market costs, the interest of the purchasers, and the power age of the Photovoltaics. It settles how much moving all over the heaps and exchanging power with the dispersion organization. All the data of the microgrids is shipped off the distribution operator through the microgrid aggregator. It uses a distributor operator as a central cloud to enhance. The distribution operator declares to the market administrator about the exchanging power.

4.3.2. Smart Cities

A smart city [23] is an urbanization district that gathers information utilizing a few computerized and actual gadgets. The data from such devices oversee incomes, assets, resources, and so forth. In contrast, the data from such gadgets support execution throughout the city. Cloud-based Internet of Things applications could assist with painful urban areas containing data assembled from residents, devices, homes, and other things. This data undergoes examination to screen and oversee transportation organizations, electric utilities, assets the board, water supply frameworks, squander the executives, wrongdoing identification, security systems, capability, advanced library, medical services offices, and different open doors. A cloud specialist organization offers public cloud benefits that can refresh the IoT climate, empowering outsider exercises to install IoT information inside electronic gadgets executing on the IoT. Fig. (**9**) represents the applications of CloudIoT in smart cities.

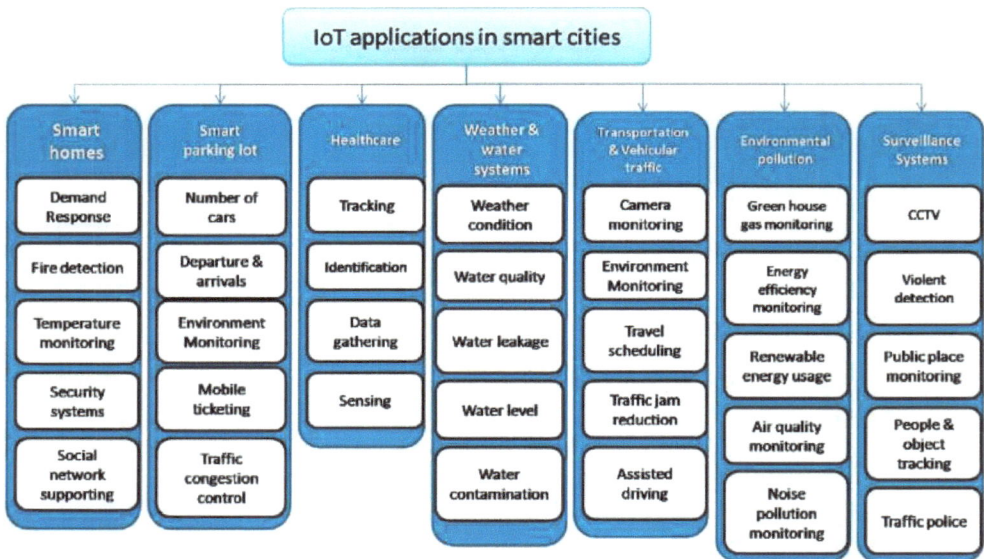

Fig. (9). Applications of CloudIoT in smart cities [24].

The work [25] examines the data security gambles in the smart city from the IoT discernment layer, investigates the common advancements in IoT, and gives related security answers for the current security dangers. The development of wise visual IoT can make keen discernment and programmed information assortment for the components of metropolitan complex, covering all parts of the metropolitan complicated. The gathered information can be pictured and normalized so directors can lead the executives of the visual metro complex. The discernment layer understands the view of the pre-set data of the item. It seems the climate of the article judges the environmental adjustment. It considers the location code. It sees the difference in the way and the substance of the report during the time spent change. The organization layer of IoT is predominantly made out of the ZigBee entryway and switch of every subsystem to understand the entrance of detecting layer hubs and direct information transmission through ZigBee and TCP/IP. The application layer of IoT epitomizes brilliant structures, intelligent homes, and shrewd networks.

CityHub [26] gives a system that makes it simple for outsiders to create and send Smart City applications. These outsiders can be resident gatherings to support nearby organizations offering hyper-neighborhood administrations or even public organizations offering new administrations to residents. The structure uses a cloud foundation and provides a center IoT capacity to oversee and communicate with Smart City infrastructure. The CityHub cloud foundation layers a cloud adminis-tration layer on the IoT system, making this accessible to application engineers. Lifecycle, the board upholds the making of new administrations and their utilization of stage and IoT assets to meet help requests. The asset use and charging capacity guarantee the effective use of assets and to fit charge out to specialist co-ops. Table **4.1** portrays the implementation details of various contribution

Table 4.1. Portrays the implementation details of various contributions.

Contribution	Implementation Details
[6]	Uses coco coir as Hydroponic Media.
[7]	Keystone is an implementation of the OpenStack Identity service. The #SmartME project is a crowd-funded initiative aiming at morphing Messina into a Software Defined City.
[9]	The testbed consists of one NVIDIA Jetson nano card, two Raspberry Pi cards, two Samsung smartphones, one HP Pavilion Laptop, and access to the Google Cloud Run platform.
[12]	Google Colaboratory was used to encode the whole water management process with Python 3.7.12. The incremental embedding of the WIN was implemented using PyTorch.

(Table 4.1) cont.....

Contribution	Implementation Details
[14]	The experimental setup has been conducted upon a desktop with an Intel Core i5-4210U 1.70GHz (c/ TB 2.70 GHz), 4GB RAM / Disco Duro 500GB, and a 64-bit PC (AMD64) Ubuntu operating system. C?? and Tool Command Language (TCL) are the language programs to implement the BSOA.
[15]	• Gateway used (Serial-USB) 802.14.5. • The work uses the Google App Engine cloud platform.
[18]	• Summaries have been generated from a Tweet dataset having over 15 million tweets, persisted and indexed in the MongoDB. • The experiment was performed on the Amazon EC2 platform using instances running Ubuntu Server 14.04.
[17]	• It uses a low-power listing (LPL) protocol.
[21]	• It uses the ZigBee communication module. • The electricity consumption datasets of air conditioners were collected from 77 different customers for 35 days.
[22]	• It uses three main feeders. • Each feeder consists of 20 MGs which supplies 30 percent of the load of the feeder. • HOMER software is used to obtain the power generation of the PV arrays.
[25]	• The simulation of the LoRa communication protocol is realized by MATLAB. • The normalized throughput analysis of the IoT communication system includes theBEB and the new back-off algorithm (REBEB).
[26]	• The testbed deployed in Oulo, Finland. • WoTKit processor is used that allows IoT application developers to map to the data sources.

4.3.3. Smart Agriculture

Farming [27, 28] assumes a principal part of the planet both as a critical wellspring of a job and its job in the worldwide food production network. Agronomists and horticultural enterprises go to Innovations to satisfy the need of the populace. Some instances include Cloud Computing, Edge Computing, Fog Computing, IoT, Big Data, Artificial Intelligence, and Drones. Sensors can offer profoundly exact estimations of yield status. It gives enhancements to reap gauging, climate expectation, increment creation, water protection, continuous information assortment, brought down activity costs, gear observing, remote checking, and precise homestead and field assessment. Heterogeneous sensors and different gadgets gather pertinent agrarian information like stickiness, tempera-ture, pH and soil conditions.

The work [29] suggests the architecture model. The stockpile layer is predomi-nantly for adequate scale information capacity and information examination. This layer is additionally liable for stacking calculations and information scientific apparatuses to Fog hubs. It can store reinforcement information for future investigation. The Fog layer is fundamental in this model. It introduces it to neighboring ranches. Haze layers will be answerable for ongoing information investigation, for example, anticipating nuisances and illnesses, yield expectation, climate forecast, and agrarian observing robotization. The handled and examined information transfers to the cloud layer for reinforcement purposes or further investigation. The third layer is the Edge, comprising end gadgets, farm haulers, sensors, and actuators. The fundamental objective of this layer is the assortment of information and its exchange to the Fog layer. Fig. (**10**) depicts the same.

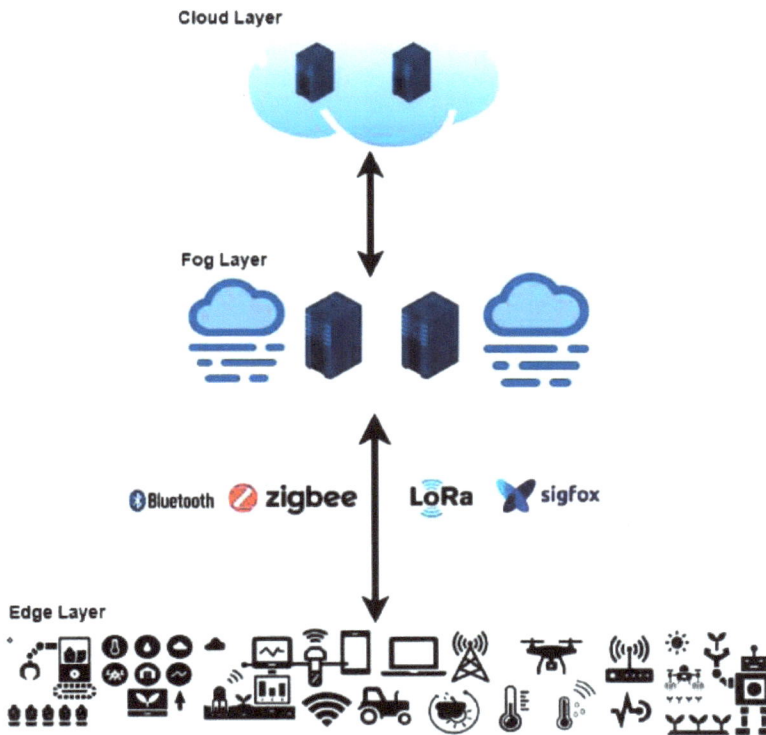

Fig. (10). Three-layered Architecture [29].

It is a cloud-empowered CLAY-MIST estimation record [30] in light of tempera-ture and relative moistness to survey the solace levels of a harvest. The calculated layer has a microcontroller board to get information from the actual layer, which comprises sensors to screen the farming field. It additionally assesses plant development. The microcontroller controls the CLAYMIST estimation list in light of information from the stickiness and temperature sensors sent in the actual layer. The document data, alongside temperature also relative stickiness, are assessed given the relative water fume in the air. The work transmits outcomes to ranchers through message notices such as SMS or Mail alerts. The application layer is the client communication layer planned to follow the expected boundaries, notice what is going on, estimate values in a whole motorized way, and screen the farming harvest field. The sequential observing framework screen the decision-production of the Thingspeck cloud given determined values. The general dampness assesses water in the air and is used in the horticulture crop observing framework. The dirt sensors assemble data about soil conditions, moisture, and supplements. The environment sensors collect data on stickiness and temperature. The server investigates and picks the infection from the simple rundown in light of information from sensors used to make the right move. On the server-side, the expert system casings and isolates the data given the recommended edge rundown and sends the broken-down proposition to the rancher about crop yields.

It is a sensor-based horticulture [31] checking framework that ought to incorporate a choice emotionally supportive network to boost creation, streamline asset use, and can diminish natural hazards. The work gathers information from relative sensors, and that information/data ships off the information assortment server. This correspondence finishes with the new Li-Fi innovation. In the wake of getting information from sensors, that data should move to a cloud server with the assistance of GPRS and WiMAX advancements. The cloud server reliably examines the information in light of necessity. Given the gathered information, the cut-off will make a choice, which needs to circulate among the bought-in clients. It accumulates data and sends a warning. This cycle is called caution with signal sound.

The work [32] is the presentation of a Smart Drone for crop the executives where the continuous Drone information coupled with IoT and Cloud Computing advances help in building a reasonable Smart Agriculture. The robot innovation utilized for the model is Sky Drone FPV2, which packs a camera module, an information module, and a 4G/LTE modem. The intelligent robot would be a Fixed wing ethereal vehicle that can convey numerous sensors, accomplish more noteworthy velocities, have longer flight time, and cover huge regions. It will have an implanted programming for flight arranging and control in light of GPS navigation, implying that the handling results are accessible following the trip to approved users. The proposed model comprises three modules. Flight and route sensors like vision, whirligig, slant, current, and GPS are constrained by the robot's status and flight boundaries. The sensors likewise help the route and screen the quick or farther climate of the robot to identify and stay away from startling obstacles. The correspondence and systems administration block is answerable for the data stream. The coordination block focuses on adjusting to the necessities of utilizing interest.

4.3.4. Smart Healthcare

The Internet of Things [33] is an affiliated organization of shrewd sensor gadgets, which frequently have restricted capacity and low handling power ability. This innovation joins different advances like the cloud to give a great degree. Artificial brainpower guides machines to make choices. The whole arrangement makes shrewd medical services checking structure. The transmission and interaction of clinical-related mixed media signals from intelligent sensors and cell phones give patients ideal help and quality medical care administrations. Fig. (**11**) portrays the IoT architecture for healthcare systems.

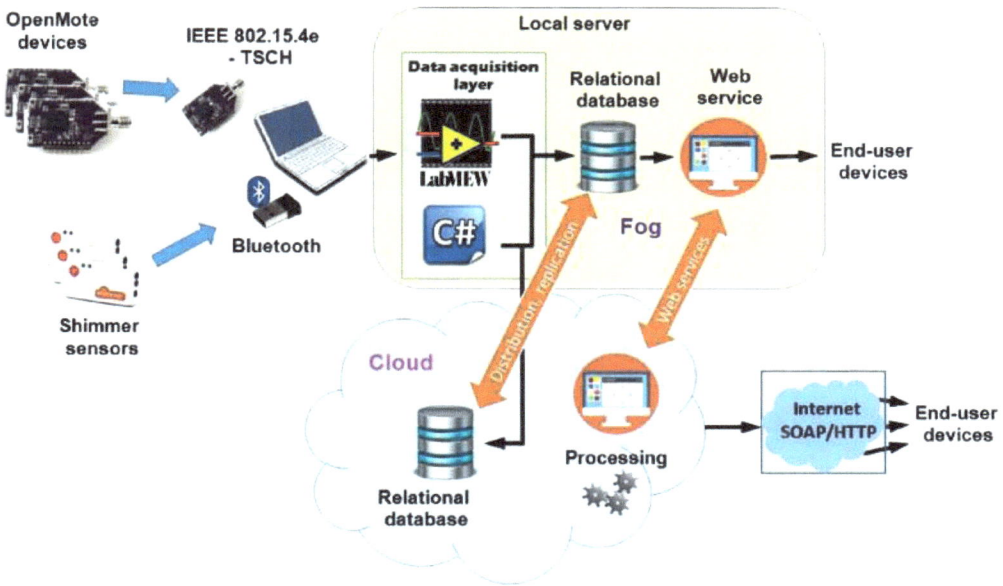

Fig. (11). IoT Architecture for Healthcare [34].

The proposal [35] is another strategy for ECG checking given Internet-of-things methods. The work accumulates ECG information utilizing a wearable observing hub and communicates to the IoT warehouse using Wi-Fi. The ECG information assembled from sensors is sent to the IoT cloud through a particular remote convention. It comprises four valuable modules. In Data cleaning, significant elements are separate from ECG flags to distinguish potential heart diseases. The ECG information frequently incorporates the time and digitized signal abundance. The IoT cloud often gives an information examination stage to separate valuable data from the ECG signal. Infection cautioning on the IoT cloud has become significant for safeguarding patients from being harmed. Given the consequences of information examination, the IoT cloud can comprehend the ongoing medical issue of the patient. The IoT cloud will tell the group of the patient and the specialist in time (on getting dubious readings). The GUI is liable for information perception and the executives. It gives simple admittance to the information in the IoT cloud. Users can sign onto the cloud to obtain envisioned ECG information progressively. A versatile application can respond promptly to client input, while website pages are more helpful regarding upkeep and update.

The work [36] comprises intelligent EEG sensors to record and sends EEG signals from epileptic patients. The mental framework can examine this information progressively and play out the best activity to offer types of assistance to patients. This transferred information can likewise be remotely seen and dissected by clinical staff individuals who can again help and guide the concerned patients. The mental framework consistently works out the patient's state continuously. The epileptic patient has to wear an intelligent EEG sensor, which comes as an agreeable and lightweight skull cap. The clinical staff individuals can additionally research and prompt the patient appropriately. The signs handled consistently founded on the seriousness of the seizure recognition and arrangement result. The mental framework warns the clinical staff, individuals and related partners through the shrewd medical care provider. The system has a LAN layer that goes about as a point of interaction to send the got signals, like EEG, from the IoT gadgets' layer to a facilitating layer comprising heterogeneous brilliant devices. The facilitating layer contains heterogeneous shrewd gadgets. It gathers information locally. The cloud involves the cloud chief, server farm, highlight extraction waiter, identification waiter, and grouping waiter. The cloud director initially confirms the occupant's enrollment with a shrewd medical care supplier. The cloud director is likewise answerable for verifying the character of all partners in the savvy medical care framework, like specialists, clinical staff individuals, clinic delegates, and patients. The cloud director controls the information stream to and from the servers and oversees correspondence, stockpiling, and other resources. The sensor flags incorporate the patient's developments and motions and look to be aware of the patient's state. The signal handling procedures extricate preprocessed data from the element extraction server. The discovery server identifies and groups seizure information and sends the location results to the cloud administrator.

The proposal [37] permits the sensor to screen the patient's side effects. It depends on mechanizing the technique for a social event patients' information is utilizing sensors associated with clinical gadgets and passing this data on to the clinical focuses cloud with the end goal of capacity, handling, and scattering using docker holder and raspberry pi. The framework includes four fundamental parts: sensors, raspberry pi, server, and users. The sensor hubs have the product to gather, encode, and send information over remote correspondence channels. These sensors are associated with raspberry pi, which reads information from the sensor and sends it to a server. The server involved a docker holder and the nearby data set for additional handling of gathered screen information and giving it to various clients like the cloud, specialists, medical attendants, and clinics to analyze and screen medical issues.

4.3.5. Smart Industry

The review [38] proposes a circulated computational part-based system. It coordinates calculation, capacity assets, and ongoing abilities through innovation and microservices. The coordination happens between nonexclusive structures and actual acknowledgement. It has four stages. Application disintegrates into microservices with the related information model. It Identifies the holders that will have the services. It associates in every compartment whether the help is offered or expected with distribution or membership. It recognizes non-utilitarian requirements. The plan design can produce the process configuration in light of the parts introduced. The work uses planning from microservices to DDS. The interaction scaled to the current level can be checked with a reproduction level plan. Fig. (**12**) represents the same.

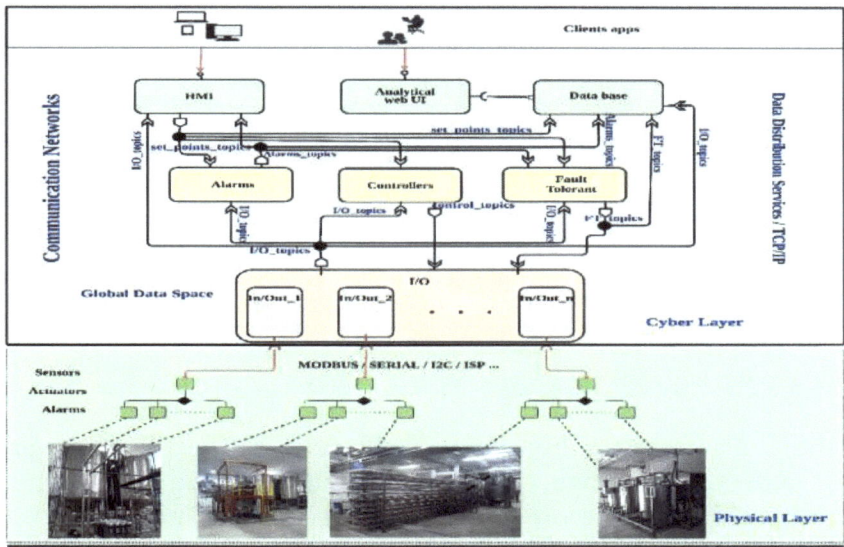

Fig. (12). IoT Architecture for Healthcare [34].

The review [39] presents LabVIEW-based web-based contamination checking of ventures for the command over contamination brought about by untreated removal of waste. The framework begins with the Arduino board bringing information from the dht11, mg-811 CO_2 sensor, and pH sensor, and information is shipped off the LabVIEW. The LabVIEW makes and stores the boundary values in the particular field in the data set on the table on the nearby waiter utilizing MYSQL. The information from the nearby server is then put away in a cloud web facilitating. The qualities put away in the tables are brought up and shown on the site and in the Android application. The data stream will be from the right to the left of the controlling segment. The controlling info is from the site and Android application by squeezing the different separate buttons. When a button shrinks, the suitable PHP scripts execute, and the information goes from the site, and the Android application to the internet-based data set tables and gets refreshed. Arduino decodes the refreshed qualities in the control table and sets the warmer, chiller, and different control valves on or off. Table **4.2** List implementation details of various contributions

Table 4.2. List implementation details of various contributions.

Contribution	Implementation Details
[35]	• It uses an AD8232 ECG sensor. • It uses a 32-bit ARM CortexM3 micro-controller operating at 72 MHz, a Flash memory of up to 512 Kbytes.
[36]	• The work uses the CHB-MIT dataset. • It uses 686 multiple-channel scalps EEG recordings from paediatric patients who were affected by intractable seizures.
[37]	• Raspberry pi is used. • It uses 40 GPIO pins • 6LowPAN protocol is used to transfer data from sensor to server.
[39]	• The work uses Xampp • It consists of an Apache HTTP server, MariaDB database, and an interpreter to decode the scripts written in PHP language. • The work uses ARDUINO MEGA 2560.

4.4. CHALLENGES OF AI AND IOT-CLOUD

Despite the IoT's resource limitations, IoT networks enable outsourced data collecting and cloud storage. The distribution of cloud computing is very effective, storage is getting more up-to-date, and some organizations are changing their data from internal records to the hubs of cloud computing vendors. The section details the challenges faced by the amalgamation system.

4.4.1. Data Privacy and Security

In cloud computing, people can store their data on computers and give public users access to it through data centers. Providing security for data access policy, which must also be stored on cloud servers, is one of the most challenging challenges. The ciphertext's contents may be partially discernible from the access structure alone. Several encryption systems are available to ensure security for data access policy. Two critical security concerns are user access management and keeping cloud data secure.

CP-ABE [40] conceals the entrance strategy utilizing a hashing calculation and gives protection from insider assault using a mark confirmation scheme. The information proprietor is mindful of encoding all information utilizing an access strategy before moving to the cloud. The information proprietor likewise utilizes a hashing calculation to stow away and present the entrance strategy with the ciphertext. The undertaking of a cloud server is to store the information proprietor's documents and permit the authorized clients to get to data. The critical age community is liable for making a mystery key for a singular cloud client. Just the genuine client whose private key fulfills the entrance strategy can decode the data. The critical age place produces and circulates secret keys to authentic cloud clients. Fig. (**13**) depicts the same.

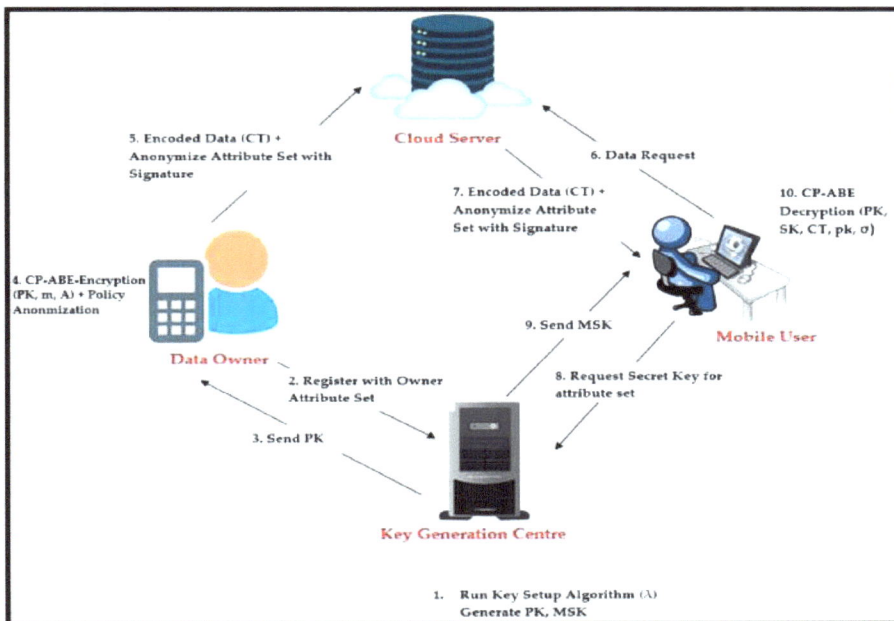

Fig. (13). Proposed CP-ABE scheme [40].

The review [41] is an AI-empowered three-party game system for ensuring information protection in the portable edge crowdsensing of IoT. It is a characterization namelessness model that successfully protects delicate information. It directs all substances to take on harmless social techniques to boost their benefits while safeguarding the security of detecting information. Information should be pre-separated into delicate and non-delicate information as indicated by the security degree and the previously expected secret. An order namelessness model preprocesses transferred detecting information to safeguard information security. A three-party game model gauges the security spillage and chance of catching news and gives a premise for developing the resulting capability. The Nash harmony benefits each game player in the versatile edge crowdsensing and the conditions under which all players pick humane ways of behaving.

The review [42] tends to the expanded interest in distributed computing and its definition, advancements broadly utilized in medical care, their concerns and conceivable outcomes, and how assurance systems are coordinated and arranged when the organization carries out the most recent developing assistance model. The E-wellbeing framework is a recently evolved space that contains electronic cycles and interchanges. It is a gathering of patient well-being information. It is computerized data that includes news, outlines, patient clinical data, prescriptions, emergency clinic or center reports, radiology photos, charging data, and other touchy patient data. Distributed computing offers the expense of successfully putting away handling vital information with proficiency and quality.

The proposed PPP-MKRS plot [43] accomplishes multi-watchword looking and their connected frequencies. It is a protection safeguarding phrase with a multi-catchphrase position. It presents streamlined separating, parallel tree record construction, and conjunctive watchword search to accomplish secure looking through productivity. A mergeable pile with a bunch of store-requested trees takes advantage of the tasks like hub inclusion and extraction with the base keys. It carries out a cycle that presents a few basic tasks. The continuous elements, including IoT entryway, cloud-server, information proprietor, and client, ensure information privacy to rethink the scrambled information records. It can assemble accessible files to empower effective and secure access commands over encoded information. Each record makes a protected looking-through file to characterize the client types and strategies. It approves information clients that execute question secret entryway, which depends on scrambled catchphrases.

The work [44] explores the fundamental issues of a constant contamination checking framework, including the sensors, Internet of Things correspondence conventions, procurement and transmission of information through correspondence channels, and information security and consistency. The framework has Wired and remote sensors for different measurement estimations, IoT passages for information assortment, IoT correspondence middleware with security highlights for sending information to IoT mists, IoT cloud answers for numerical insights, and manufactured brainpower models for information investigation and information science strategies. Fig. (**14**) portrays the same.

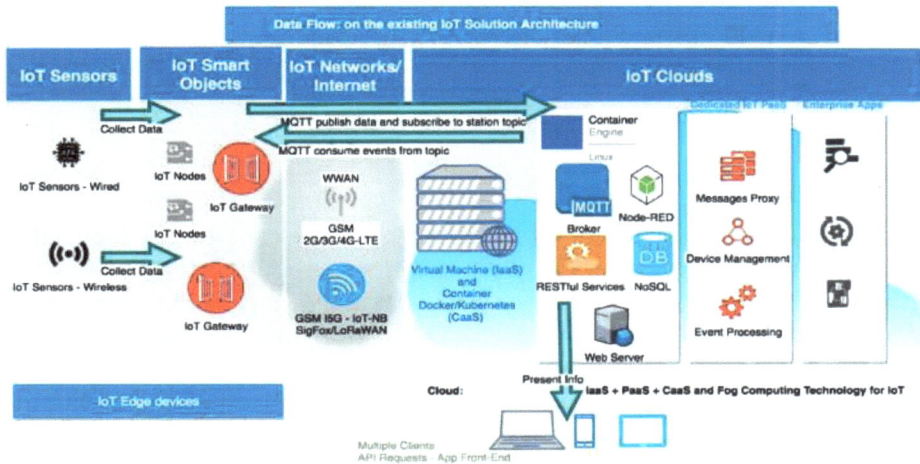

Fig. (14). System architecture [44].

The solid engineering for the IoT edge layer framework is called AI4SAFE-IoT [45]. This design has AI-controlled security modules at the edge layer for safeguarding the IoT foundation. The principal method has a three-layer structure covered by an unavoidable security layer for the edge layer. Edge gadgets generally manage IoT applications through web administrations in the application layer. CoAP is a plaintext convention like HTTP. The digital danger Attribution module in the application layer is liable for crediting the malignant action that dwells on the edge layer gadgets by a profile matching motor to its unique pernicious entertainer. It also suggests the definitive ruling against the danger/assault. The organization layer of the IoT design gives a standard-based component to impeding dubious traffic. The intrusion detection module benefits from a prepared motor under ordinary, noxious traffic profiles. The equipped AI motor can utilize the current profiles from current TCP/IP conventions or, on the other hand, current traffic streams in the organization layer of the edge layer gadgets to prepare. Each end-point widget in the edge layer should send its caught information to the IoT cloud back-end structure.

The system [46] uses Black Network conventions and acute administration to get the most powerless and regularly unstable IoT interchanges. The system uses various leveled, conveyed designs with pooled assets to forestall weak links and sandbox assault influences. This ordered progression permits AI-empowered administration devices close to the IoT edge to utilize limited information in the Big Data assortments. The examination uncovers that the proposed system gives versatile well-being and security to the executive's structure that records a smart city's dynamic, consistent, and steadily evolving life. The Secure Smart City works at two levels - the organization level and the application level. The organization level comprises IoT gadgets, IoT entryways restricted registering gadgets, joins for interIoT correspondence, cloud-based information assortment, capacity, and examination. All organization-level interchanges are gotten utilizing Black Networks. The correspondence parcels in Black Networks are entirely encoded, of fixed length, and viable with the primary convention. This paper presents novel IPv6 Black parcels and surveys the excellent Bluetooth Low Energy Black bundles. The application level is essential for the board and examination in the cloud: get, store, dissect, file, and erase. Manufactured brainpower effectively deals with the organization and application levels for critical security administration, dissemination, arrangement of the board, and observing and controlling the well-being and security of the intelligent city framework. Information investigation prompts reaction and gives redone resident administrations in light of information gathered rather than straightforward predefined rules. The Secure Smart City structure utilizes a dispersed design to restrict the impacts of disappointments and assaults and gives strength to keep up with high uptime and privately redid administrations.

4.4.2. Quality of Service

One enabling method to dissolve the ossification is cloud computing, founded on virtualization technologies. Internet service providers may be given elastic virtualized node and link resources in a cloud computing environment. Implementing virtualization based on cloud computing is still hampered by several technological problems.

The review [47] has handled and separated information and works on the nature of the administration of IoT organizations. It is a calculated model of circulated haze figuring, and an AI-based information handling and examination model is the ideal usage of cloud assets. Fog registering comprises three-level engineering incorporating a sensor layer, a haze figuring layer, and a cloud layer. The sensor layer includes the advancement of IoT hubs containing miniature regulators and different sensors for estimating air toxins. The small regulator is a correspondence module for sending information to the haze layer. In the sensor layer, it is fixed and portable, contingent upon the spatial degree of the urban community checking and the inclusion required. The mist hubs will be spatially dispersed zone-wise to successfully deal with the air poisons information sent by the sensor layer in the disseminated layer. The zonal haze hubs set at various chosen geological areas will remotely get the data from the sensor layer through wifi or GPRS technology. The cloud layer receives the information from the circulated mist hubs for long-haul stockpiling and high-level information logically. The verifiable information involves grouping, time series investigation, prescient demonstrating, and recognizing stowed-away patterns or examples. Fig. (**15**) depicts the same.

Fig. (15). System Architecture [47].

The framework [48] can gather AQ information from a few locales. The collected information is handled and sent to an IoT server. The entryway processes the information and posts the amassed information with timestamps to the outside world over the Internet. The framework equipment comprises most of the sensor hubs and passages. Every sensor hub screens the groupings of six gases notwithstanding, encompassing temperature and relative dampness. The sensor hub imparts remotely with the entryway through XBee PRO radio modules. A devoted firmware is in the sensor hub. The proposed IAQM framework incorporates sensor hubs and doors. Every part has committed firmware. The actual layer comprises the radio module. The information connects layer includes the passage, gadget director, and correspondence convention.

The work [49] is a comprehensive Deep Neural Network-driven IoT creative medical care strategy called Gray Filter Bayesian Convolution Neural Network given regular examination. The motivation behind IoT-driven sensors involving Cyber-Physical Systems for the medical care framework is to change the medical services framework by gainfully expanding the nature of administration to a patient. In the cloud space, information from the actual distance is pre-handled with the assistance of dim sifting and relies upon collected duplicating activity. The pre-handled highlights apply Bayesian Logistic Sigmoid Activation capabilities to recognize ideal human action. The errand of actual space stays in aggregating the information from IoT-driven sensors with enrollment. Likewise, a unique patient ID is designated to the related patient for future correspondences, guaranteeing unending systems administration capacities to the patients. Physical space manages three sorts of clients: specific patients, clinics, and physicians. Cyber Space is responsible for looking at the information gathered from the actual area for clinical information examination that relies upon the thought of the on-request IoT sensors to acquire cultural involvement with the arising savvy medical care framework. It comprises three sections. Profound brain networks perform the clinical information investigation as it has the benefit of acting without being uncommonly arranged.

The proposed intelligent structure framework [50] has three levels of engineering. In IoT Layer, detecting and correspondence capacities are inside the actual things of working on getting them prepared for IoT. In the fog layer, the haze door server is kept up, which can take some neighborhood choices in light of the sensor's information. This layer is answerable for gathering, separating, and preprocessing the info. It likewise fills in as a web door that interfaces IoT with the web utilizing VPN. Information moves from the fog layer to the warehouse for capacity and calculation in the cloud layer.

Polluino [51] is a framework for observing air contamination. It includes an assortment of ecological information by utilizing a few outside sensors. It gathers and communicates information collected by numerous sensor modules. A sensor, the executive's stage has three principal entertainers: sensor proprietors, Cloud suppliers, and information consumers. The proprietors of the sensors can distribute information gathered from all their accessible gadgets to get a profit from the venture. Sensors involve over the Internet free of charge or at an expense. Shoppers can choose sensors from which to gather information within a given period. This model has an IoT framework and administration. In the PaaS approach, the Cloud supplier offers runtimes, data sets, middlewares, systems, dealers, and different administrations for IoT gadget communications. In the IaaS approach, the observing framework has sensor proprietors, who send sensors into the climate and make the administration foundation by depending on Cloud supplier IaaS administrations.

The structure [52] further develops QoS by giving decreased idleness and burden adjusting at the fog layer. The proposed system expects to total the information close to its age to diminish the information move. The fog layer comprises various hubs grouped into a few bunches. The gateways are packs given their topographical area, so the adjoining mist hubs are in the same group. Each batch is checked and constrained by a haze hub called group chief. Bunch Chief is an extraordinary mist hub able to adjust load among all devices inside the group. It guarantees that every gateway is neither under-stacked nor overburdened. The cluster supervisor ensures that it should achieve the errand in the least time. This contextual investigation concerns the wellbeing checking framework where medical care chooses biomedical information examination. It involves ubiquitous frameworks and the transmission of information continuously climate instead of sending it to the cloud.

4.4.3. Context Awareness

For a long time, cognitive assistants have been regarded as one of the top computer information technologies for assisting people in their daily lives. They must handle a significant amount of data of a wide range to give consistent and reliable decision support, which varies from broad issues to specific tasks within a small domain. Over the past ten years, context-aware systems have become a significant class of intelligent systems. Any information explaining an entity's situation in such scenarios is context. Researchers and developers were obliged to develop effective ways to model and process contextual information due to the rapid expansion of personal mobile devices like smartphones, tablets, smart-watches, and other wearables. Fig. (**16**) portrays a system architecture.

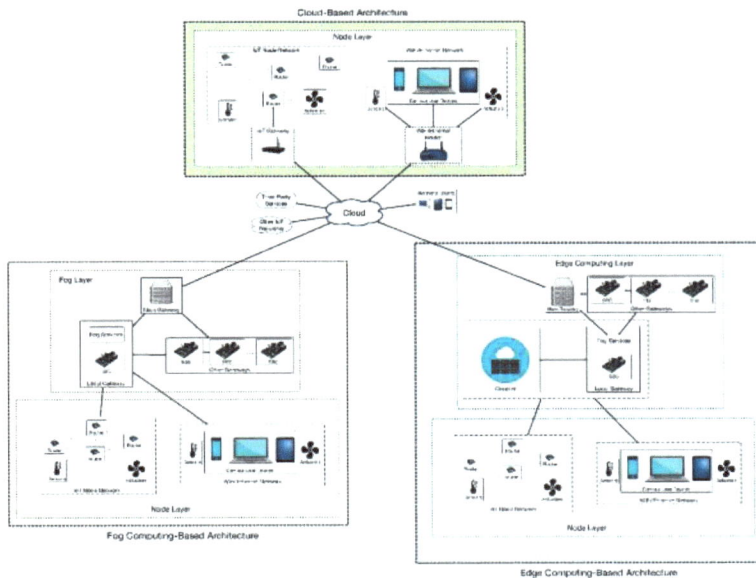

Fig. (16). System Architecture [53].

The proposed prefetch plot [54] targets give proposals concerning the documents that should be stored, considering the setting behind every individual solicitation. It separates data from the upcoming solicitations, permitting it to provide better forecasts. The work process can have two periods. The preparation stage performs disconnection. The proposal and pre-bringing location are set each time a solicitation is received and served on the web. The disconnected stage starts with preparing an expectation model utilizing an informational index connected with demands performed at a prior time. The approaching solicitations are components of succession. The principal component of the grouping is the direct solicitation from a particular client, and the last component is the most recent gotten demand from a similar user. By checking this cycle, we at last concocted a grouping of mentioned records alongside the timestamp of each solicitation. The model is a seven-layer model comprising six LSTM layers and a final thick layer. The internet-based stage respects the step set off once a grouping of solicitations is shipped off the capacity cloud by a solitary user. Once the solicitation is gotten and the mentioned information matches the prefetched information, their actual trade is launched straightforwardly from the prefetch part. The disconnected stage rehashes every day, while all approaching solicitations are put away in a devoted data set to re-apply the above-shown plot with the new information. This information base incorporates verifiable knowledge of committed medical care experts' solicitations to the cloud.

CoCaMAAL model [55] tries to resolve such issues and help situated engineering for brought together setting age. The framework includes five fundamental cloud-arranged components. It can serve enormous quantities of AAL clients. AAL clients go about as sensor information suppliers and putting mindful help buyers. The arrangement of AAL frameworks fluctuates in light of target client prerequisites. Every one of the AAL frameworks comprises various BSN establishments and checking frameworks. The CAP cloud contains the registering rationale and cycle of switching low-level crude information over completely to extract setting portrayal, which is unmistakable to all design parts. The CAP cloud utilizes combination and thinking systems to surmise settings from sensor information. The specialist co-op cloud contains data, for example, side effect identification for various infections and the kinds of activity required. The CaM cloud has the framework to handle setting information, putting away and recovering settings, *etc*. The model likewise has different interpersonal organizations of specialists and patients' loved ones to break down, envision, and talk about clinical information at whatever point. The wearable sensors and encompassing gadgets have the proper remote or wired network to a neighborhood workstation in the AAL climate. Every sensor and device has a unique identifier in the nearby framework so that the workstation can recognize approaching information from various sensors and gadgets. An information gatherer program in the workstation occasionally gathers sensor information. The program then passes the gathered example with gadget data to the cloud door utilizing an advanced testing rate. Each gadget test contains a total arrangement of data. The collected information is transferred to the cloud servers using a cloud passage.

4.4.4. Security and Compliance

From intelligent wearable technology to industrial systems, the Internet of Things brings many advantages to our daily lives. The cloud-based IoT architecture is developing into a trend in the IoT market when combined with leading technologies like the cloud. Security and compliance are two of the main issues for cloud-based IoT environments.

Distributed computing gives adaptable engineering where information and assets are scattered in different areas and are open to other modern conditions. Distributed computing has changed the utilization, putting away, and sharing of assets like information, administrations, and applications for everyday applications. Distributed computing gives versatility and regular reports on programming and equipment for many modern applications. The cloud offers the dissemination of heterogeneous information and assets alongside virtual conditions. Web of Things - based cloud framework is a broad organization that incorporates a few IoT-upheld applications and gadgets. The framework includes servers, capacity, hidden foundation, ongoing handling, and tasks. IoT-based cloud framework likewise incorporates guidelines and administrations for getting, making due, and associating different IoT applications and gadgets. Fig. (**17**) depicts the IoT-based cloud attack model.

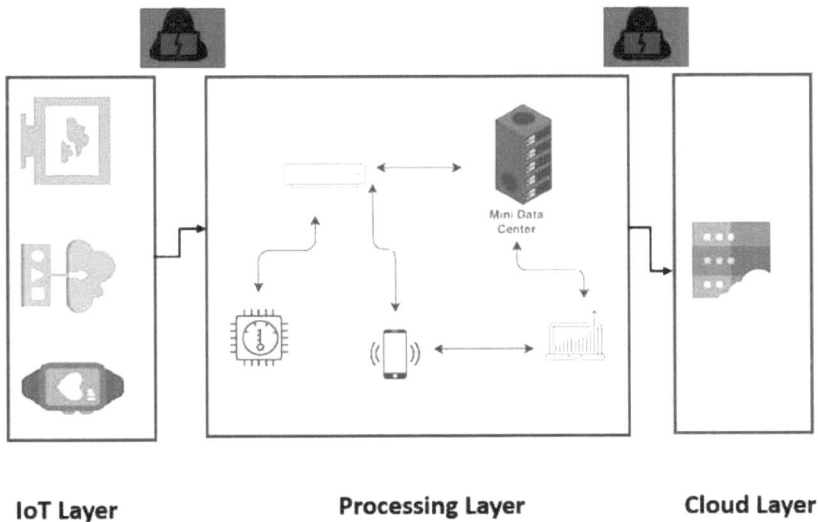

IoT Layer   Processing Layer   Cloud Layer

Fig. (17). IoT-based cloud attack model [56].

The SCCAF [57] works with cloud administration to help clients to choose an ideal cloud specialist organization that fulfills their security prerequisites. It is a protected and consistent nonstop appraisal system to assess cloud administrations' security and consistency levels in the life cycle. It contains three primary cycles. The cloud service customers set the security level of choices as per the conformance between the guaranteed security arrangements and the security measurements characterized by the cloud service customers. Then, the cloud service customers choose the ideal cloud service provider to send cloud administration, given the security evaluation result. Cloud service customers can choose the ideal cloud service provider to give cloud administration. During the utilization of cloud administration, the cloud service customers assess the consistency level of the cloud administration provided the conformance between the asserted cloud service level agreements and the genuine service level agreements. After the consistency appraisal finishes, the cloud service customers can lay out consistency resistance rules given the effect of consistency level on their real business. Fig. (**18**) represents the same.

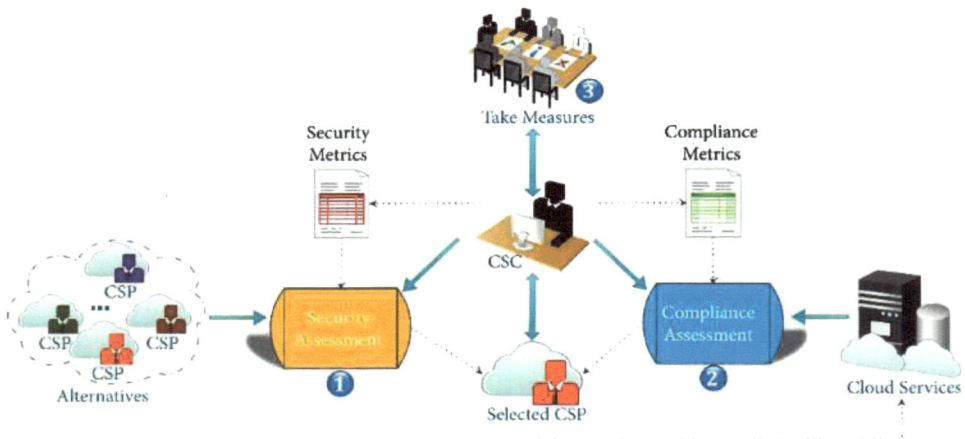

Fig. (18). SCCAF Architecture [57].

The work [58] characterizes configuration signals for the security engineering and components of future, virtualized, randomly affixed, and in the end, cut IoT frameworks. The configuration signals are gotten from the plan and execution of a secure virtual climate for a conveyed and cooperative AI framework that uses alleged AI pipelines. The pipelines apply bound virtual components and administrations and work with the cutting of the framework. The virtual climate is short as the virtual reason. Keyword Spotting involves a Deep Neural Network model recognizing watchwords in spoken sentences. This pipeline incorporates data sourcing, Data Preparation, Training, and Target Benchmarking. The steps get and pre-process information and prepare and benchmark the DNN model. Each step is implanted in a relic and launched as a Docker compartment. The result of an antique is a contribution to the succeeding one. The development of the preparation is an AI model that can be changed over into code, which transmits to IoT gadgets with satisfactory computational capabilities. The holders are put away by the MP in the Bonseyes' Private Docker archive. The significant level of security moves into specialized security arrangements.

4.4.5. Quick Response Times

Our capacity to gather information from the physical world has dramatically increased because of the Internet of Things technology, which links many physical objects to the Internet. Thanks to the data flood these IoT gadgets provide, we have a tremendous opportunity to investigate the physical world, which paves the way for intelligent life. For IoT systems centered on the Cloud, data created by an IoT device must first be transferred to the Cloud for processing before being returned to the device with the results. The same issues arise with a Cloud-centric IoT system because all accurate IoT data must be transmitted to the Cloud to retrain the model to attain optimum accuracy. Fig. (**19**) suggest an edge architecture.

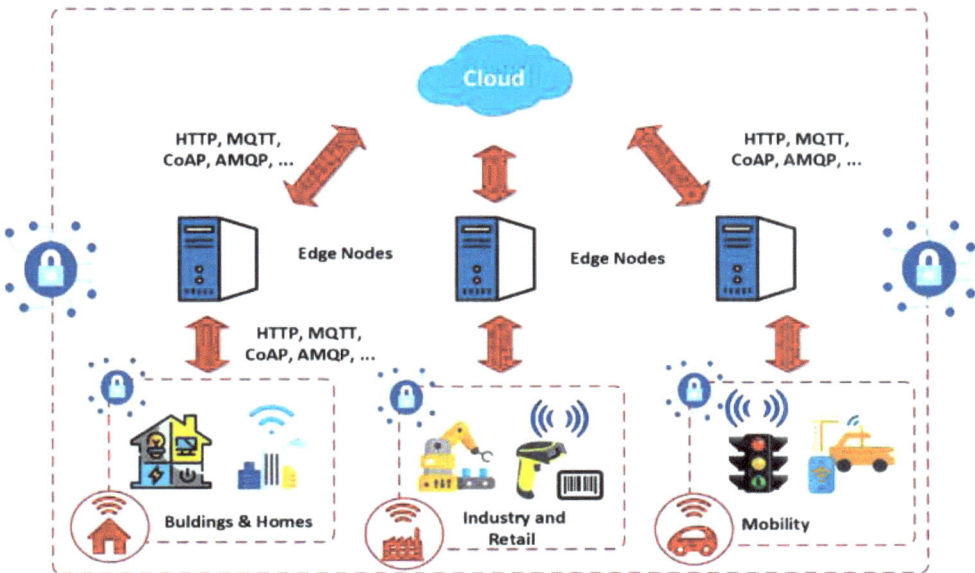

Fig. (19). Edge computing architecture [59].

The work [60] is three-layer engineering for proficient undertaking booking for application, for example, medical care in intelligent homes. The IoT layer comprises clever terminal gadgets called sensor gadgets or IoT gadgets liable for gathering IoT information and transferring it to the upper layer for additional handling. The haze processing layer comprises various mist hubs with better figuring and putting away ability. Haze hubs might be switches, switches, and virtual Network capability running a server utilizing Network Virtualization innovations. The haze processing layer gets IoT information and errand created by the IoT gadgets and distributes registering assets per the undertaking's necessities without disregarding the Service level arrangement. The fog recording layer likewise comprises additional vital gadgets alluded to as mist regulators that control every one of the hubs inside a group of hubs. It goes about as a passage for the mist group. The accessible hubs effectively speak with the cloud server farm, assuming they need it.

The review [61] is contextual analysis, a delicate deferral application that runs in a circumstance where the registering capacity of mist waiters is limited, and the web association is temperamental. It is a touchy postponement application that utilizes the Wireless Body Sensor Networks for information assortment. It joins the proposed strategies to dissect the gathered information by the Wireless Body Sensor Networks, meaning to anticipate the human body's response to various environmental factors and working circumstances. This application checks the well-being status of laborers in extreme weather patterns, such as the climate in sea environments. The proposed approach is utilizing a brilliant merchant who could foresee the handling time and the size of the consequence of a got-to task. Using a wise strategy for task circulation among haze and cloud servers turns out to be more noticeable in sea conditions as in these situations, factors like postponement, server responsibility, and solicitation appearance rate change constantly over the long run. The client sends various errands to the agent. The intermediary haphazardly sends the got undertakings to the mist and cloud servers. Fog and cloud servers process the projects. They log the information from the intermediary and the size of the consequence of the errand. Every one of the servers trains an Artificial Neural Network in which the information is the merchant's information, and the result is the handling time and the size of the result. The Artificial Neural Networks will be shipped off to the broker. The agent disseminates the errands based on the assessed reaction times and sizes concerning the pre-characterized arrangements.

4.4.6. Enhancements in Current BI Software Solutions

For top leaders in the organization to make effective decisions based on what is happening now and predict what will happen shortly, executive hospitals must figure out how to transform the raw data stored in relational databases into relevant information. Healthcare practitioners, analysts, and executive management levels disagree on using BI systems in healthcare settings. Executive leaders prefer to use highly aggregated data when making strategic decisions. Organizations use BI as a strategic endeavor to monitor and improve the performance of their competitive strategy. This ambitious aim requires analysis, software, money, technical leadership, and process.

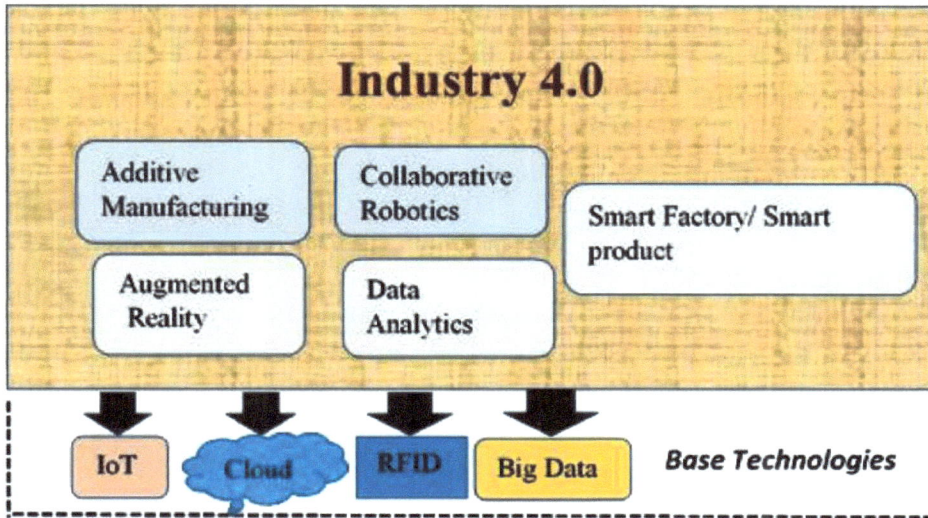

Fig. (20). Edge computing architecture [59].

Business Intelligence Systems [62] is a mix of specialized devices and procedures that give verifiable data to its clients for examination, inquiry, and revealing. These help the executives and huge decision-production for upgrading the effectiveness of business processes. It empowers associations not exclusively to get intensity but also heightens income by further developing independent direction. It has a few particularly conspicuous qualities that consider leaders to take on this development in contemporary organizations. It makes scientific cycles about market positions, abilities, activities, and objectives of the organization simple by changing the inner and outer information into essential data that directs the organization to remain maintainable and cutthroat. It has various divisions of the industry to help promote successful efforts, screen the ways of behaving of clients, and examine the productivity of multiple items. Fig. (**20**) depicts the same.

The building approach [63] depends on cloud-local devices for opportune information assortment, handling, and curation, depending on the powerful launch of information pipelines while tending to security, protection, and classification worries across the physical and virtual entities. RAMI 4.0 offers a support-situated reference design that traverses all components and data innovation parts throughout the item life cycle. Upgrade all current RAMI 4.0 layers, mirroring that AI is a cross-cutting concern influencing all usefulness in IT-producing frameworks. AI-increased assembling requires novel information handling and data demonstration types, and AI will consider more independent and mechanized business knowledge. The human-in-the-know layer gives strategies, models, and devices to work with the joint effort among human and AI-based virtual elements inside an assembling site, consequently helping people to make the ideal choices. Manufactured intelligence calculations, danger examination results, sending recipes and best practices across assembling locales by coordinating novel ideas, for example, secure unified learning and AI-on-request conspires. Fig. (**21**) represents the same.

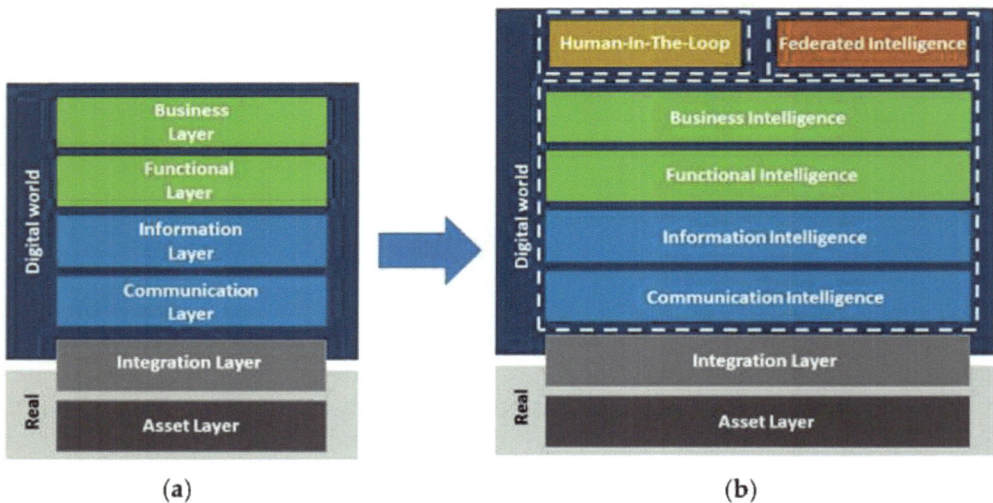

Fig. (21). Reference model of Industry 4.0 [63].

The exploration [64] directed in this study utilizes Design Science Research as an exploration worldview center around making a curio that tackles a certifiable issue. It has three principal cycles. The Relevance Cycle associates the plan interaction with the application climate by giving open doors or problems as necessities. This cycle additionally provides a technique for assessing the curio by testing in the application space. The Rigor Cycle interfaces an information base and the plan interaction. It carries out a thorough analysis to help the plan interaction and to extricate information to return to the information base. The Design Cycle is the iterative course of assessing inputs from the Relevance Cycle, separating techniques and hypotheses to help the plan from the Rigor Cycle, also planning, executing a relic, testing the curio, utilizing the Importance Cycle against the prerequisites and adding to the information base using the Relevance Cycle.

The review [65] proposes an Interactive IoT Data Visualization for Business Intelligence strategy to examine and limit the issues of reception and self-administration of information assets. An IoT-based information representation strategy helps Interactive decision-production to procure information assets from immense business knowledge sources. During their choices, the outcomes contrasted with the run-of-the-mill visuals or tables demonstrate the choice. The information representation intelligence is the secret to conveying subtleties to subjects before having their preference due to hostility to intelligent depictions. The work consolidates the semantic information quality check to search for the exercises' worldly succession information. The frameworks are active in the machine and assembling, observing, mechanizing information detecting, item quality checking, and lactation-based shrewd transportation. It conveys a rich arrangement of intuitive representations and complete investigation reports for significant endeavors. It imagines and follows different sensors that gather data. The proposed IIoT-DVBI model consolidates information securing and run-time thinking to get to the next level of quality control and proactive maintenance. The representations present the anticipated development of the framework concerning dangers, expenses, and assets. Every action checks consecutively, and the connected data is gathered and perceived through the information perception technique. The boundaries dissected in a business climate incorporate quality, cost, and need the significance of promoting factors. These Factors are observed during contribution, advancement, deal, and surveys. The sensor-based framework remembers investigation for ceaseless anonymized fall watching and movement examination, including stationary behavior. The remote movement sensors study individuals' cooperation in the climate and further examine their ways of behaving, like estimating the time away from home and development inside the residing spaces. In the creation period, examining the result is fundamental to observing. The IoT figuring information base puts away the data gathered for different information the board and perception investigation for the quality look at worth examination process. Table **4.3** represents the implementations of various contributions.

Table 4.3. Represents the implementations of various contributions.

Contribution	Implementation Details
[40]	• The work uses Intel Core i5-4440 CPU @ 3.10 GHz processor with 8 GB RAM running on Microsoft Windows-10 64-bit operating systems. • It used Android 7.0.1 Honor mobile with an Octa-core processor and 3 GB RAM as the IoT device.
[44]	• The MongoDB database is hosted by the mLab platform through Amazon web services. mLab offers a sandbox with a 500 MB MongoDB instance. • IoTP4mSCp IoT gateway is used.
[47]	• It has a dataset of a random selection of 50,000 samples.
[48]	• The Libelium sensor platform was selected for the sensor nodes. • The study uses Raspberry Pi2 model B minicomputer.
[50]	• The prototype is built using Arduino Uno, Sensors, Bluetooth Module, WIFI module, fog gateway server, the cloud platform. • The Arduino IDE is a cross-platform Java application that serves as a code editor and compiler.
[52]	• It has an Arduino-based sensor device.
[54]	• The system uses 2xCPU Intel Xeon CPU E5-2620 v2 @ 2.10 GHz, 8 GB of DDR3 memory, and 60 GB of Hard Disk Drive (HDD).
[57]	• The experiments are conducted by using MATLAB R2017b and performed on a DELL desktop computer with configuration as follows: Intel Core i5 2.7 GHz CPU,8 GB RAM and Windows 10 operating system.
[63]	• Multi-layer perceptron ANNs are used in MATLAB.
[64]	• The SARIMA model will then be repeatedly trained on a window of the data, predict 24 hours and determine if the actual values are anomalous. • The LSTM model is trained with 3000 and 5000 rows of data extracted into 24 features.

4.5. FUTURE OF AI AND IOT-CLOUD

4.5.1. Fog Computing

It is suggested that fog computing enables computing right at the network's edge, which can bring new applications and services, particularly for the future of the Internet. Fog nodes are the buildings or infrastructures that supply resources for services at the network's edge. They can be resource-rich machines or resource-poor ones, such as set-top boxes, access points, routers, switches, base stations, and end devices.

The goal of fog computing [67] is to collaboratively provide elastic computation, storage, and communication in remote environments to a sizable number of clients nearby. Fog computing is a geographically distributed computing architecture with a resource pool that consists of one or more ubiquitously connected heterogeneous devices at the edge of the network and is not exclusively seamlessly backed by Cloud services. It bridges end devices and the cloud, bringing networking, processing, and storage capabilities closer to the end devices. Anywhere with a network connection can use them. Fog nodes can be any device with computation, storage, and network connectivity, including industrial controllers, switches, routers, embedded servers, and security cameras. Fog as a service, where a service provider deploys an array of fog nodes across its geographic footprint and serves as a landlord to many tenants from different vertical markets, is made possible by integrating fog computing with the IoT. Local networking, computing, and storage resources are available on each fog node. It will make it possible for new business models to provide client services. Large businesses run clouds with the financial resources to construct and maintain sizable data centers. FaaS will allow large and small companies to deploy and run private or public computing, storage, and control services at various scales to satisfy the needs of multiple customers. Fig. (**22**) portrays the fog-IoT applications.

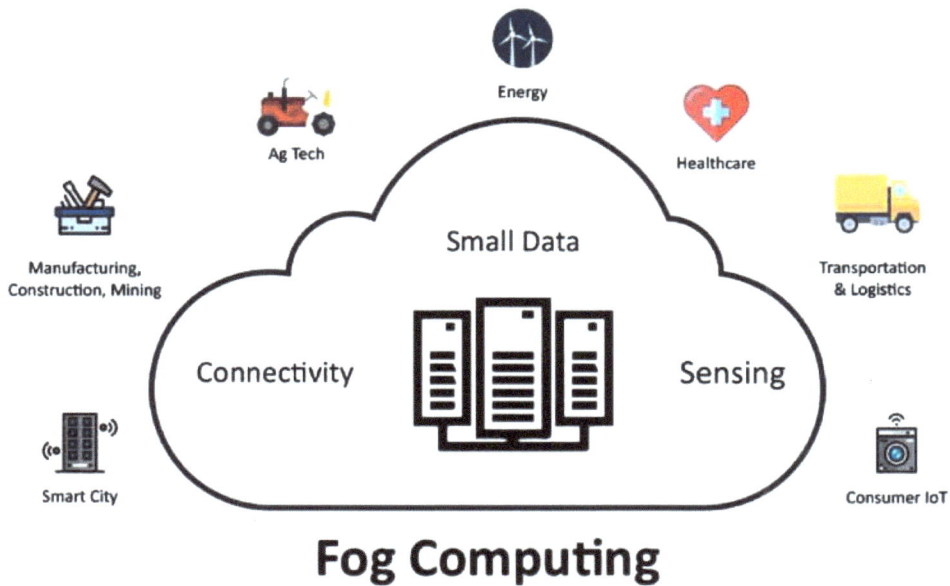

Fig. (22). Fog-IoT Applications [66].

4.5.2. Quantum Computing

Quantum information [69] serves as the foundation for quantum computers. Information is represented by quantum states in these computers, which use quantum physics' quantum effects. The fundamental idea of reversible computation serves as the foundation for quantum calculations. Quantum algorithms use the basics of quantum computational complexity. There are two necessary layers to it. While classical and quantum processing technology has similar functional goals, both domains are distinct at the physical level. The DiVincenzo requirements and specific physical layer properties establish the biological underpinnings of quantum computing systems. Fig. (**23**) represents the Integrating of quantum optical networks and optical quantum computing.

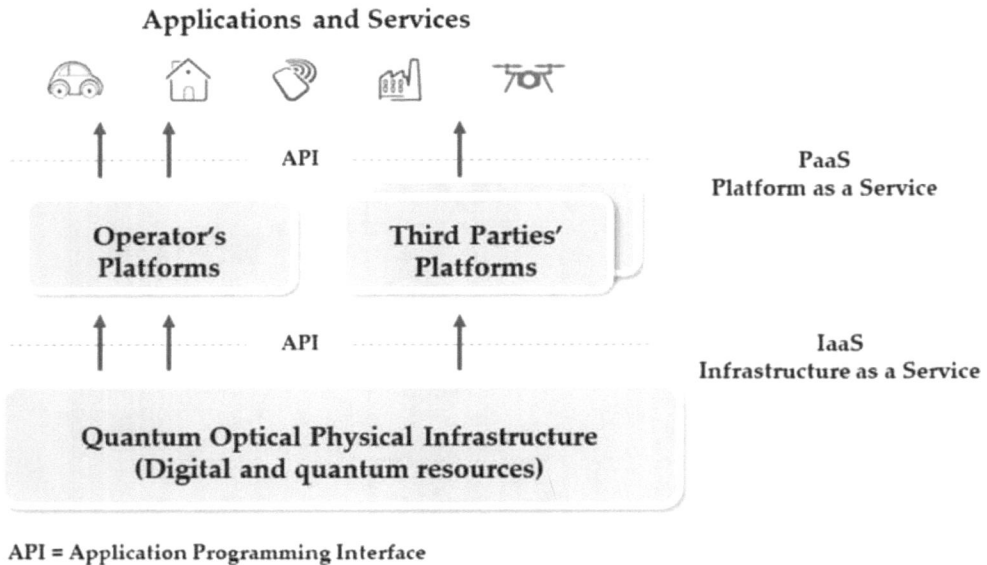

Applications and Services

API

PaaS
Platform as a Service

Operator's Platforms

Third Parties' Platforms

API

IaaS
Infrastructure as a Service

Quantum Optical Physical Infrastructure
(Digital and quantum resources)

API = Application Programming Interface

Fig. (23). Fog-IoT Applications [68].

4.5.3. Software-defined Networks

Software-defined networking [71] can simplify network management by giving programmers a network-wide view and direct control over the underlying switches from a logically centralized controller. Several new capabilities are part of software-defined networking. It includes introducing new network functions quickly at software speed instead of hardware or firmware product cycles and more seamless network integration with enterprise IT processes through programmable service-oriented APIs. Regarding capacity and capabilities, software-defined computing creates an abstraction of heterogeneous computing resources. The software-defined environment integrates various components' control planes and brings software-defined computation, networking, and storage together. Unified control planes offer detailed resource abstractions that make it possible to put together appropriate systems for their intended use. They also provide programmable infrastructures for dynamic optimization in response to shifting business needs. Fig. (**24**) portrays the SDN perspective.

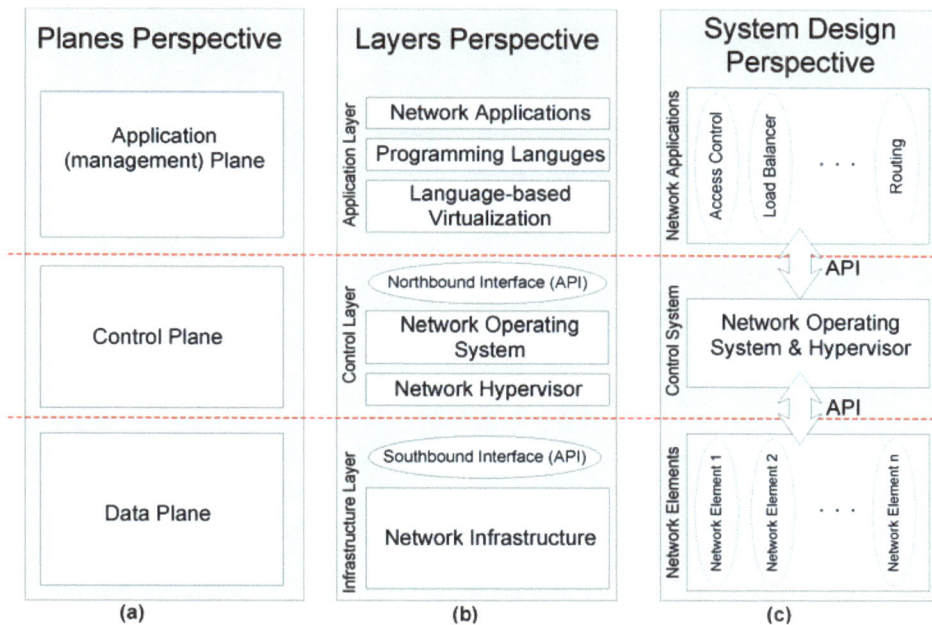

Fig. (24). SDN perspective [70].

4.5.4. Business Data Analytics

The system infrastructure's [73] responsibility is to store, extract, transform, and load data. Once the data is available, it can find important information using data analytics techniques. There are three categories of data analysis techniques: prescriptive, predictive, and descriptive. Business analytics must be strongly related to business strategy and integrated into organizational processes to generate superior analytics-driven insights that enable timely action. It requires every effort from manufacturing and new product design to credit authorization and customer relationship management. Big data analytics finds the best suppliers, assesses supplier performance based on cost and quality, improves supply chain visibility and integration, manages transportation, raises production yield, and enables optimum inventory planning and source input. Fig. (**25**) represents the Big data analytics framework.

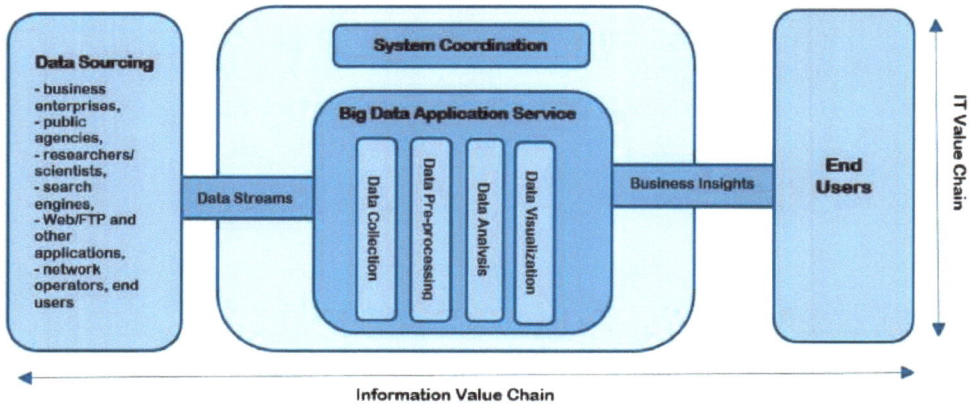

Fig. (25). Big data analytics framework [72].

4.5.5. Data Science

Artificial intelligence approaches have expanded quickly in recent years, which typically enables devices to perform intelligently in the area of computers with smart mobile phones. The target mobile applications can be made intelligent and more efficient using popular AI techniques, such as machine learning and deep learning methods, natural language processing, knowledge representation, and expert systems. IoT can process and store data among its many other capabilities. The ability to efficiently process large datasets and improve the behavior of any application by informing it of the surrounding contextual information, such as temporal context, spatial context, social context, environmental or device-related context, *etc.*, remains a crucial challenge in this emerging research domain. Fig. (**26**) portrays steps in Data Science.

Data science [75] is a systematic endeavor that develops and organizes knowledge through verifiable universe-related explanations and hypotheses. Consequently, it can imply a concentration on data and, indirectly, statistics, which is a systematic study of the organization, characteristics, and analysis of data and their use in inference, including our confidence in such belief. It is a collection of fundamental rules that underpin and direct the systematic extraction of knowledge and information from data. It is used for general customer relationship management to assess customer behavior. Data science is used in the finance sector for operations, fraud detection, trading, and labor management. Principles, procedures, and methodologies for comprehending phenomena are included in data science.

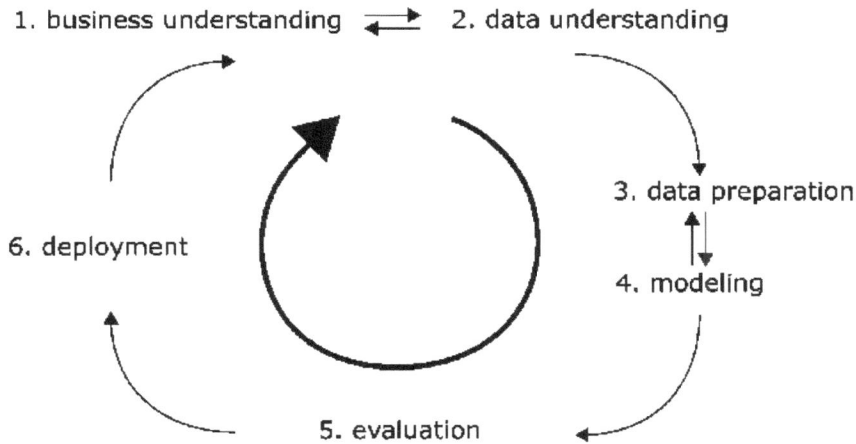

Fig. (26). Steps in Data Science [74].

CONCLUSION

Numerous opportunities for utilizing and integrating information technology in all spheres of life, have been broadened by the emergence of Cloud computing, the Internet of Things, and Artificial Intelligence.

Drones, nano- and micro-sensors, bionic robots, remote cameras, intelligent sorting, energy-efficient processing equipment, statistical modules, and algorithms are some of the methods and apparatus that will lessen human interaction and boost aquaculture output. Therefore, cutting-edge technologies will be crucial for future operations that require less human labor, efficient maintenance, and efficient use of resources.

REFERENCES

[1]   N. Ambika, Aiding iot and cloud to control covid-19: a systematic approach.*Pervasive Healthcare.* Springer: Cham, 2022, pp. 349-365.
[http://dx.doi.org/10.1007/978-3-030-77746-3_21]

[2]   T. Mastelic, A. Oleksiak, H. Claussen, I. Brandic, J.M. Pierson, and A.V. Vasilakos, "Cloud computing", *acm comput. surv.,* vol. 47, no. 2, pp. 1-36, 2015. [csur].
[http://dx.doi.org/10.1145/2656204]

[3]   M. Mohamad Noor, and W.H. Hassan, "Current research on internet of things (iot) security: a survey", *Comput. Netw.,* vol. 148, pp. 283-294, 2019.
[http://dx.doi.org/10.1016/j.comnet.2018.11.025]

[4]   M.H. Devare, Convergence of manufacturing cloud and industrial iot.*applying Integration Techniques and Methods in Distributed Systems and Technologies.* IGI Global: US, 2019, pp. 49-78.
[http://dx.doi.org/10.4018/978-1-5225-8295-3.ch003]

[5] T. Alam, "Cloud-based iot applications and their roles in smart cities", *Smart Cities,* vol. 4, no. 3, pp. 1196-1219, 2021.
[http://dx.doi.org/10.3390/smartcities4030064]

[6] F. Ferrández-Pastor, J. García-Chamizo, M. Nieto-Hidalgo, J. Mora-Pascual, and J. Mora-Martínez, "Developing ubiquitous sensor network platform using internet of things: application in Precision Agriculture", *Sensors (Basel),* vol. 16, no. 7, p. 1141, 2016.
[http://dx.doi.org/10.3390/s16071141] [PMID: 27455265]

[7] D. Bruneo, S. Distefano, F. Longo, G. Merlino, and A. Puliafito, "Iot-cloud authorization and delegation mechanisms for ubiquitous sensing and actuation",
[http://dx.doi.org/10.1109/WF-IoT.2016.7845494]

[8] A. Nagaraj, *Introduction to Sensors in IoT and Cloud Computing Applications.* Bentham Science Publishers: UAE, 2021.
[http://dx.doi.org/10.2174/97898114793591210101]

[9] N. Janbi, R. Mehmood, I. Katib, A. Albeshri, J.M. Corchado, and T. Yigitcanlar, "Imtidad: a reference architecture and a case study on developing distributed ai services for skin disease diagnosis over cloud, fog and edge", *Sensors (Basel),* vol. 22, no. 5, p. 1854, 2022.
[http://dx.doi.org/10.3390/s22051854] [PMID: 35271000]

[10] L. Gupta, T. Salman, M. Zolanvari, A. Erbad, and R. Jain, "Fault and performance management in multi-cloud virtual network services using AI: A tutorial and a case study", *Comput. Netw.,* vol. 165, p. 106950, 2019.
[http://dx.doi.org/10.1016/j.comnet.2019.106950]

[11] M. Abdel-Basset, G. Manogaran, and M. Mohamed, "Retracted: internet of things (iot) and its impact on supply chain: a framework for building smart, secure and efficient systems", *Future Gener. Comput. Syst.,* vol. 86, pp. 614-628, 2018.
[http://dx.doi.org/10.1016/j.future.2018.04.051]

[12] H. Mezni, M. Driss, W. Boulila, S. Ben Atitallah, M. Sellami, and N. Alharbi, "Smartwater: a service-oriented and sensor cloud-based framework for smart monitoring of Water Environments", *Remote Sens. (Basel),* vol. 14, no. 4, p. 922, 2022.
[http://dx.doi.org/10.3390/rs14040922]

[13] M.M. Badawy, Z.H. Ali, and H.A. Ali, "Qos provisioning framework for service-oriented internet of things (iot)", *Cluster Comput.,* vol. 23, no. 2, pp. 575-591, 2020.
[http://dx.doi.org/10.1007/s10586-019-02945-x]

[14] B.Q. Cao, B. Li, and Q.M. Xia, "A service-oriented qos-assured and multi-agent cloud computing architecture", *in IEEE international conference on cloud computing,* 2009 Beijing, China
[http://dx.doi.org/10.1007/978-3-642-10665-1_66]

[15] J. Cubo, A. Nieto, and E. Pimentel, "A cloud-based internet of things platform for ambient assisted living", *Sensors (Basel),* vol. 14, no. 8, pp. 14070-14105, 2014.
[http://dx.doi.org/10.3390/s140814070] [PMID: 25093343]

[16] J.L. Shah, H.F. Bhat, and A.I. Khan, Integration of cloud and iot for smart e-healthcare.*healthcare Paradigms in the Internet of Things Ecosystem.* Academic Press, 2021, pp. 101-136.
[http://dx.doi.org/10.1016/B978-0-12-819664-9.00006-5]

[17] T. Dinh, Y. Kim, and H. Lee, "A location-based interactive model of internet of things and cloud (iot-cloud) for Mobile Cloud Computing Applications", *Sensors (Basel),* vol. 17, no. 3, p. 489, 2017.
[http://dx.doi.org/10.3390/s17030489] [PMID: 28257067]

[18] A. Beheshti, F. Schiliro, S. Ghodratnama, F. Amouzgar, B. Benatallah, J. Yang, Q. Sheng, F. Casati, and H. Motahari-Nezhad, "iprocess: enabling iot platforms in data-driven knowledge-intensive processes", *International Conference on Business Process Management,* 2018 Sydney, NSW, Australia

[http://dx.doi.org/10.1007/978-3-319-98651-7_7]

[19]   I. Marcu, G. Suciu, C. Bălăceanu, A. Vulpe, and A.M. Drăgulinescu, "Arrowhead technology for digitalization and automation solution: smart cities and Smart Agriculture", *Sensors (Basel)*, vol. 20, no. 5, p. 1464, 2020.
[http://dx.doi.org/10.3390/s20051464] [PMID: 32155934]

[20]   Y.Y. Chen, Y.H. Lin, C.C. Kung, M.H. Chung, and I.H. Yen, "Design and implementation of cloud analytics-assisted smart power meters considering advanced artificial intelligence as edge analytics in demand-side management for smart homes", *Sensors (Basel)*, vol. 19, no. 9, p. 2047, 2019.
[http://dx.doi.org/10.3390/s19092047] [PMID: 31052502]

[21]   W. Song, N. Feng, Y. Tian, S. Fong, and K. Cho, "A deep belief network for electricity utilisation feature analysis of air conditioners using a smart IoT platform", *Journal of Information Processing Systems*, vol. 14, no. 1, pp. 162-175, 2018.

[22]   H. Golpîra, and S. Bahramara, "Internet-of-things-based optimal smart city energy management considering shiftable loads and energy storage", *J. Clean. Prod.*, vol. 264, p. 121620, 2020.
[http://dx.doi.org/10.1016/j.jclepro.2020.121620]

[23]   M.M. Rathore, A. Paul, A. Ahmad, N. Chilamkurti, W.H. Hong, and H. Seo, "Real-time secure communication for smart city in high-speed big data environment", *Future Gener. Comput. Syst.*, vol. 83, pp. 638-652, 2018.
[http://dx.doi.org/10.1016/j.future.2017.08.006]

[24]   S. Talari, M. Shafie-khah, P. Siano, V. Loia, A. Tommasetti, and J. Catalão, "A review of smart cities based on the internet of things concept", *Energies*, vol. 10, no. 4, p. 421, 2017.
[http://dx.doi.org/10.3390/en10040421]

[25]   Z. Lv, L. Qiao, A. Kumar Singh, and Q. Wang, "Ai-empowered iot security for smart cities", *aCM Trans. Internet Technol.*, vol. 21, no. 4, pp. 1-21, 2021.

[26]   R. Lea, and M. Blackstock, "City hub: a cloud-based iot platform for smart cities", *in 6th international conference on cloud computing technology and science*, 2014 Singapore
[http://dx.doi.org/10.1109/CloudCom.2014.65]

[27]   E. Alreshidi, "Smart sustainable agriculture (ssa) solution underpinned by internet of things (IoT) and artificial intelligence (AI)", *Int. J. Adv. Comput. Sci. Appl.*, vol. 10, no. 5, pp. 93-102, 2019.
[http://dx.doi.org/10.14569/IJACSA.2019.0100513]

[28]   B.B. Bhanu, K.R. Rao, J.V.N. Ramesh, and M.A. Hussain, "Agriculture field monitoring and analysis using wireless sensor networks for improving crop production", *in Eleventh international conference on wireless and optical communications networks (WOCN)*, 2014 Vijayawada, India
[http://dx.doi.org/10.1109/WOCN.2014.6923043]

[29]   Y. Kalyani, and R. Collier, "A systematic survey on the role of cloud, fog, and edge computing combination in Smart Agriculture", *Sensors (Basel)*, vol. 21, no. 17, p. 5922, 2021.
[http://dx.doi.org/10.3390/s21175922] [PMID: 34502813]

[30]   M.S. Mekala, and P. Viswanathan, "Clay-mist: iot-cloud enabled cmm index for smart agriculture monitoring system", *Measurement*, vol. 134, pp. 236-244, 2019.
[http://dx.doi.org/10.1016/j.measurement.2018.10.072]

[31]   M.S. Mekala, and P. Viswanathan, "A novel technology for smart agriculture based on iot with cloud computing", *in International Conference on I-SMAC (IoT in Social.*, 2017 Palladam, India
[http://dx.doi.org/10.1109/I-SMAC.2017.8058280]

[32]   S. Namani, and B. Gonen, "Smart agriculture based on iot and cloud computing", *3rd International Conference on Information and Computer Technologies (ICICT)*, 2020 San Jose, CA, USA
[http://dx.doi.org/10.1109/ICICT50521.2020.00094]

[33]   F. Alshehri, and G. Muhammad, "A comprehensive survey of the internet of things (iot) and ai-based smart healthcare", *IEEE Access*, vol. 9, pp. 3660-3678, 2021.

[http://dx.doi.org/10.1109/ACCESS.2020.3047960]

[34]   G. Gardašević, K. Katzis, D. Bajić, and L. Berbakov, "Emerging wireless sensor networks and internet of things technologies—foundations of Smart Healthcare", *Sensors (Basel),* vol. 20, no. 13, p. 3619, 2020.
[http://dx.doi.org/10.3390/s20133619] [PMID: 32605071]

[35]   Z. Yang, Q. Zhou, L. Lei, K. Zheng, and W. Xiang, "An iot-cloud based wearable ecg monitoring system for smart healthcare", *J. Med. Syst.,* vol. 40, no. 12, p. 286, 2016.
[http://dx.doi.org/10.1007/s10916-016-0644-9] [PMID: 27796840]

[36]   M. Alhussein, G. Muhammad, M.S. Hossain, and S.U. Amin, "Cognitive iot-cloud integration for smart healthcare: case study for epileptic seizure detection and monitoring", *Mob. Netw. Appl.,* vol. 23, no. 6, pp. 1624-1635, 2018.
[http://dx.doi.org/10.1007/s11036-018-1113-0]

[37]   K. Jaiswal, S. Sobhanayak, B.K. Mohanta, and D. Jena, "Iot-cloud based framework for patient's data collection in smart healthcare system using raspberry-pi", *International conference on electrical and computing technologies and applications (ICECTA),* 2017 Ras Al Khaimah, United Arab Emirates
[http://dx.doi.org/10.1109/ICECTA.2017.8251967]

[38]   H. Serrano-Magaña, A. González-Potes, V. Ibarra-Junquera, P. Balbastre, D. Martínez-Castro, and J. Simó, "Software components for smart industry based on microservices: a case study in pH Control Process for the Beverage Industry", *Electronics (Basel),* vol. 10, no. 7, p. 763, 2021.
[http://dx.doi.org/10.3390/electronics10070763]

[39]   K.B. Swain, G. Santamanyu, and A.R. Senapati, "Smart industry pollution monitoring and controlling using labview based iot", *in third international conference on sensing, signal processing and security (ICSSS).,* 2017 Chennai, India
[http://dx.doi.org/10.1109/SSPS.2017.8071568]

[40]   P. Chinnasamy, P. Deepalakshmi, A.K. Dutta, J. You, and G.P. Joshi, "Ciphertext-policy attribute-based encryption for cloud storage: toward data privacy and Authentication in AI-Enabled IoT System", *Mathematics,* vol. 10, no. 1, p. 68, 2021.
[http://dx.doi.org/10.3390/math10010068]

[41]   J. Xiong, M. Zhao, M.Z.A. Bhuiyan, L. Chen, and Y. Tian, "An ai-enabled three-party game framework for guaranteed data privacy in mobile edge crowdsensing of IoT", *IEEE Trans. Industr. Inform.,* vol. 17, no. 2, pp. 922-933, 2021.
[http://dx.doi.org/10.1109/TII.2019.2957130]

[42]   R. Sivan, and Z.A. Zukarnain, "Security and privacy in cloud-based e-health system", *Symmetry (Basel),* vol. 13, no. 5, p. 742, 2021.
[http://dx.doi.org/10.3390/sym13050742]

[43]   B.D. Deebak, F.H. Memon, K. Dev, S.A. Khowaja, and N.M.F. Qureshi, "Ai-enabled privacy-preservation phrase with multi-keyword ranked searching for sustainable edge-cloud networks in the era of industrial IoT", *Ad Hoc Netw.,* vol. 125, p. 102740, 2022.
[http://dx.doi.org/10.1016/j.adhoc.2021.102740]

[44]   C. Toma, A. Alexandru, M. Popa, and A. Zamfiroiu, "Iot solution for smart cities' pollution monitoring and the security challenges", *Sensors (Basel),* vol. 19, no. 15, p. 3401, 2019.
[http://dx.doi.org/10.3390/s19153401] [PMID: 31382512]

[45]   H. HaddadPajouh, R. Khayami, A. Dehghantanha, K-K.R. Choo, and R.M. Parizi, "Ai4safe-iot: an ai-powered secure architecture for edge layer of internet of things", *Neural Comput. Appl.,* vol. 32, no. 20, pp. 16119-16133, 2020.
[http://dx.doi.org/10.1007/s00521-020-04772-3]

[46]   S. Chakrabarty, and D.W. Engels, "Secure smart cities framework using iot and ai", *Global Conference on Artificial Intelligence and Internet of Things (GCAIoT),* 2020 Dubai, United Arab Emirates

[http://dx.doi.org/10.1109/GCAIoT51063.2020.9345912]

[47]   M. Ahmed, R. Mumtaz, S.M.H. Zaidi, M. Hafeez, S.A.R. Zaidi, and M. Ahmad, "Distributed fog computing for internet of things (iot) based ambient data processing and Analysis", *Electronics (Basel),* vol. 9, no. 11, p. 1756, 2020.
[http://dx.doi.org/10.3390/electronics9111756]

[48]   M. Benammar, A. Abdaoui, S. Ahmad, F. Touati, and A. Kadri, "A modular iot platform for real-time indoor air quality monitoring", *Sensors (Basel),* vol. 18, no. 2, p. 581, 2018.
[http://dx.doi.org/10.3390/s18020581] [PMID: 29443893]

[49]   R. Patan, G.S. Pradeep Ghantasala, R. Sekaran, D. Gupta, and M. Ramachandran, "Smart healthcare and quality of service in iot using grey filter convolutional based cyber physical system", *Sustain Cities Soc.,* vol. 59, p. 102141, 2020.
[http://dx.doi.org/10.1016/j.scs.2020.102141]

[50]   J. Dutta, and S. Roy, "Iot-fog-cloud based architecture for smart city: prototype of a smart building", *7th International Conference on Cloud Computing, Data Science & Engineering-Confluence,* 2017 Noida, India
[http://dx.doi.org/10.1109/CONFLUENCE.2017.7943156]

[51]   G.B. Fioccola, R. Sommese, I. Tufano, and G. Ventre, "Polluino: an efficient cloud-based management of iot devices for air quality monitoring", *in 2nd International Forum on Research and Technologies for Society and Industry Leveraging a better tomorrow (RTSI).,* 2016 Bologna, Italy

[52]   R. Akhare, M. Mangla, S. Deokar, and V. Wadhwa, Proposed framework for fog computing to improve quality-of-service in iot applications.*Fog Data Analytics for IoT Applications.* Springer: Singapore, 2020, pp. 123-143.
[http://dx.doi.org/10.1007/978-981-15-6044-6_7]

[53]   T.M. Fernández-Caramés, and P. Fraga-Lamas, "Towards next generation teaching, learning, and context-aware applications for Higher Education: A Review on Blockchain, IoT, Fog and Edge Computing Enabled Smart Campuses and Universities", *Appl. Sci. (Basel),* vol. 9, no. 21, p. 4479, 2019.
[http://dx.doi.org/10.3390/app9214479]

[54]   C. Symvoulidis, G. Marinos, A. Kiourtis, A. Mavrogiorgou, and D. Kyriazis, "Healthfetch: an influence-based, context-aware prefetch scheme in citizen-centered Health Storage Clouds", *Future Internet,* vol. 14, no. 4, p. 112, 2022.
[http://dx.doi.org/10.3390/fi14040112]

[55]   A. Forkan, I. Khalil, and Z. Tari, "Cocamaal: a cloud-oriented context-aware middleware in ambient assisted living", *Future Gener. Comput. Syst.,* vol. 35, pp. 114-127, 2014.
[http://dx.doi.org/10.1016/j.future.2013.07.009]

[56]   W. Ahmad, A. Rasool, A.R. Javed, T. Baker, and Z. Jalil, "Cyber security in iot-based cloud computing: a comprehensive survey", *Electronics (Basel),* vol. 11, no. 1, p. 16, 2021.
[http://dx.doi.org/10.3390/electronics11010016]

[57]   "Sccaf: a secure and compliant continuous assessment framework in cloud-based iot context", *Wireless Communications and Mobile Computing.,* 2018.

[58]   V. Mehri, D. Ilie, and K. Tutschku, "Designing a secure iot system architecture from a virtual premise for a collaborative AI lab", *Workshop on Decentralized IoT Systems and Security (DISS),* 2019 San Diego, CA
[http://dx.doi.org/10.14722/diss.2019.23006]

[59]   J.M. Corchado, P. Chamoso, G. Hernández, A.S.R. Gutierrez, A.R. Camacho, A. González-Briones, F. Pinto-Santos, E. Goyenechea, D. Garcia-Retuerta, M. Alonso-Miguel, B.B. Hernandez, D.V. Villaverde, M. Sanchez-Verdejo, P. Plaza-Martínez, M. López-Pérez, S. Manzano-García, R.S. Alonso, R. Casado-Vara, J.P. Tejedor, F. Prieta, S. Rodríguez-González, J. Parra-Domínguez, M.S. Mohamad, S. Trabelsi, E. Díaz-Plaza, J.A. Garcia-Coria, T. Yigitcanlar, P. Novais, and S. Omatu,

"Deepint.net: a rapid deployment platform for smart territories", *Sensors (Basel)*, vol. 21, no. 1, p. 236, 2021.
[http://dx.doi.org/10.3390/s21010236] [PMID: 33401468]

[60]   H.K. Apat, B. sahoo Compt, K. Bhaisare, and P. Maiti, "An optimal task scheduling towards minimized cost and response time in fog computing infrastructure", *in international conference on information technology (ICIT).*, 2019 Bhubaneswar, India

[61]   M. Abedi, and M. Pourkiani, "Resource allocation in combined fog-cloud scenarios by using artificial intelligence", *Fifth International Conference on Fog and Mobile Edge Computing (FMEC)*, 2020 Paris, France
[http://dx.doi.org/10.1109/FMEC49853.2020.9144693]

[62]   S. Ahmad, S. Miskon, R. Alabdan, and I. Tlili, "Towards sustainable textile and apparel industry: exploring the role of business Intelligence Systems in the Era of Industry 4.0", *Sustainability (Basel)*, vol. 12, no. 7, p. 2632, 2020.
[http://dx.doi.org/10.3390/su12072632]

[63]   P. Trakadas, P. Simoens, P. Gkonis, L. Sarakis, A. Angelopoulos, A.P. Ramallo-González, A. Skarmeta, C. Trochoutsos, D. Calvo, T. Pariente, K. Chintamani, I. Fernandez, A.A. Irigaray, J.X. Parreira, P. Petrali, N. Leligou, and P. Karkazis, "An artificial intelligence-based collaboration approach in industrial iot manufacturing: Key Concepts, Architectural Extensions and Potential Applications", *Sensors (Basel)*, vol. 20, no. 19, p. 5480, 2020.
[http://dx.doi.org/10.3390/s20195480] [PMID: 32987911]

[64]   J.E.W. Holm, L.W. Moolman, and G.P.R. van der Merwe, Cloud-based business intelligence for a cellular iot network*in: IEEE AFRICON* Accra: Ghana, 2019.
[http://dx.doi.org/10.1109/AFRICON46755.2019.9134020]

[65]   L. Zhang, B. Vinodhini, and T. Maragatham, "Interactive iot data visualization for decision making in business intelligence", *Arab. J. Sci. Eng.*, pp. 1-11, 2021.
[http://dx.doi.org/10.1007/s13369-021-05889-w]

[66]   H. Atlam, R. Walters, and G. Wills, "Fog computing and the internet of things: a review", *Big Data and Cognitive Computing*, vol. 2, no. 2, p. 10, 2018.
[http://dx.doi.org/10.3390/bdcc2020010]

[67]   Z. Mahmood, Fog computing: concepts, frameworks and technologies, switzerland: Springer, 2018.

[68]   A. Manzalini, "Topological photonics for optical communications and quantum computing", *Quantum Reports*, vol. 2, no. 4, pp. 579-590, 2020.
[http://dx.doi.org/10.3390/quantum2040040]

[69]   E.G. Rieffel, and W.H. Polak, *Quantum computing: A gentle introduction.* MIT Press: Cambridge, Massachusetts, 2011.

[70]   E. Ahvar, S. Ahvar, S.M. Raza, J. Manuel Sanchez Vilchez, and G.M. Lee, "Next generation of sdn in cloud-fog for 5g and beyond-enabled applications: opportunities and Challenges", *Network*, vol. 1, no. 1, pp. 28-49, 2021.
[http://dx.doi.org/10.3390/network1010004]

[71]   P. Goransson, C. Black, and T. Culver, *Software defined networks: a comprehensive approach.* Morgan Kaufmann: Burlington, Massachusetts, 2016.

[72]   S. Mathrani, and X. Lai, "Big data analytic framework for organizational leverage", *Appl. Sci. (Basel)*, vol. 11, no. 5, p. 2340, 2021.
[http://dx.doi.org/10.3390/app11052340]

[73]   T.A. Runkler, *Data analytics., Fachmedien Wiesbaden.* Springer, 2020.
[http://dx.doi.org/10.1007/978-3-658-29779-4]

[74]   L. Beinrohr, E. Kail, P. Piros, E. Tóth, R. Fleiner, and K. Kolev, "Anatomy of a data science software toolkit that uses machine learning to aid 'bench-to-Bedside' Medical Research—With Essential

Concepts of Data Mining and Analysis Explained", *Appl. Sci. (Basel)*, vol. 11, no. 24, p. 12135, 2021. [http://dx.doi.org/10.3390/app112412135]

[75]   F. Provost, and T. Fawcett, *Data Science for Business: What you need to know about data mining and data-analytic thinking.* O'Reilly Media: Sebastopol, California, 2013.

CHAPTER 5

Use Cases

Abstract: Intelligent sensors sense the environment and collect information about the environment. IoT gathers information from various sources and saves it in data warehouses. The cloud provides abundant space for these devices to store data. It uses many artificial intelligence algorithms to provide adequate service. This chapter details various cases of different amalgamations of the sub-systems.

Keywords: Artificial intelligence, Cloud systems, Intelligent sensors, Internet of things, Machine learning, Virtualization.

5.1. INTRODUCTION

The Internet of Things (IoT) is no longer a fad in the technological world due to the proliferation of cutting-edge applications; it is rather a revolution already in full swing. IoT applications can cover all facets of our lives as intelligent devices and sensors become increasingly ingrained in our environment. IoT applications emerge as technological enablers in various domains, including smart homes and cities, agriculture and farming, healthcare, logistics and manufacturing. The information-based economy has been significantly altered by connecting multiple objects to the Internet. Future information technology ecosystems will rely heavily on information flow. "Internet of Things" refers to the connectivity of various end devices, sensors, and objects to the Internet. IoT task management, data processing, and decision-making systems will face severe difficulties due to the anticipated high number of sensors connecting to the Internet. IoT sensor data management and processing will cause latency, making it impossible to provide the same services to users. The tasks in the workflow are monitored and tracked by IoT sensors, and Industry 5.0 is added for image processing production verification. A global infrastructure environment known as cloud computing offers sophisticated task resources and IT services. Defining and designing mechanical components for data processing and task management of such massive IoT data is essential and pertinent as more devices and IoT sensors join the ecosystem. Its features include the cloud's ability to connect to numerous cloud services, the elasticity of resources, and lower hardware costs. Due to the availability of resources, the user may receive more services of higher quality, enhancing their experience. AI will reside at every edge in the future's hybrid clouds, multi-cloud, and mesh networks. For mobility, IoT, and other edge environments, prominent AI platform vendors have invested significantly in 5G-based services.

Fig. (**1**) portrays the Interplay between IoT and Cloud layers.

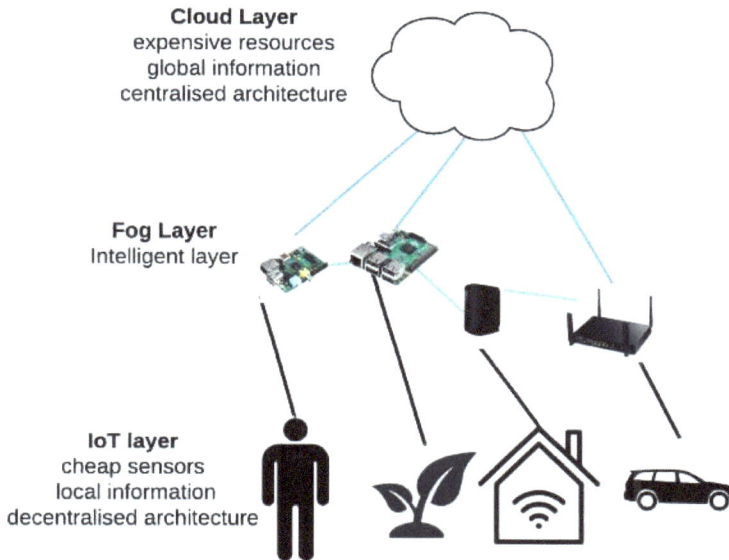

Fig. (1). Interplay between IoT and Cloud Layers portrays the Interplay T and Cloud layers.

5.2. USE CASES OF IOT-AI

The IoT Architecture [1] has three layers. The discernment layer interacts with the actual world to oblige the data from a source. A wide range of data is gathered in this layer. Sensors and specialized remote gadgets are the critical parts of this layer. Network Layer works with straightforward information transmission utilizing the current correspondence medium, for example, versatile, Wireless sensor hubs, Radio access organization, and other specialized devices. The service Layer has the essential capability, for example, information on the board, application backing, security, and execution.

The review [2] comprises an Industry 5.0 savvy studio that searches for further developing administrator security and activity following. Such an application case utilizes a fog processing design made up of AI-empowered IoT hubs. In the wake of portraying the application case, it assesses energy utilization and dissects the effect of the carbon impression it might have on various nations. Fog Computing Layer has AI-empowered IIoT hubs that run AI calculations locally. The cloud acts like in the edge registering-based architecture. The picked situation has partaken in a Joint Research Unit and possibly of the biggest shipbuilder on the planet (Navantia). The raw pipes are put away in the Reception Area. If the lines convey with soil or oil, they are cleaned in the Cleaning Area before being put away in the Reception Area. Each line cuts in the Cutting Area as per the expected aspects. Pipes are bowed in the Bending Area. Pipes are cleaned and moved to the manufacturing area, where embellishments are in the application. Lines are stacked into beds, stuffed, and afterward put away in two unique regions of the studio Fig. (**2**).

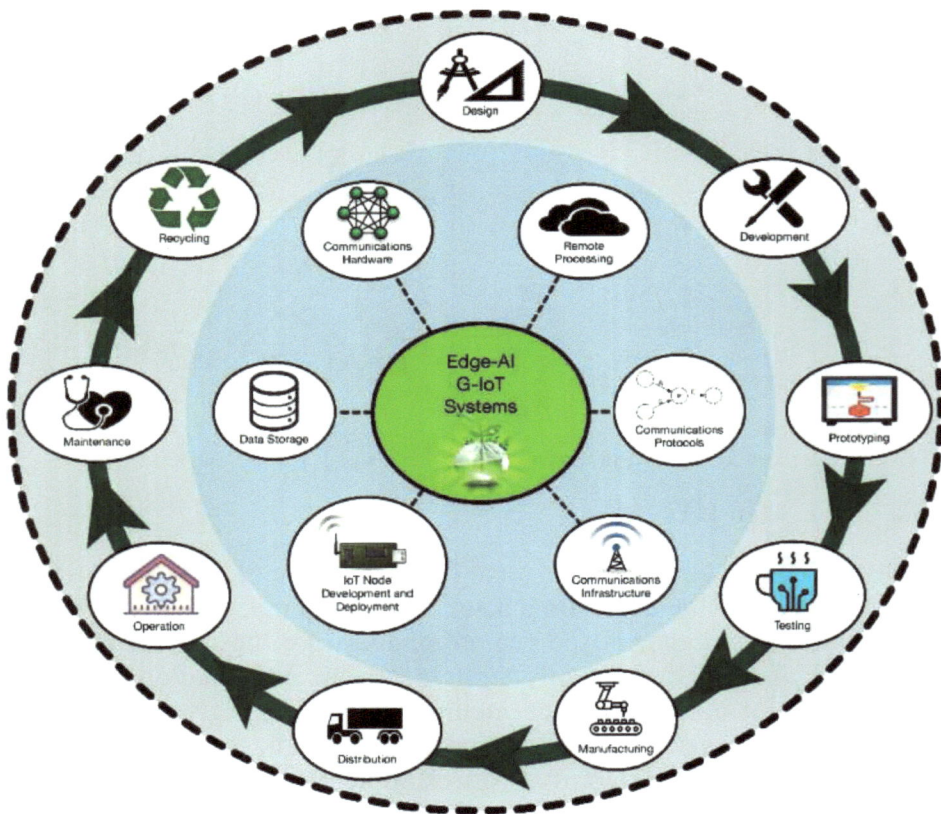

Fig. (2). Edge AI G-IoT life cycle [2] depicts the same.

The work [3] expects to accomplish a brilliant home robotization framework with absolute highlights. It is a protected and incorporated model, interfacing IoT gadgets and machines to carry out brilliant home mechanization with a voice-based order and control approach. It uses the consistent network of IoT stages to distinguish devices over a safely conveyed network. The proposed brilliant home computerization framework guarantees the security and protection of every client by interfacing and designing the IoT gadgets utilizing OpenVPN and a cell phone to control the devices. It distinguishes different discourse sounds and voice-based orders to work with other IoT gadgets to understand the exciting benefit of having both accommodation and security. Minimal-expense inserted regulators process each order and send it to the fitting device inside the brilliant home climate through its hand-off regulator. It remotely interfaces a cell phone to the Raspberry Pi to send the client's discourse orders. The proposed coordinated voice-acknowledgment framework executes client orders to work, screen, and control different gadgets in a smart home.

The work [4] utilizes a programmed cycle to remove subjects of examination interest and saw that the main ebb and flow lines of exploration zeroed in on persistent-based arrangements. Scientometrics is the investigation of the quantitative parts of the creation, spread, and utilization of logical data. It is fully intent on accomplishing a superior comprehension of the instruments of analytical exploration and its development. It utilizes scientometric planning and text mining using VOSviewer programming, created at Leiden University in the Netherlands. It gathers bibliographic information and offers visual guides that address bibliographic coupling, co-references, co-origin, and co-event of creator keywords. The programming involves the Leiden calculation to find many associated groups in networks. It gives a low-layered representation in which articles are situated so that the distance between any sets of items mirrors their similitude.

5.3. USE CASES OF CLOUD-AI

The suggestion [5] is a portable planning framework mounted on an electric tricycle, and a method for making on-road leaving measurements that permits government organizations and strategy creators to confirm and change leaving arrangements in various city districts. It joins georeferenced red-green-ble-profundity symbolism from two minimal expense 3D cameras with advanced 3D item location calculations for removing and planning left vehicles. The MM payload incorporates both route and planning sensors and a PC for information pre-handling and stockpiling. The GNSS and IMU-based route unit SwiftNav Piksi Multi comprises a multi-band and multi-star grouping GNSS RTK beneficiary board and a geodetic GNSS receiving wire. The GNSS beneficiary board additionally incorporates the customer grade IMU Bosch BMI160. It utilizes an RGB-D camera Intel RealSense D455. The subsequent camera will recognize parking spots and vehicles that are, in many cases, situated on the right-hand roadside in metropolitan regions. A brain network pre-prepared on a non-open dataset identified the countenances and vehicle tags in the information pictures. A Gaussian channel obscures the distinguished items, and an anonymized form of the information picture is saved. All vehicle identification calculations used in this venture require point mists as information. Fig. (**3**) depicts the same.

Fig. (3). Graphical Abstract [5].

The suggestion proposes a cloud-based structure and the stage for start-to-finish advancement and lifecycle of the executives of manufactured brainpower applications. ModelOps [6] is an original system and phase for the lifecycle of the board of computer-based intelligence application curios. It spins around the central idea of pipelines: a progression of errands that produce, screen, and further develop manufactured intelligence models. It utilizes the concept of pipelines to communicate the rationale applied in complex mechanized model preparation workflows. Users express pipelines as a coordinated non-cyclic diagram where each hub addresses an undertaking, and each edge characterizes the control stream between errands. It tracks metadata across the lifecycle and depicts metamodel elements that theoretically center the ideas of computer-based intelligence activities resources, records, pipelines and undertakings, and occasion triggers. It regards conditions as top-notch residents in the metamodel.

The work [7] is intelligence Deduction Motors for independent driving applications given profound learning modules, where preparing undertakings are conveyed flexibly over both Cloud and Edge assets, fully intent on lessening the expected organization transmission capacity and moderating protection issues.

The initial two stages respect information definition and information standardization and cleaning. These characterize the computer-based intelligence induction motor design, where we appropriately arrange the layers of the DNN and select the info preparing information as indicated by the pre-handled datastreams. The prepared model is changed over naturally to an organization. The changed-over model addresses the computer-based intelligence Derivation Motor, coordinated and tried in various driving scenarios. Phase 1 comprises characterizing the issue space and gathering the essential information for the preparation cycle. The data is pre-handled, commented on, standardized, and sifted in this stage. In Stage 2, they plan the DNN design, actuation capabilities, construction of the hidden layers, and result hubs. Step 3 arrangements with tuning the DNN, or at least all hyperparameters essential for the preparation stage. Fig. (**4**) depicts the same.

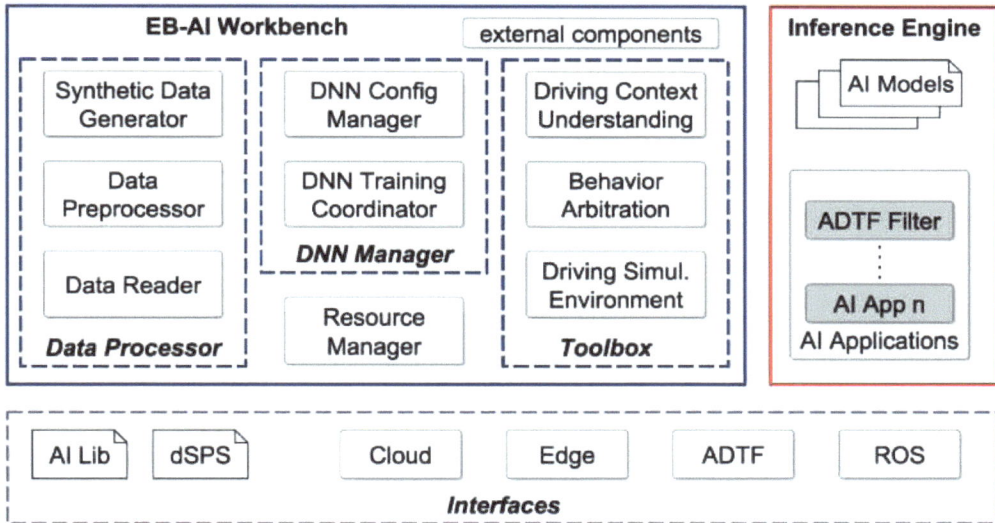

Fig. (4). EB-AI Cloud architecture [7].

It is a reasonable structure [8] to satisfy the DT's joint effort necessities by utilizing the mix of blockchain, prescient investigation procedures, and DT innovations. The proposed system means engaging more insight DTs in light of blockchain innovation. The information-driven blockchain-based cooperative DTs engage more savvy and cooperative answers for DTs because of DLT and appropriated agreement choice-making. It has information-driven record-based cooperative DTs for prescient examination and agreement-based navigation. Information Driven fosters a philosophy for making and refreshing data-driven record-based cooperative DTs. It shows the proactive investigation approach by creating disconnected and online prescient models utilizing the information record-based verifiable DTs information and live streaming DTs data. The consensus-Based Dynamic part fosters a disseminated agreement calculation to develop the DTs joint effort further. The proposed reasonable structure intends to promote a cooperative DTs framework to give conveyed decision-production to avoid possibly undermining the creation framework. Fig. (**5**) depicts the same.

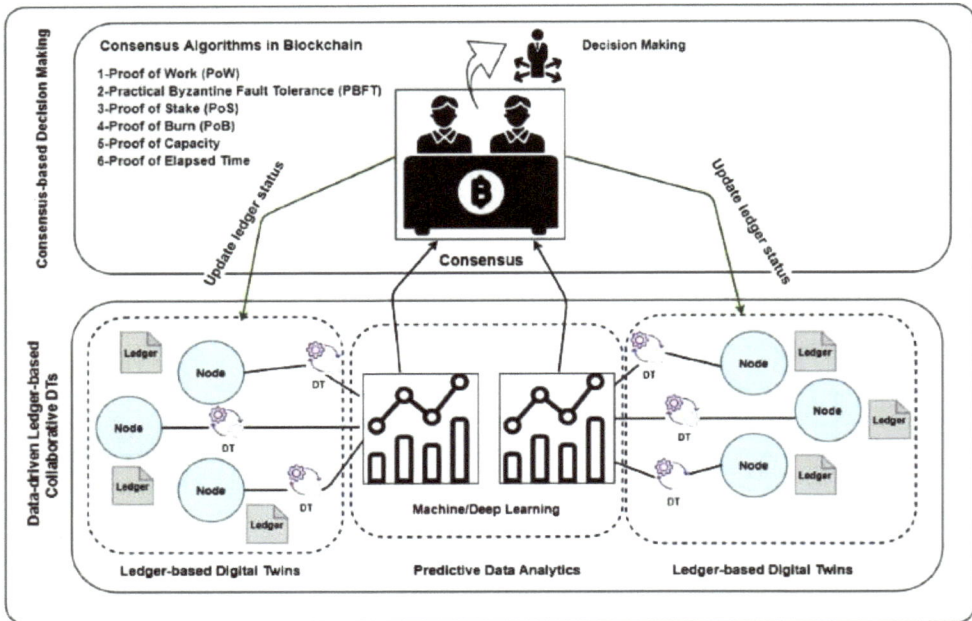

Fig. (5). Conceptual Framework [8].

The work [9] is a nonexclusive brilliant cloud-based framework. The horticulture ranches utilize the Web of Things observing from a distance. Subject matter experts and ranchers break down the ongoing and put away information. The cloud is a focal computerized information store where data gathers from different sources in gigantic volumes and assortment, like sound, video, picture, text, and advanced maps. The grouped information allocates to the virtual machines where this information is accessible by the end clients using essential server farms. The ranchers then utilize this computerized data to work on their cultivating abilities and refresh them as pre-debacle recuperation for brilliant agri-food. It will give general and explicit data about global business sectors and their yields. The securing layer contains different sensors used to gather information introduced in various areas. The news got in information gathering gadgets are of multiple configurations like sound, video, pictures, maps, texts, and so on. The data trade layer is liable for sharing the information from the obtaining layer to the application layer through the datacenter and runtime information. The application layer is answerable for showing the outcomes to the end clients as GUI. The work utilizes 100,000 records gather at run time in different configurations like sound, video, picture, text, and guides. These records are of shifting sizes from 0.1 MB to 1 GB. The reproduction is performed on a Center i9 Intel Quad-center framework with 16 GB Slam and 4 TB HDD. Fig. (**6**) depicts the same.

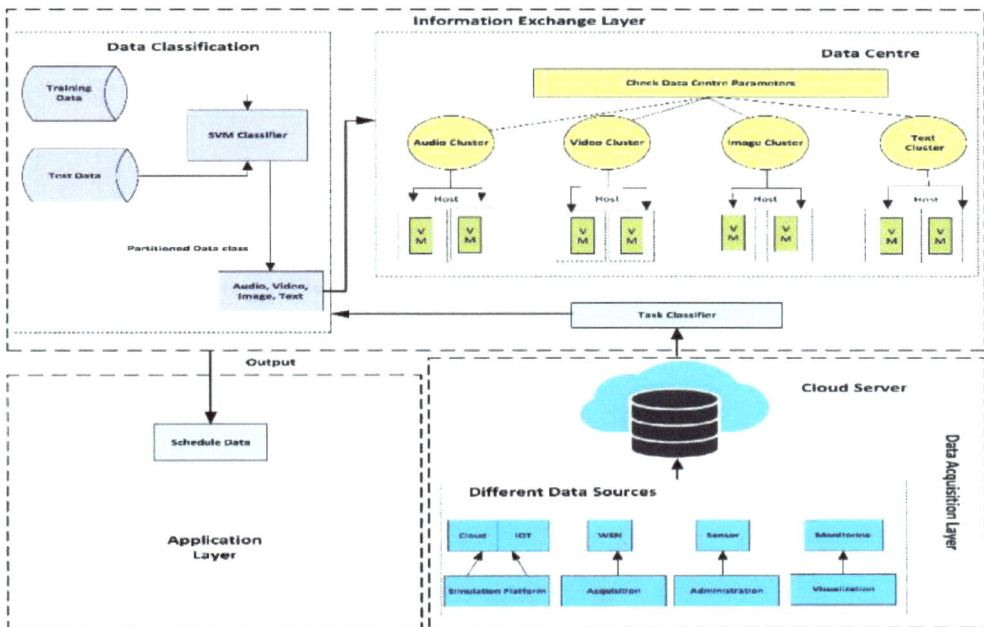

Fig. (6). Agricloud working [9].

DePaaS [10] is a bound-together stage expected to be utilized by SDP specialists and programming industry experts. DePaaS will be on a public cloud as an openly consumable help. It will comprise several SDP models that can be gotten to by programming improvement groups utilizing a front-end application. SDP models are based on highlight sets from public datasets, and cross-project/cross-rendition/cross-discharge abandons information hung on DePaaS. The stage has an administrator who directs the DePaaS scene by dealing with security, model accessibility, and dataset accessibility and adjusts the boundaries of the DePaaS work process. The stage has an arrangement for free scientists to notice the presence of SDP models. This job is planned to assist with spreading consciousness of SDP among the two specialists and practitioners. The administrator comes as an inherent element of the DePaaS platform. The supplier transfers the SDP model by giving subtleties like model depiction, reasonable use settings, proposed datasets, tunable boundaries, model execution values, known issues, and so forth. The sprinter runs the SDP work process. The stage handholds the client's excursion through the SDP process. The model execution is assessed. The source dataset, highlight sets, upsides of the tunable boundaries, and execution boundaries are protected for future examination and improvements. The design parts are gathered into five layers. The security comprises modules that register end clients, keep up with their profiles, and force job-based protection across the DePaaS stage at the application level. The data and list of capabilities layer comprise modules that oversee the transfer, approval, and combination of datasets. The executive's layer comprises modules that manage the transfer, license, and incorporation of SDP models. SDP Run Administration Layer contains numerous modules that guide the business professional to perform one run of programming deformity prediction. The persistence layer comprises a data set and double records, which are executable documents of the SDP models. DePaaS modules access the DePaaS stockpiling through the Information Programming interface, which isolates information and executable code. Fig. (7) depicts the same.

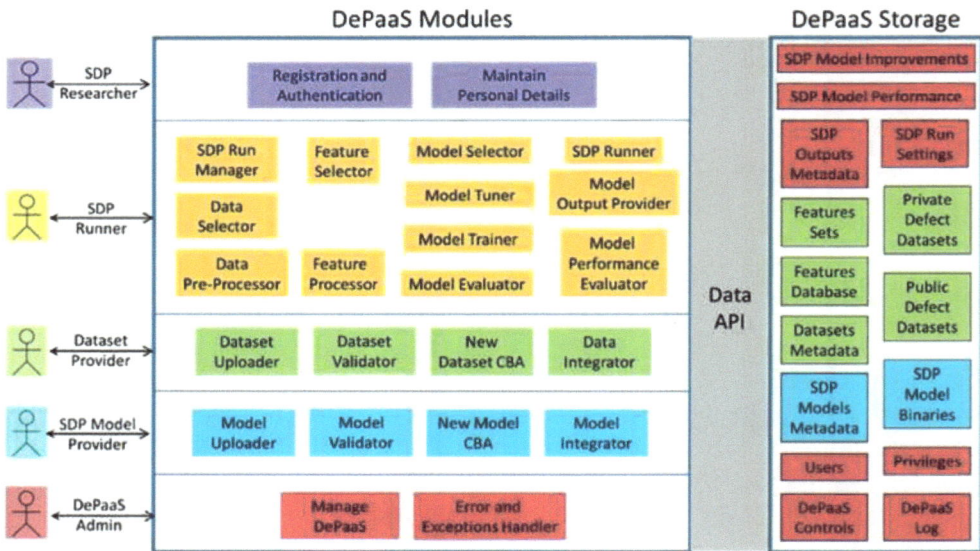

Fig. (7). Architecture of DePaas [10].

The work [11] is a 5G NPN engineering approach critical to empowering innovations. The framework layer comprises the center and edge/local organization capabilities virtualization foundations, the phone site stage, transport network portions, and synchronization components. NFVI is a critical part of the organization's capabilities in virtualization engineering that depicts the equipment and programming parts on which virtual organizations. The cell site stage incorporates restrictive frameworks, where the product is combined with the equipment and supports the arrangement of actual organization functions. The O-RAN design depends on the deterioration of components into NFs. At the MOA layer, different modules give insight and computerization to the organization and administration of the board and coordination. The NFV orchestrator is answerable for dealing with the organization's administration lifecycle. The orchestrator has three primary modules. The safe provisioner arrangements the hub. The SLA chief is responsible for ensuring the SLAs of the various occupants. The help situation chief chooses the ideal areas for the administration for execution. The cut supervisor is liable for providing E2E cuts in the figure, organization, and access network domains. Network telemetry is a constant information assortment in which gadgets push information to a suitable location. O-RAN working gatherings have determined RAN parts have ML usefulness across network spaces, taking care of both disconnected and web-based preparing and surmising. Fig. (**8**) represents the same.

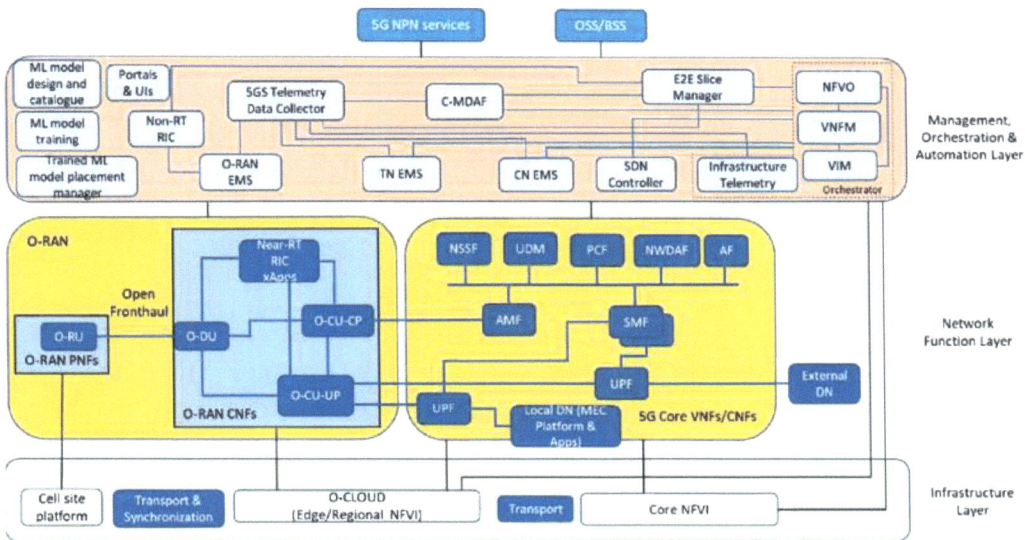

Fig. (8). System architecture [11].

The review center [12] detects Light Discovery and Running strategies and Sound Route and Going. Inside the BLAINDER add-on, various profundity sensors stacks from presets can carry out altered sensors and produce natural circumstances. Virtual LiDAR and Sonar sensors combine with strong 3D displaying and liveliness abilities. They permit the age of semantically named preparing information for ML calculations. Objects are demonstrated utilizing cross sections, parametric surfaces, or helpful strong math in Blender and conceptualized into a scene. The standard Blender work process permits a severe level of versatility however requires a ton of 3D demonstrating mastery and time to coordinate an adequate number of varieties into the preparation models for synthetic intelligence. Fig. (**9**) represents the same.

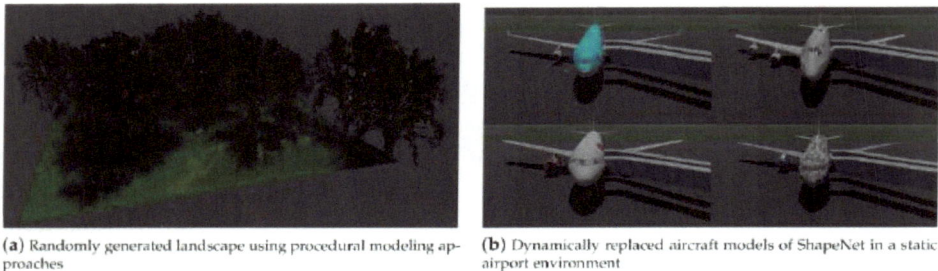

(**a**) Randomly generated landscape using procedural modeling approaches

(**b**) Dynamically replaced aircraft models of ShapeNet in a static airport environment

Fig. (9). Semi-static scene varied by aircraft model [12].

The review [13] proposes an edge-haze cloud design with versatile IoT edge hubs carried on independent robots for warm oddities located in aluminum plants. The focal unit of the general framework is an IoT hub carried on by our independent robot assessor. The IoT hub incorporates all sensors required for review. No matter their level, correspondence between all sub-frameworks utilizes a distributed buy-in design. Low-level sub-frameworks contain ones for engine control, controller, line-following, and hindrance aversion. Engine control gets order signals from mid-level sub-frameworks like self-driving or low-level ones like controller and hindrance evasion, with clashes settled through fundamentally basic settings. Engine control likewise distributes robot speed input to bought-in sub-frameworks. Mid-level sub-frameworks handle confinement and conduct cloning and are, in this manner, liable for independent driving. Significant-level sub-frameworks are application layer frameworks adaptable to the examination prerequisites and the modern climate challenges. Long-haul examinations of inconsistencies are finished by offloading to the cloud. Fig. (**10**) represents the same.

The TacPic framework [14] was created as a web-based stage to make material informational, given the picture contributions of clients who don't have related knowledge in material photograph advancement or 3D printing. The TacPic framework allows clients to transfer pictures to a site and uses manufactured intelligence distributed computing on the Amazon Web Administrations stage. It portions and marks the photographs. The text name changes into braille words. The surface delivery and union of the picture and text are performed before it is changed into a solitary document prepared for 3D printing. These modules are liable for the accompanying errands: Customization Connection point, Component Discovery and Extraction, Example Division, Braille Age, 3D Reproduction, and 3D Review Connection point. The improvement of the framework used in a Python climate. The calculations depended on the Python execution inside numerous libraries, specifically TensorFlow, OpenCV, and NumPy. The TensorFlow library performed object discovery and example division on pictures. The OpenCV library plays out the image-handling calculations. The NumPy library was utilized for picture enrollment and 3D STL age. This is applied to the AWS stage for simple incorporation with various elements. It is gainful if the calculation is sent inside an electronic or versatile application. The AWS Versatile Holder Library stores the multiple measures. Fig. (**11**) depicts the same.

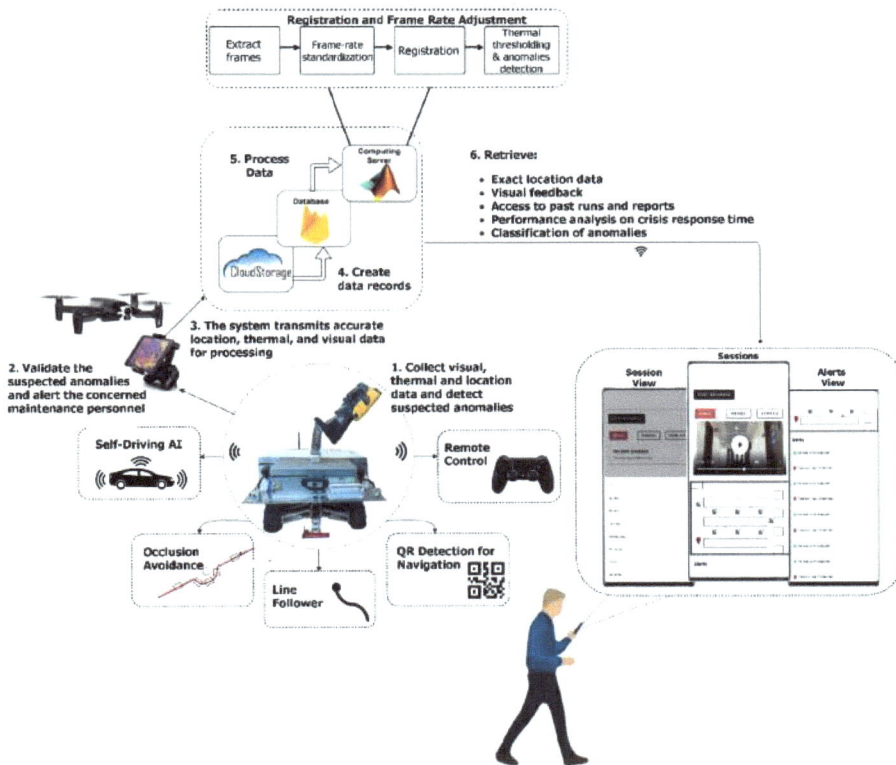

Fig. (10). Proposed architecture [13].

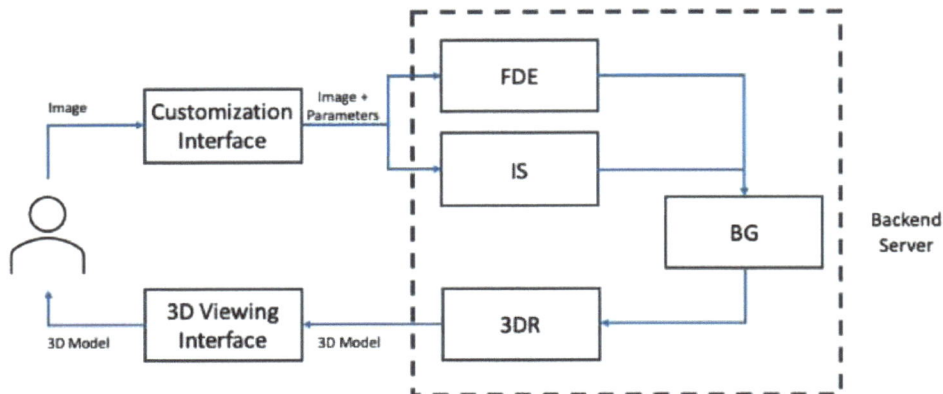

Fig. (11). TacPic System [14].

The EBP impact [15] on diesel motor execution required a test seat with fitting sensors and instrumentation. Data trailed the arrangement of information structures for artificial intelligence-based computation set the groundwork for ANN preparation and testing. Simulated intelligence executes in limited-state machine models in a methodology. ANNs were point by point in the viewpoint of computational requirements for cloud-manufactured intelligence versus edge-simulated intelligence. The cloud-simulated intelligence executions depended on MathWorks MATLAB internet being the ideal decision of Gaussian regressor, the Tensorflow backend Keras and Expanded Inclination Supporting, and the ANS Place ANNHUB. The motor presentation estimates in the Motor Testing Research Center of the Street Vehicle Foundation, Brasov, on a DC 300 kW/3000 rpm dynamometric test seat delivered by MEZ-Vsetin. The seat instruments with temperature sensors for fumes gas, air, and cooling liquid, pressure sensors for charge air, surrounding air, oil pressure, and EBP, flowmeters for air and fuel, a tachometer for motor rotational speed, and a fumes gas opacimeter. The fuel control framework changed the motor burden, and the dynamometer altered the momentum. The EBP applies by a mechanical choke valve introduced on the exhaust arrangement of the test seat, 2 m downstream of the turbine. The change of the EBP is physical, with moderate positions aligned after the most excellent EBP values were fixed at evaluated speed and entire burden. The fume gas temperature was estimated using a K-type thermocouple embedded in the fumes gas pipe through a pike coupling. Fig. (**12**) portrays the same.

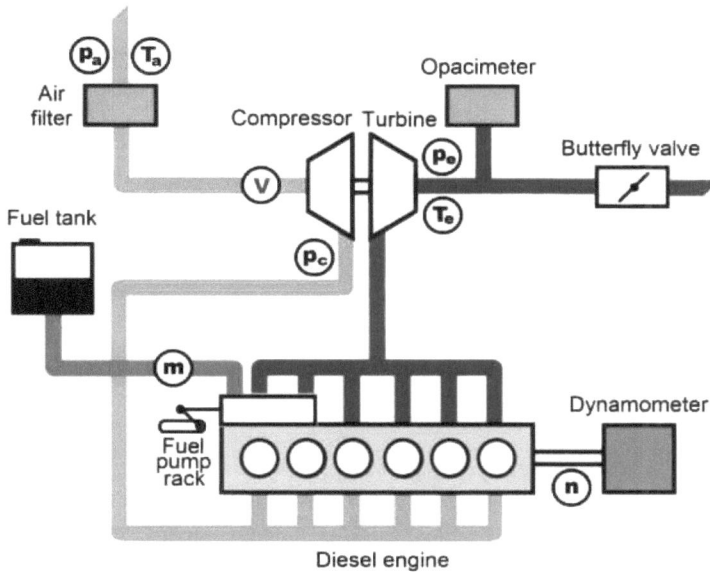

Fig. (12). Diesel Engine Test Configuration [15].

5.4. USE CASES OF AI AND IOT-CLOUD

The cloud [2] gathers information from far-off IoT sensors and can send orders to IoT actuators. The cloud can likewise associate with outsider administrations and far-off clients to whom it offers executives programming. Cloudlets consider giving continuous delivery or figure concentrated administrations, which require conveying perfect quality PCs in the neighbourhood organization. The fog hubs lessen the requirement for trading information to the higher layers of the design. After dissecting the past models, it makes G-IoT frameworks. Their equipment and software mould the turn of events and organization of productive G-IoT gadgets. Central Processing Units are universally applicable handling units that offer an acceptable compromise between execution and power utilization. It enhances fast and equal processing. Graphics Processing Units offload realistic calculations from the CPUs. Fig. (**13**) depicts the same.

The work [16] considered IIoT comprising modern gadgets, base stations prepared with edge server usefulness, and remote cloud. Modern mobile devices screen the current boundaries. It conveys the gathered information to the server farm for collection. The AI-empowered IIoT administration incorporates self-observing, request determining, issue identification, and labor force the executives. The choice is taken care of back to the IIoT gadgets and executed automatically. The preparation period of machine learning calculations, like CNNs, stresses the computational capacity of edge servers and the correspondence asset in the spine network, which were preparing information from a remote cloud. Edge and distributed computing work helpfully to serve IIoT gadgets with general and brief registering administration through the edge layer and robust and complete figuring administration through the cloud layer. Edge Layer obliges lightweight keen registering administration for IIoT. Cloud Layer gives substantial and entire figuring administration for IIoT at the expense of idleness and correspondence burden. The edge layer and cloud layer connect. The edge layer might require the help of the cloud layer to prepare its AI model, while the edge layer works as a hand-off to move information from IIoT gadgets to the remote cloud.

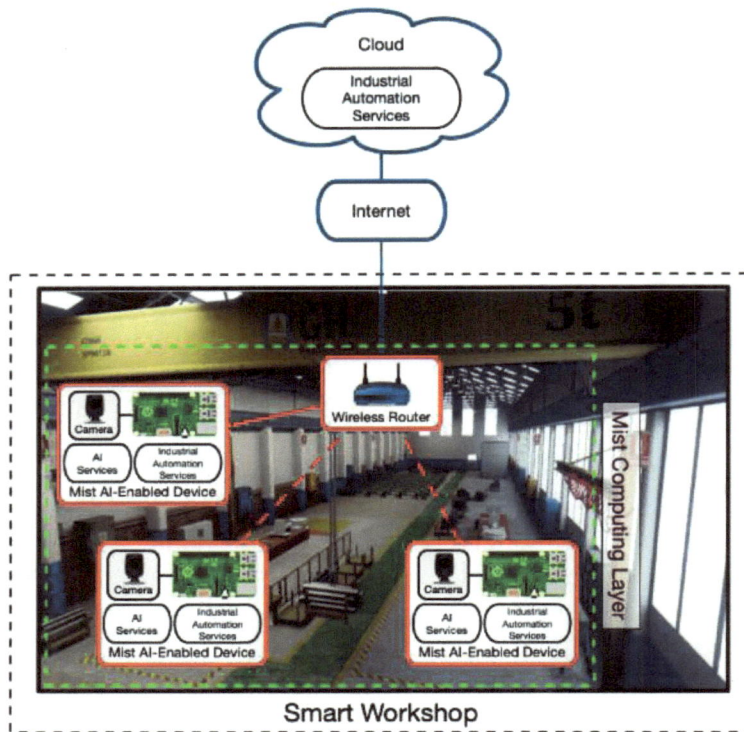

Fig. (13). Mist-computing-based communication architecture [2].

To catch information from the actual world and Customers, passage to handle data from the IoT gadgets and send it over the web to far-off servers/cloud/server farms for programming applications. These programming applications [1] are planned in light of administrations expected by clients from retail to big business and dwell in server farms with programming applications. The perception layer communicates with the actual world to oblige the data from the source. A wide range of data is gathered in this layer. The network Layer works with straightforward information transmission utilizing the current correspondence medium, for example, portable, Wireless sensor hubs, Radio access organization, and other specialized gadgets. The administration Layer has the essential capability, for example, information on the board, application backing, security, and execution.

The exploratory arrangement [17] includes a little group of single-board registering hubs outfits with four edge gas pedal stages: Intel Movidius NCS2 VPU, Google Edge TPU, Nvidia Jetson Nano GPU, and Nvidia TX2 GPU. It considers a Raspberry Pi3 hub to act as an illustration of an asset-compelled edge gadget and an x86 server with a 3.0GHz Xeon Skylake CPU to illustrate a cloudlet-style edge server. The responsibility comprises three normal vision-based picture handling and discourse-based sound handling errands that emerge in many edge-based AI applications. Picture characterization aims to dole out a text mark to a picture given its items. Object discovery includes deciding all objects of interest available in print by figuring a bounding box around each such entity and afterward relegating a probabilistic mark to each object. Keyword spotting includes handling a sound stream to distinguish and perceive the event of a bunch of watchwords.

The proposed framework [18] uses three datasets from PhysioNet prepared on a profound learning workstation and afterward moved to virtualized miniature regulators associated with IoT sensors. It is a heartbeat grouping method that can be sent and coordinated with sensors to give them the capacity to produce quicker results utilizing the AI-supported rationale in-sensor framework. The consequences of ECG investigation can be sent from the IoT sensor to the consideration suppliers for persistent observation. It considers a mechanized profound learning-based one-layered CNN that needs no commotion sifting and manual element extraction. The CNN model gains discriminative examples naturally from the crude ECG signal. The Automated Classification step utilizes a solitary 1-D convolution layer, trailed by completely associated layers. The dropout layer helps the organization to decrease overfitting with the goal that it doesn't retain the preparation information. The clump standardization method is applied before the initiation capability to normalize the contribution to the following layer and settle the educational experience. The work is a lattice scan with k-overlap cross-approval for hyper-boundary tuning. Every ECG signal in each of these datasets portrays a text header record, a twofold document, and a paired comment record. It creates four different beat classes keeping the guideline of AAMI EC57:1998.

The suggestion [19] is the Elastic Intelligent Fog idea, an improved IoT administration layer stage for haze hubs with cutting-edge highlights, for example, semantics enablement, the virtualization of standard IoT administration capabilities, and the enablement of AI. This improved stage can be powerfully launched at the haze hubs and channel superfluous information to pursue speedy choices. The focal cloud obliges different capabilities that empower shrewd AI administrations utilizing IoT information, the executives and semantic innovations. This focal cloud likewise gives the application programming connection points utilized by AI applications to use pre-characterized AI and IoT parts provided by a stage-administration layer with a home in different information centres. The mist cloud virtualizes network, IoT, and AI capabilities to offer common types of assistance to places near clients. The haze hub has a lightweight AI motor that can determine the setting and operational data through overseeing sensors. Contiguous, shrewd haze hubs added IoT administrations can be acquainted with clients, for example, an insightful traffic stream checking administration. Simulated intelligence motors like face acknowledgment, abnormality discovery, and constant circumstance examination are in the information stream investigation process. The work utilizes EiF is caution walkers about acceptable residue levels and gives ecological data given AI executed on a haze gadget. The assistance can give hyper-neighbourhood bits of knowledge into current and determined street/ground satisfactory residue conditions, asphalt temperatures, and essential data at a geo-area level granularity.

The work [20] investigates advanced business change from the perspective of four innovation fields. Afiniti utilizes AI to anticipate examples of the relational way of behaving for organizations searching for outcomes in human collaboration. Afiniti uses AI, extensive information examination, and AI calculations to break down the human form of conducting and involves the results for better-matching clients with specialists. It gathers information from various vectors of correspondence, call history, and CRM records for clients all over the planet. It then joins communication-level outcomes from the client's information. It utilizes particular ML calculations to distinguish different buyers' ways of behaving and foresee results from their authentic conduct.

The proposal [3] is a novel model that consolidates minimal expense, versatility, and accessible design start-to-finish security of IoT alongside voice-controlled order tasks of different gadgets in a smart home. For each device in a smart home, the proposed model furnishes a coordinated voice control framework with a solid association with the IoT organization. The activity accomplishes by launching start-to-finish security utilizing particularly tweaked VPN innovation. The suitable organization executes cell phone-based discourse acknowledgment for order and control of the devices. The proposed intelligent home mechanization framework guarantees the security and protection of every client by interfacing and designing the IoT gadgets utilizing OpenVPN and a cell phone to control the devices. Clients want to communicate with the framework in non-local English using a machine-clever programming stage. It is customized in Python with API orders to speak with basic cell phones that don't need a refined voice framework. Minimal-expense implanted regulators process each order and send it to the suitable gadget inside the shrewd home climate through its transfer regulator. We utilize the Raspberry Pi stage as it gives a few choices to associate IoT gadgets, home machines, and sensors essentially and effectively. Fig. (**14**) represents the same.

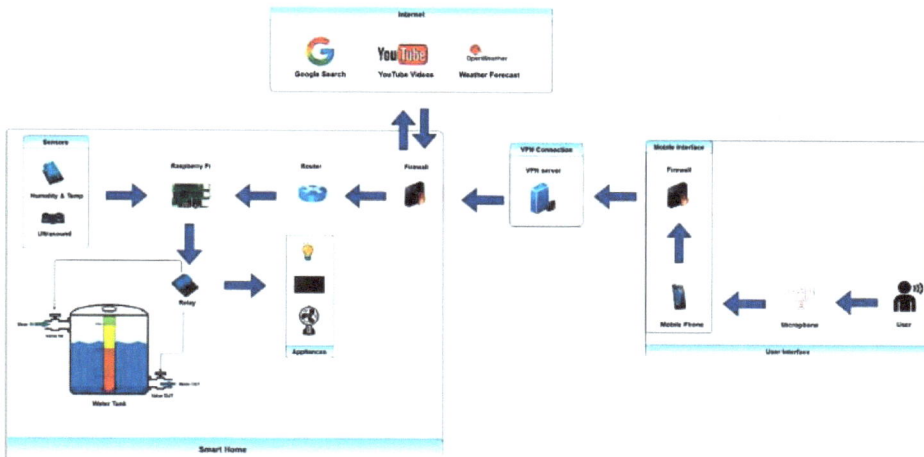

Fig. (14). Smart house automation [3].

The proposal [21] is a sensor-prepared van to empower remote skin-checking administrations to help provincial individuals impacted by skin disorders. The framework plans to give minimal-expense skincare administrations to individuals who are more defenceless against skin issues in country regions. The objective is additionally to gather information on skin sicknesses for scientists to investigate and group area-based skin illnesses. The Smart Skincare Van fits different skin sensors and gear for straightforward well-being tests. Picture sensors, dampness level, ph level, dryness level, tewl level sensors, *etc.*, may be different skin sensors. These sensors gather data from the predetermined country region about temperature, mugginess, level of contamination, and so forth. With the guidance of medical services laborers, skin patients went to the wise skincare van and enlisted. The application downloads on their cell phone, and a unique ID and secret key are given to the patient after enlistment. The equivalent, indistinguishable ID ensures the patient's protection services. Fundamental data and body examination are finished if the enlistment cycle is finished. Skincare Van sensors catch skin pictures and skin boundary values. The clinical information and history of the patient are gathered and communicated to the cloud stage, notwithstanding the natural boundary data. The report put away in the cloud is then examined, ordered, and determined for illness. Once the sickness is analysed, a seriousness record is related to the disease given the seriousness class. The expectations are communicated to the enrolled medical clinic after this system creates the auto-determination result. The patients are furnished through a portable application with drug suggestions and the following arrangement data. After examining the outcomes, the examination group endeavours to think of specific forecasts and deductions, connecting skin sicknesses and natural boundaries.

Hub RED [22] is a stream programming device that empowers the making of different highlights, including web administrations, UIs, variation, and middleware logic. UI execution layer integrates graphical interaction points through which the various entertainers can pronounce the use of items and conditions and start-up the particular components of their store network. A middleware and combination layer make separate changes and transformations, starting with one information source and then onto the next. It involves the Semantic help to enhance approaching information, takes care of storing network-related explanations and forwards this information to the Data Management block for utilization in the AI process. Semantic administration block consolidates the AffectUs cosmology that corresponds to ideas from the production network, for example, stages, sorts of areas, and connections among actors. It involves the OWL philosophy for surmising and thinking, the SPARQL 1.1 is into question, and the mix with automatic guidelines on the Node-RED site and extra custom principles for the Jena reasoner in the Knowledge Base. The computerized reasoning block intends to deduce critical measurements of each stage and recognize inconsistencies by assessing clarified factual information.

CONCLUSION

Nowadays, most sophisticated applications employ computer intelligence to make decisions based on random, vague data analysis. Artificial Intelligence is the name given to this intelligence in computers. The Internet of Things (IoT) is a network of physical devices connected to perform various tasks like data transfer and process control like sensors, actuators, controllers, *etc*. The Internet of Things (IoT) has recently been proposed for use in numerous fields, including smart cities, industrial automation, medical device monitoring, *etc*. By connecting all devices and storing data in the cloud, the method can be applied to various fields.

REFERENCES

[1]   H. Ramalingam, and V.P. Venkatesan, Conceptual analysis of Internet of Things use cases in Banking domain.*TENCON 2019-2019 IEEE Region 10 Conference.* TENCON: Kochi, India, 2019.
[http://dx.doi.org/10.1109/TENCON.2019.8929473]

[2]   P. Fraga-Lamas, S.I. Lopes, and T.M. Fernández-Caramés, "Green iot and edge ai as key technological enablers for a sustainable digital transition towards a smart circular economy: an industry 5.0 use case", *Sensors (Basel)*, vol. 21, no. 17, p. 5745, 2021.
[http://dx.doi.org/10.3390/s21175745] [PMID: 34502637]

[3]   S. Venkatraman, A. Overmars, and M. Thong, "Smart home automation—use cases of a secure and integrated voice-control system", *systems*, vol. 9, no. 4, p. 77, 2021.
[http://dx.doi.org/10.3390/systems9040077]

[4]   I. Rodríguez-Rodríguez, J.V. Rodríguez, N. Shirvanizadeh, A. Ortiz, and D.J. Pardo-Quiles, "Applications of artificial intelligence, machine learning, big data and the internet of things to the covid-19 pandemic: a scientometric review using text mining", *Int. J. Environ. Res. Public Health*, vol. 18, no. 16, p. 8578, 2021.
[http://dx.doi.org/10.3390/ijerph18168578] [PMID: 34444327]

[5]   S. Nebiker, J. Meyer, S. Blaser, M. Ammann, and S. Rhyner, "Outdoor mobile mapping and ai-based 3d object detection with low-cost rgb-d cameras: the use case of on-street parking statistics", *Remote Sens. (Basel)*, vol. 13, no. 16, p. 3099, 2021.
[http://dx.doi.org/10.3390/rs13163099]

[6]   W. Hummer, V. Muthusamy, T. Rausch, P. Dube, K. El Maghraoui, A. Murthi, and P. Oum, "Modelops: cloud-based lifecycle management for reliable and trusted ai", *ieee international conference on cloud engineering (IC2E)*, 2019 Prague, Czech Republic
[http://dx.doi.org/10.1109/IC2E.2019.00025]

[7]   S. Grigorescu, T. Cocias, B. Trasnea, A. Margheri, F. Lombardi, and L. Aniello, "Cloud2edge elastic ai framework for prototyping and deployment of ai inference engines in autonomous vehicles", *Sensors (Basel)*, vol. 20, no. 19, p. 5450, 2020.
[http://dx.doi.org/10.3390/s20195450] [PMID: 32977409]

[8]   R. Sahal, S.H. Alsamhi, K.N. Brown, D. O'Shea, C. McCarthy, and M. Guizani, "Blockchain-empowered digital twins collaboration: smart transportation use case", *machines*, vol. 9, no. 9, p. 193, 2021.
[http://dx.doi.org/10.3390/machines9090193]

[9]   M. Junaid, A. Shaikh, M.U. Hassan, A. Alghamdi, K. Rajab, M.S. Al Reshan, and M. Alkinani, "Smart agriculture cloud using ai based techniques", *energies*, vol. 14, no. 16, p. 5129, 2021.
[http://dx.doi.org/10.3390/en14165129]

[10]   M. Pandit, D. Gupta, D. Anand, N. Goyal, H.M. Aljahdali, A.O. Mansilla, S. Kadry, and A. Kumar, "Towards design and feasibility analysis of depaas: ai based global unified software defect prediction framework", *Appl. Sci. (Basel)*, vol. 12, no. 1, p. 493, 2022.
[http://dx.doi.org/10.3390/app12010493]

[11]   P. Trakadas, L. Sarakis, A. Giannopoulos, S. Spantideas, N. Capsalis, P. Gkonis, P. Karkazis, G. Rigazzi, A. Antonopoulos, M.A. Cambeiro, S. Gonzalez-Diaz, and L. Conceição, "A cost-efficient 5g non-public network architectural approach: key concepts and enablers, building blocks and potential use cases", *Sensors (Basel)*, vol. 21, no. 16, p. 5578, 2021.
[http://dx.doi.org/10.3390/s21165578] [PMID: 34451020]

[12]   S. Reitmann, L. Neumann, and B. Jung, "Blainder—A blender ai add-on for generation of semantically labeled depth-sensing data", *sensors (basel)*, vol. 21, no. 6, p. 2144, 2021.
[http://dx.doi.org/10.3390/s21062144] [PMID: 33803908]

[13]   M. Ghazal, T. Basmaji, M. Yaghi, M. Alkhedher, M. Mahmoud, and A.S. El-Baz, "Cloud-based monitoring of thermal anomalies in industrial environments using ai and the internet of robotic things", *Sensors (Basel)*, vol. 20, no. 21, p. 6348, 2020.
[http://dx.doi.org/10.3390/s20216348] [PMID: 33171714]

[14]   A.R. See, and W.D. Advincula, "Creating tactile educational materials for the visually impaired and blind students using ai cloud computing", *Appl. Sci. (Basel)*, vol. 11, no. 16, p. 7552, 2021.

[http://dx.doi.org/10.3390/app11167552]

[15] V. Fernoaga, V. Sandu, and T. Balan, "Artificial intelligence for the prediction of exhaust back pressure effect on the performance of diesel engines", *Appl. Sci. (Basel),* vol. 10, no. 20, p. 7370, 2020.
[http://dx.doi.org/10.3390/app10207370]

[16] W. Sun, J. Liu, and Y. Yue, "Ai-enhanced offloading in edge computing: when machine learning meets industrial iot", *ieee netw.,* vol. 33, no. 5, pp. 68-74, 2019.
[http://dx.doi.org/10.1109/MNET.001.1800510]

[17] Q. Liang, P. Shenoy, and D. Irwin, *AI on the edge: Rethinking AI-based IoT applications using specialized edge architectures.,* arXiv preprint: new york, .

[18] S. Sakib, M.M. Fouda, Z.M. Fadlullah, and N. Nasser, Migrating intelligence from cloud to ultra-edge smart IoT sensor based on deep learning: An arrhythmia monitoring use-case.*International Wireless Communications and Mobile Computing.* IWCMC: Limassol, Cyprus, 2020.
[http://dx.doi.org/10.1109/IWCMC48107.2020.9148134]

[19] J. An, W. Li, F.L. Gall, E. Kovac, J. Kim, T. Taleb, and J. Song, "Eif: toward an elastic iot fog framework for ai services", *ieee commun. mag.,* vol. 57, no. 5, pp. 28-33, 2019.
[http://dx.doi.org/10.1109/MCOM.2019.1800215]

[20] S. Akter, K. Michael, M.R. Uddin, G. McCarthy, and M. Rahman, "Transforming business using digital innovations: the application of ai, blockchain, cloud and data analytics", *Ann. Oper. Res.,* pp. 1-33, 2020.

[21] S. Juyal, S. Sharma, and A.S. Shukla, "Smart skin health monitoring using ai-enabled cloud-based iot", *international conference on technological advancements in Materials Science and Manufacturing,* 2021 Uttarakhand, India
[http://dx.doi.org/10.1016/j.matpr.2021.01.074]

[22] G. Kousiouris, S. Tsarsitalidis, E. Psomakelis, S. Koloniaris, C. Bardaki, K. Tserpes, M. Nikolaidou, and D. Anagnostopoulos, "A microservice-based framework for integrating iot management platforms, semantic and ai services for supply chain management", *ICT Express,* vol. 5, no. 2, pp. 141-145, 2019.
[http://dx.doi.org/10.1016/j.icte.2019.04.002]

SUBJECT INDEX

www.ingramcontent.com/pod-product-compliance
Lightning Source LLC
Chambersburg PA
CBHW041700210326
41598CB00007B/480